A WOMAN'S JOURNEY

HELEN DOPSA

"Life goes on and we start with new books."
— JOZSEF DOPSA

Copyright © 2020 by Helen Dopsa

Print ISBN 978-0-6482842-9-1

ebook ISBN 978-0-6482842-2-2

All rights reserved.

No part of this book may be reproduced in any form or by any electronic or mechanical means, including information storage and retrieval systems, without written permission from the author, except for the use of brief quotations in a book review.

INTRODUCTION

Today is the 6th of January 2018 and I am starting my story. I am now approaching my seventy-eight birthday, in just three days. I keep thinking back, what was my life all about? What had happened, what was going on, how did I get here? I'd like to dedicate this story to my daughters Pearly and Georgie, so they learn a little bit about me. A little bit of history I heard from and about my parents and family. How my life evolved to what it is today. This is not something that I want to do to make people feel responsible or obligated or reproached, no nothing like that. This is something for me to put down, as facts, as I know them, as the story of my life. I hope they will eventually hear it or read it and will understand about their mother a little bit better. I feel sometimes that we aren't very close; sometimes it seems we're very far apart. We don't seem to be as close as I dreamed and as I'd like it to be. That is possibly what I have created, unintentionally with what life has thrown at me. How I 've been all my life, not how I'd like to be. So, please forgive me if this seems painful or remote. The intentions have been always pure.

I

So, let's begin from the beginning. According to stories told by my Father and Mother, I was born in a very cold winter day when Budapest had "an unusual amount of snow," on the 9th of January 1940 in the Sacred Heart Hospital. I was told that my father was over the moon, that finally he had a baby, a daughter. I found out later Mother wasn't that pleased; she wanted a son, however that's what's happened.

The story is that my parents had been married ten years before I came along, as my mother had become very anaemic and had been so weak that my father had to care for her, even carry her. Then a couple of years before my birth, a gypsy woman told them to make 'iron wine' (red wine cooked up with sugar and spices with the iron ring from the range cooked in it) and drink a glass three times a day. Which as a last resort they did. Within 6-8 month she was well again and I was conceived. This 'cure' had one drawback, my mother become quite plump; however she was always a very well proportioned, pretty woman: no one could call her fat.

At that time, my father, Jozsef Dopsa, was a well-to-do businessman, with his own workshop and about 8-10 people working for him, manufacturing very special embroidered dance slippers that were mainly used with national costumes. Everyone liked to have them as special footwear, and they were also exporting them all over the world. He was a qualified shoe-maker, so was my Grandfather. It was quite a successful business. My parents always had some young woman living with us, to help my mother with housework and then with children. Mother was very much involved in the business and she was also the first and only woman in Hungary who was a qualified shoemaker in the 1930s.

I was told that when they brought me home, Budapest had a very cold winter and a lot of snow. We lived not far from a main road in a house where the business was also situated, a quiet suburban street. There wasn't any snowplough working in the side streets at that time. Our street had about 30-40 centimetres of snow and the taxi couldn't drive to the house. So my father got all his men, (I think he had at that time six or so working for him) and they shovelled the snow away from the main road to our house, so the taxi could drive us home. I had a royal reception I believe, which is a nice story to remember and to know that it was such a joyous occasion, at least to my Father.

My parents had quite an unusual start to their life with regard to the way they got together.

They were both born and bred in Kiskunfélegyháza (this is a very hard word to spell or pronounce in English). It was a medium size town in Hungary and was the district centre for quite some time. It is situated in the centre of Hungary to the south of Budapest, half way between the Danube (Duna) and the Tyson (Tisza), the two largest rivers in Hungary. It is where the first Hungarians the Huns, with Prince Árpád, settled in the 9th century.

On my mother's side, my grandfather was a farmer and my grandmother of course looked after the family. They had a large family; the first six did not live past their early childhood. My grandmother wanted one of her daughters or sons to be part of the church so the boys went into Priest school and the girls went into a Covent. By the time they got to school age, every one of those children had died before their tenth or twelfth birthday. It was a very heart-breaking time, and my grandfather decided, "No more church school," so the children that followed did not attend. They had six more children, so all together twelve. There were two girls and four boys, who all grew up to be healthy and to reach a good old age. Unfortunately, my grandfather passed on fairly young and I did not get to know him. When he died, his youngest child, my uncle, was only about ten months or one year old I believe, so my grandmother was left in the country town with six children to bring up and no man to support her. She just carried on with the farm as much as she could, leasing the land and the vineyard. She branched into rearing chickens, ducks, and geese to sell.

The ducks and geese were mostly for their feathers as that was very much in demand for feather beds and pillows. She managed quite well with the business of selling the feathers, fattening the ducks and geese to be sold, as well as chooks and the eggs. The ducks and geese had to be always force fed with corn so their liver would grow big, because ducks/geese livers is a delicacy and in great demand, locally as well as internationally. Hungary exported a lot of duck livers all over the world, especially to France and Germany and does so even today. So my grandmother was part of that industry and a very self-assured smart lady.

She had educated all her sons to be tradesmen. My eldest uncle 'János bácsi' (the word bácsi means uncle in Hungarian) became a boot maker, but later on he joined the post office. He advanced to the position of Postmaster in the town and had two sons. My second uncle 'Laci bácsi' was a plumber with one son, the third uncle 'Imre bácsi' was a tailor but got into some business of selling grain and wine and didn't marry till very late and had no children. The youngest 'Joska bácsi' became a farmer. Unfortunately he got lost, possibly died, in the Second World War in Russia, leaving two young sons – Laci and Öcsi – and a very sick wife behind. My aunty had heart and breathing problems and died fairly young, leaving the two young boys for the family to look after. They become tradesmen themselves. Unfortunately they have all now passed away. Öcsi was really called Jozsef, same as my brother, that's why he got called Öcsi which means younger.

I remember the good times we spent on summer holidays, playing in the fields and vineyard, taking the geese to the meadow, climbing trees, collecting fruit, helping at the harvest and the wine making.

Then there were the two youngest daughters: My mother Ilona (in English, Helen) Everyone called her Ica which is just one of the variations on the name. The baby of the family was my aunty Maria (we called her Maca, a variation on Maria) who was my godmother. The girls, after finishing school, learned how to do all the housework, look after the boys and other skills like sewing, handiwork etc. My mother, as a young woman, earned a living and helped with expenses by doing very fine embroidery. She was embroidering fine table linen and silk lingerie, expensive underwear slips, bras, and panties for rich ladies, (mainly Jewish ladies and the town's elite) who had the money for fine things and appreciated the exquisite work. She was creating the most beautiful things for 'glory boxes' for sale, (as well as for my aunty at the same time) but didn't make one for herself and declared she wasn't going to get married!

Mum was about eighteen when she met my father, her sister was eighteen months younger but she already had a fiancé and she wanted to get married as soon as possible.

My mother met my father on a summer picnic. That's what usually happened after the harvest. The young people would take a large flat-bed cart with four Clydesdale horses, big heavy carthorses, and drive some distance to the Tisza (Hungary's second largest river) for a summer picnic and swimming. My father was a friend of one of my uncles: there was a whole bunch of them going for a summer picnic and on the way back home, my father said to my mother, "Well, I think I'm going to marry you."

My mother was most indignant and she said, "No way Joska, I will not marry anybody, especially not you! You are a shoe maker, that's not a trade."

My father at the time was working with his father – they had a big business, making handmade shoes and also specialised slippers.

They courted for a short while, I am not quite sure how long, but by 1930 they were married. My mother was born in 1911 and my father in 1906 so, she was nineteen when my father asked my grandmother for her daughter's hand.

Grandmother was very happy about it. But mother was adamantly refusing to get married. In the end she had to get married because my aunty wanted to marry, and as she was the younger, she couldn't get married because that would be unseemly to get married before the older sister. So, the whole family decided and mother just had to follow orders.

The story about how they got to the church to register the marriage was the best story told by Mum. The rule at the Catholic Church was that you had to go into church to register your intention to marry and for six Sundays, it had to be announced to the town, "That Mr Jozsef Dopsa and Miss Ilona Szabo want to get married and if anybody has any objection they had to come forward."

Mother protested all the way as they went to the Church to register. There was my mother going on one side of the street with my grandmother, telling her off, all the way. My grandmother was threatening my mother: "If you don't go, I will take off my slippers and beat you all the way to church."

My grandmother used to wear traditional clothing for a countrywoman: long dark skirt and leather slippers. All the while, my father was walking on the other side of the street, watching them.

In due course they got married. My mother accepted that it had to be this way. She told me later that she loved my father, but was just afraid of marriage.

The story goes that she was an absolute innocent, because on their first night together, my mother made up the bed in the room for my father and another in the kitchen for herself. They only had one room and a kitchen, which was a norm in Hungary in a country town (even today it is counted as a nice home to have for a young couple). My grandmother's house had three rooms and that was the boys' room, the girls' room and grandma's, which was also the living room and a kitchen. So, my father said, "God what do you think you're doing? You are my wife now."

And she replied, "Do you think that I will go and sleep with you as well? I know that I have to cook and wash and clean after you, but you want me to sleep with you as well? That is disgusting!"

Apparently, she didn't really know what it meant to "sleep" with a man, she just knew that it wasn't very nice and that nice girls didn't do things like that.

It took my father six weeks to convince her and coax her into his bed. Later, he had a big discussion with my grandmother and told her off. How could she let a girl marry without any knowledge of what married life would be? If she had married a brute of a man, who forced himself on her straight away, she would have been ruined for life. My father took it on himself to instruct my mother about what it means to be married.

Eventually they settled into married life and my mother and father were devoted to one another. It's unbelievably beautiful how much they loved each other. So much so, that my mother, after becoming a widow at the age of thirty-seven, never married again. She always said there is not another one like your father. She lived to be eighty-six before she passed on. It's hard for me to think or imagine what it would be like to have a marriage and a partner that is so in tune with you.

Anyway they lived very happily for ten years together before my arrival. Their only sorrow was that they didn't have any children as yet. My mother became very anaemic early on in the marriage. She was so very badly affected and so weak that my father had to help to wash her, to feed her, carry her in his arms, even to the toilet. She couldn't do anything for herself; she was nearly totally helpless, virtually at death's door. My father was terribly worried about her and took her to all the doctors, but they couldn't do anything for her. Nothing seemed to be working.

Then the story goes that a gypsy called at the door, because the gypsies go around in Hungary even today, calling at doors to tell you your fortune, or help you around the house with some small jobs, in exchange for food or money.

My father always gave hand-outs for beggars and gypsies and when this gypsy woman came and my father was carrying my mother into her chair, she said to my father, "You know what you have to do, she will be well, she will be healthy soon," and gave him the recipe. "You have to make iron wine." The old-fashioned kitchen stoves had cast-iron tops with a number of rings that you could adjust to the size of the pot. She said; "Get one of those rings, scrub it nice and clean and then take a big pot with one or two litres of red wine. Put that iron ring into it add a bit of sugar, lots of cinnamon and cloves. Boil it up, let it stand until it cools down and get her to drink it, three times a day, a small glass full."

My father was at his wit's end. He decided it couldn't hurt and followed the instruction. He made the iron wine and got my mother to drink it. She didn't like wine, but with the sugar in it and all the spices, it wasn't too bad. The alcohol had mostly evaporated by then, so she was drinking that wine for six weeks.

After six weeks she was able to stand up and in six months she was her normal self. In the time while she was sick, she was just skin and bones and lost a lot of weight. When improvements set in, she started putting weight back on, but a bit more than before and become a little chubby. They used to call her 'turtle dove' because it's a nice, plump bird. She never was thin again, never could be. She could never get very fat either. She was around seventy, eighty kilos. If she put on weight she ended up at ninety kilos. I remember when I was about fifteen, she decided that she was ninety eight and now she would eat as much as possible to make it to a hundred kilos. She never made it and gave it up, and then she went back to her normal weight. She was plump, but very pretty, because she was always in proportion.

A couple of years later, she eventually got pregnant and ten years after their wedding, they had me.

They had waited a long time and my father's feelings were understandable, he was over the moon that eventually he had a child and that it was a girl. He had always wanted a girl. Apparently he spent hours and hours designing ball gowns and street gowns, for me to wear when I was grown up. When I'm a five year old I'm going to wear this pretty dress, then when I'm ten I'm going to wear that and when I go to my first ball, I'm going to wear this dress. He had a perfect portfolio of dress design and shoe designs for my future. He was absolutely thrilled that he had a daughter and my mother was happy to have a child of course, but she wasn't as happy because she wanted a boy. However, fifteen months later she had her wish and my brother was born, so the family was complete, everybody was quite happy.

In the ten years my parents worked in the business together, my mother wanted to learn to be a shoemaker so she would have a trade, not just be a housewife. This came in handy later on in her life.

So, my father taught her and she passed her exam as a qualified shoemaker. She was the first and only woman in 1936, who was a qualified shoemaker, in the whole of Hungary. She loved the business she worked in with my father. That's why they always had a young woman staying with us, to help with the housework and later, look after us. Some of them later became apprentices and worked in the business. They become part of the family; we had quite a few who even called my parents Mum & Dad. I remember three of them and particularly one lady 'Annus' who had a very tough family life. Her father was a good for nothing drinker and her mother was not very useful. They had three or four children and she came to us as a live-in apprentice, to sew the tops of the shoes and eventually she stayed with my parents. They provided everything for her wedding. She called my mother "Mum" and my father "Dad" all her life. Her husband 'Pista' loved my parents as well and I loved them too. They were wonderful to me when I was growing up. They were like a big sister and brother. They looked after me and we had lots of fun. Many people always called my parents Pops and Mum and even years later, if anyone of them were around the area, they always come to say 'hello'. My parents were always very community-minded in that respect.

Once, my mother was visiting my grandmother after my brother's birth. He was about three or four months old but he was apparently a very demanding child. He always cried, always wanted attention. Annus was living with us at the time and she with my father looked after us babies. My father was bathing my brother. My brother had been screaming for hours before the bath. Didn't want his bottle, didn't want this or that. So, my father put him into the bath and in the warm water, he suddenly stopped and went quiet and relaxed, let himself totally go. My father had the shock of his life; he thought my brother had died. It took them ages to wake him up. My father nearly had a nervous breakdown thinking that he killed his son, but it was exhaustion – my brother then slept through the night!

These kinds of stories were told over and over again while I was growing up.

My mother, occasionally, remembered to tell me a story about our life with Apuka (Daddy). One of my favourites is that my father used to pick me up and put me on the cutting table to dance with me. A shoemaker's cutting table is chest high, to make work easier, because they have to put a lot of pressure onto the knife to be able to cut the leather. When I say chest high, my father was six foot one, so that table had to suit him. He would pick me up and put me on the table to dance. 'Dancy, dancy, dancy' and I'd love it of course. By the time I was about eleven months old, I was walking and talking. I was apparently a very active child. I was in and out of the workshop. I had full reign of everything and everyone. The workshop was at the front part of our house, and the cutting table was near the wall. Then beside it stood the sewing machine where they sewed the tops of shoes, with the chair beside that. In front of those were low stools, and a long low table, where the men sat to work on the shoes.

So the men were working merrily in front of this

table, when I decided to drag my little stool to the chair. I climbed onto the chair, then from the chair to the sewing machine, from the sewing machine to the cutting-table and started to merrily dance and dance and dance.

I think my mother or father had noticed and called out. I must have stepped off the table and fell into the lap of one of the men, (who had the knife pointing towards his chest to cut the sole of the shoe). They all had a fright and so did I. My mother made sure that the arrangement of the sewing machine and chair and so forth was pulled apart. It wasn't joined together anymore, so I couldn't climb up again. That was a near miss.

These are some of the stories I've been told by my mother, when she was in a good mood and wanted to remember things.

Now back to the time that I can remember. My brother was born in April 1941. The autumn of 1942 would have been about October-November, which is late autumn in Hungary, fairly cool. My father decided to move the family from Budapest back to their home town, Kiskunfélegyháza, where my mother and father were born. All our relatives lived there, grandma and my uncles and my aunty, from my mother's side. My Father's parents, brother and sister stayed in Budapest. He decided to sell and close up the business and move the family back to the country, because as he said, "The Germans are creating havoc in the world. There is a big war coming and I won't have my family starving. In a country town, there is always food to have and opportunities to manage a living." So, we packed up and we moved.

That move is what I remember most vividly. I was about two and a half years old, but when I think back, I can still see it like it was yesterday. The truck was an open flat-tail truck, like you'd use to move hay etc. The furniture was packed up into the back. My mother sat with the driver in the cabin, nursing my brother in her lap. I was sitting on the top of the truck in a big armchair, on my father's lap. He was telling me stories and showing me things to look for, such as birds and animals. I remember it was cool, but I wasn't cold sitting on Apuka's lap, I was having a wonderful time.

Well, that hundred and ten kilometres probably took us about four of five hours to get there.

Even today, many a time I have that picture of me sitting on my father's lap, amidst furniture, on the top of the truck and trudging along in that autumn weather. I still can see it. I still can feel it. I get emotional even now when I remember it.

Anyway we rented or bought (I don't know) a house next door to my grandma, (my mother's mother) that had two rooms and in-between in the middle was the kitchen and a big backyard. We had grandma's place as well, so we had lots of fun coming and going. Grandma still had ducks and geese and my brother and I had a great time playing and enjoying ourselves. We had cousins there as well. My big cousin Jancso, (whose family lived with Grandma) must have been about ten as he was eight years older than me. His big brother was much older and in high school, so it was really good fun for a couple of years, until the war came closer to Hungary.

My father decided that he would not open a business, as times were getting more difficult, so he became a travelling salesman. He started selling necessary bits and pieces into the surrounding small towns, not travelling too far away. He was selling shoelaces, elastic, sewing needles, sewing cottons, cigarette lighters, and all sorts of bits and pieces. He had a little tray that he would arrange his goods on, with ties, belts and various things hanging off it. He would put it on his neck, just like you would see in the old American films, where the young ladies, who worked in the bars, carried the cigarettes, on these trays. Well, his was a bigger tray that he carried and from which he sold many things, so he kept his family supported. I presume that was his main income of course, I had no idea at three or four how or what my father was making money from, but we lived quite comfortably.

On the opposite side of the street to us lived a couple of young girls, sixteen and eighteen and my mother had a couple of old girlfriends nearby, so we had a lot of people coming and going. It was lot of fun for us children.

Then, in 1943 my grandfather, (my father's father) died. I remember because that was the reason why we got dressed in best clothes and went in a car, back to Budapest, for his funeral. That's the first time I remember seeing my grandmother, (my father's mother) and his brother and his sister. His sister was already married and my uncle was at university.

On a side note:

My uncle could only go to university because my father researched and set up the family tree. By that time, the Germans had taken over Hungary. The new rules were you had to prove that you were not Jewish or had Jewish connections, to get into university. Because my grandfather and my father were in business the Jewish connection was assumed, he had to prove that we were not Jewish, so my uncle could have a place in the university.

So, my father decided to do their family tree, which he traced back to the beginning, all the way back to the first Kuhn's coming and settling in Hungary, and to one of the leaders called 'Dobos Vezeer'. (Dobos means 'drummer general').

Apparently, our family comes from the very first Hungarians (the Huns and Kuhns) that come over from the Ural Mountains (that's now Russia) from the 'stepper' and settled in Hungary in around the year 900. One of my ancestors was a high-ranking warlord, with the first Hungarian army that arrived in Hungary. That was a real buzz for the family to find out. Unfortunately all these documents, along with all my Father's books, got lost in the bombing.

My uncle got his place in the university. He was a very smart man who studied mechanical engineering and had top marks all along, so that wasn't a problem once his ancestry was confirmed.

The next thing I remember (not long after the funeral) was that the planes started to come and the bombs started to drop. My father wasn't called into the army. He was young enough, but he had an enlarged heart and that locked him out from the army. He was a boxer in his youth and that was when it was found out. That eventually was the cause of his passing.

The German army came and rushed through the towns, and shortly after the Hungarian soldiers rushed through the towns too. So, we as children didn't really take much notice of it. The only thing we knew is that when the siren went we had to go to the cellar. That was actually just a small dug out bunker that my father made in the backyard.

He dug it out and built it up a little on the top to a hump, so you could stand up in it. We had bedding, water and food plus kerosene lamps and candles, so we could spend some time in there, in reasonable comfort if needs be. It was quite big, originally it was used to be storage for potatoes and vegetables for the winter. So, when the siren went, Mum collected my brother and I, plus a couple of the young girls from nearby houses to come with us down to the cellar. My father went out to patrol the streets, finding people that needed help or were in trouble. Those bombs hit the railway station quite a few times (we didn't live very far from it) and my father helped to clear out the rubble. It was, for my mother, always a very anxious time, because she was always worried that something might happen to my father in these raids. He could have got shot, he could have been hit with a bomb, but he went out just the same, doing his humanitarian service.

Then the time came when the Russian army arrived, that must have been 1944, because the war officially ended in 1945 and that is the part of the war that I most vividly remember.

My new brother 1941

My parents wedding 1930

My parents and brother 1942
(before we left Budapest)

With Anna the girl my parents taken in to the family

With my Father 1940

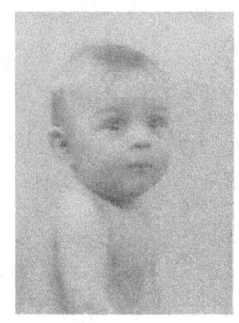

at 6 month old

2

Following on from where I left off, somewhere in 1943/44, I don't remember much of the German army marching through. Then came the Hungarian army after them (or so I was told.) I was obviously too small, so I really didn't take much notice of it. All I really remember mostly from these times is when the Russian army arrived in the town and took over. There were soldiers put into every house to accommodate them. Our house had two rooms, and three army officers commandeered the second room. My mother had to look after them by cooking, cleaning, washing for them, serving them meals and generally looking after them like a housekeeper. A lot of the officers were reasonably educated and nice people. They appreciated my mother's cooking, which was always excellent, and they brought us all the ingredients that we didn't have around the house.

I found out later on that they had taken it from other people in the town - because the Russians wanted to eat well, we also had good food all the time.

This 'reasonable' time quickly changed when the second wave of the army came, as they were more rough and ready. They looked like peasant-type people, they didn't know basic hygiene and were very rough and tough. My grandmother had women soldiers put into her spare room, and one of them wanted to cook something. Grandma would not give up her pots, so the solder went out to the back where old stuff was piled up. She found a 'potty' and used it to cook - she did not recognise it for what it was. They called everyone 'burzuy' (rich), because we did not have the animals living inside the house with us. Lots of things they did not recognise.

That was the time when they started collecting the men to take them for work. As it turned out, not for work but as political prisoners, transported to Russia. We were very scared that my father would be taken, so we hid him up in the loft: a space between the ceiling and the roof where we normally kept the straw.

My mother made like a little cubbyhole behind the straw, with comfortable bedding, a kerosene lamp and lots of books for my father. The idea was that he would be happy up there, reading quietly and wouldn't want to be on the street and maybe getting caught. It was my job to run up on the ladder and take him his breakfast, lunch and evening meal, and when I went up there, he would eat his dinner or lunch or whatever and read stories for me. I spent most of my day up in the loft with him, which was really very pleasant and very quiet, and I loved it. As it happens, he taught me to read as soon as I was about two I believe, I had my first book given to me for my 3rd birthday, but by then I could read the stories by myself.

He instilled in me the love of books and stories from a very young age. I've always loved learning and I always loved books, for as long as I can remember. Books were and are my life. So, we spent possibly a couple of weeks up in the loft, until these people went through and left the town. Then it settled back to 'normal' (if you call that normal,) with the soldiers living in the house.

We always had officers living in our house, and at one stage I remember about 4 or 5 very rough looking soldiers coming into the house. Our room was the front room, and we had two big wardrobes that were part of the bedroom furniture. My mother had been given a big tapestry of Jesus at the last supper, for a wedding present. It was a very big one, and must have covered the bed head completely, over the big twin beds. She was always very protective of it, so we packed it up and put it behind the wardrobes.

For some reason or another, the soldiers must have realized that it was there. One evening they herded us into the room, my parents and my brother and I, and held a gun at my father's head and started to yell at us. They could only say "picture, picture, picture" and my father didn't really know what they wanted. Then they started pointing behind the wardrobes and my father said, "It looks like they want your picture!"

My mother started to carry on saying, "Oh no, we cannot give it to them."

My father said very quietly, "Make up your mind. Which is more important, that I stay alive or you keep your picture?"

So with that, my mother collapsed onto the floor, didn't say anything and my father dragged out the picture and put it on the wall where it usually hung above the bed. We expected they would take it, maybe sell it or, destroy it, as we did not know what they wanted it for.

The next minute these 5 or 6 rough-looking soldiers dropped their guns down, bowed their heads, went on their knees by the bed, and prayed! It was the most extraordinary feeling for me - I was a small child, 4 or 5, something like that, but I can remember them kneeling there and praying. My mother and father were absolutely flabbergasted about what just happened.

So, the picture stayed up and the soldiers came every night and prayed in front of that picture.

The following wave of the army meant we had 3 or 4 different lots staying with us. There were again officers in the room and my mother looking after them and it was Christmas, I think it must have been 1944 my memory isn't too clear. I remember it was a cold evening, and I was sitting in the window ledge, cuddling my book, because this old house had what you called a mud-packed wall, which is about 60-70 centimetres thick. It's packed up and it holds the heat and the cold very well and provides a nice seat.

All, of a sudden, I heard some commotion in the backyard, and a pig started to squeal. We had a pig, and I don't know how we got it, but it was ready for slaughter. The next thing I know, these officers rushed out to the backyard, screaming and yelling, and a shot was fired. As I watched, one of the soldiers was trying to drag a fairly large sized pig across the paling fence: obviously he didn't have a pig so he'd decided to take our pig. But he had miscalculated and didn't realise our house had officers staying in it. That was the usual way to provide for the families they lived with by taking from someone else.

So, our officers dashed out, grabbed him, and beat him up. I was sitting in that window and watched that man, horribly beaten up by these officers, and then they put the pig back in the pen. A few minutes later they walked back in as if nothing happened, and after dinner that night, they gave me a beautiful doll as a present, and I started to cry. I didn't want that doll; I didn't want to see them. I was very, very unhappy. Somehow, in my mind, they got that doll for me because they realized I had seen the beating, and I never played with that doll. I didn't really want it. I don't know how my mother explained the story, but I was put to bed very quickly, very smartly. These are the kind of memories that stay with you from the wartime.

Another memory, which is pretty horrid, is, when we were in a bunker, with some of the neighbour's teenage girls (during the bombing, we had bedding there and lights and everything, and we used to go down there and hide while the bombing was going on, or when the solders had their drinking rampages). The soldiers had been out drinking and carrying on in the street. They pulled the covering open and 2 burly, big Russian soldiers, (who were terribly drunk and not very steady on their feet,) brandished their guns, and demanded to take the girls. They used to say, "For just a little bit of work, just a little bit of work," which of course they didn't want them to work at all. They would have been assaulted and raped as so many were.

They started pulling the girls out, and my mother jumped up and stood in front of this huge Russian soldier, (my mother being 5 foot nothing, a plump little lady), and with both of her fists, started hammering on the huge soldier's chest and screaming at them, "Get out of here, get out of here, you useless so and so!"

She screamed and yelled, and after a couple of minutes, obviously they must have gotten scared because they went away. When my father heard the story he was most upset. He said, "What a stupid thing. They could have beaten you up, killed you or anything!"

But she said, "I wasn't going to let the girls be taken away and assaulted or raped. I wasn't going to let them do that to my friends."

So, it was a bit of an exciting night, that night in the bunker.

So, these are the kinds of things I remember from my life as a 4 or 5-year-old.

In September '45, I went and attended school by the nuns, who at that time were not in their habits. They were wearing street clothes, but it was convent school, and I was supposed to start school there. I don't think I attended more than a few weeks, then we moved back to Budapest. Obviously, by then the war had officially finished. Peace was declared for Hungary on the 4th of April 1945, Hungary was freed, but attached to the Soviet block, so they said, "This is freedom." After that time, I don't know how much later, we moved back to Budapest.

Some years earlier, after my grandfather passed away, my father promised to complete his orders and commitments. So when we moved back to Budapest, my father was going to finish off all the orders and work, do a final inventory and sell all that was to be sold. Then he was going to distribute what was there, between his brother, sister and my grandmother.

Both my mother and father worked in the business for a while. We didn't have our own place and there was very little possibility for us to have a flat of our own. Our grandparents had a house but it was bombed during the war. Only one room and a pantry was somehow left undamaged, but most of the house was bombed. My father had his library in that house, with more than 1,000 books, which were all burnt.

He was heart-broken but as he said, "Life goes on, and we start with new books."

Anyway, we were sharing a large flat with a Jewish family, who came back. Luckily their flat was still intact, there was no damage, and they had three rooms. So, we got one room and a kitchenette from them, and we shared the facilities. There were four of us, plus one of the girls from the old town, who had come to help my mother with the housework and look after us, so Mum could go to work with my father.

As soon as we got there, I was enrolled in school, and I loved it. It wasn't too far to go; the school was slightly damaged but there were quite a few classrooms still intact. There were quite a lot of children in the class, and I suppose there weren't enough teachers. I can remember the Red Cross providing us with a breakfast of porridge, (which I'd never had in my life before). There were big plates of porridge with sugar in it, that was absolutely marvellous. I loved it. I don't know what else we had, but the porridge stayed in my mind. That kind of porridge I've never really been able to create again, because that was something special, cooked in the big pot and fairly gooey, but I loved it.

Food was quite a problem after the war. I remember that during the war, (while we lived in the country) several times my mother packed up backpacks and a basket. We put her up on the top of the train to travel to Budapest, to take food to my grandma as well as my uncle and aunty. She had a few horrific times on those trips, but we had food and they were very much in need of it, a lot of people had gone hungry in the cities.

While we were sharing in the house something very unpleasant happened to me. I had always been a pretty dumb little kid, because I always did what I was being asked to do. Anybody bigger than me could ask me to do something and I would do it happily. The couple had a teenage son, who must have been about 13 or 14. He was a big boy as far as I was concerned, and he sometimes gave me dollies and played games with me. Sometimes he helped me by getting my books ready or helped me to sort out my bits and pieces, that I'd collected as toys.

Anyway, we were quite good friends, and he said to me one day, "Ica," (everybody called me Ica which is a cosy name for Helen), "Ica go into our room, my mother's bag is on the chair, and get me a note from it." (I wouldn't have known what kind of a note it was or what is represented,) "Just get that note for me, and I will get some dollies."

So, I never thought anything of it and went and got the money out of the purse. I gave it to him and continued to happily play with my toys. A very short time later, my mother absolutely went off her rocker. She screamed and yelled, "What have I brought up, a dirty little cheat, and a thief. Stealing money from the neighbours, how dare you!" She grabbed me, shook me, and started hitting me. Luckily for me, my father just dashed in and grabbed me out of her hands. She virtually had to be restrained by my father. She was quite hysterical and absolutely horrified by the idea that I had stolen.

Apparently, what happened is the lady found out that the money was missing, accused her son, and of course he'd then said said, "No, no, no, Ica did it."

My father said, "Hang on a minute, and ask her what happened."

"No, no, no she's stolen money!" My mother was really wild and screamed and yelled at me. Then, my father turned around and said. "What did actually happen?"

I said, "The boy said to go and get that note and give it to him and I did."

My father was really very upset about it, and I think he had quite an argument with my mother about it. My father did not subscribe to the fact that my mother hit me first without checking out the truth. There was definitely no hitting, no discrimination without proper cause, no screaming and yelling at kids. So, he was really very strict about it, and he was upset and had an argument with my mother, I believe he had a few words with the lady as well. Within a very, very short time, possibly a week or so, we were moving house because he said, "We're not going to share with anyone, and I'm not going to allow the family to be put into this situation."

So he found a flat for us, which was at the edge of the town. We were the last house on the corner, and after our house were the market gardens.

The front section of this house had been bombed. It was an L-shaped house, which had two rooms in the front and then two rooms in the L shape. The owners, an old couple, had propped up part of the front section, creating one room in which to live. The back part, that was not damaged, had one room and a kitchen that was for us. The toilet and water were outside. We rented it from them.

Some time before we moved in, (this was late Autumn, early Winter,) there must have been a big frost, because the water pipe burst and the water sprayed the walls, the fences and the backyard. Everything froze. We couldn't get into the back yard because the gate opened inwards and it looked like a frozen lake, (it wasn't actually a garden, just a bitumen yard). We couldn't open the gate because everything was covered in about 5 centimetres of ice, so my father had to go and borrow a pickaxe, jump the fence, hack out enough from the ice so we could open the gate inwards. Then he got to hacking around the kitchen door. Then the next thing he did was organize for a little wood/coal stove, (actually just a tin construction of a small stove) then he made a big fire in that stove so the rooms heated up. We didn't sleep there that night because it wasn't possible.

But my father stayed and heated the flat all night, hacking off the ice as it melted off the walls. We then moved into that flat. My father, mother, brother and I slept in the one bedroom and the young girl Manci, (she was about 17 or 18) slept in the kitchen on a little couch. We settled into living there.

That was the flat that some years later, (around 10-11 years later) I left Hungary from. My mother was still living in that flat with my brother for years after I left. That was the way we lived.

I was going to school, which was a long way away. It was two tram stops and a big hike from the flat to the main street, so it was quite a long walk but we managed to get to school, and started living a normal life. My father then started his own business; he liquidated everything for my Grandmother and finalized Grandfather's business commitments. Then he started his own business, and my mom and dad worked very hard to start it up, picking up old contacts etc..

After the business started, things started to get better. We had a good domestic market and they were exporting, as well as serving old clients. So it was looking reasonably good in my eyes. I was a very happy little girl.

Our first Christmas (in 1946) in our own place in Budapest, if I remember rightly), was especially a very, very happy one. My father, on Christmas Eve, as it started to get dark, (which in Europe was by 4-5 pm) used to take us, my brother and I, and walk us around the town in Budapest. We would look in windows where the lights were on and we could see the Christmas trees, where Father Christmas had already been. We went into the churches where my father would explain to us all the paintings and architecture. We didn't really go in for praying, he wasn't really religious, he just appreciated the art, the peace and beauty of the churches.

We would walk around for a couple of hours in town and by the time we got home, the room-door was locked. We couldn't get in and that was because we had to have dinner and the explanation was that we couldn't get in because Father Christmas must be busy in the bedroom and had locked the door. So, we were all in the kitchen having our dinner, and just as we were about to finish, the bell rang. Little bells rang in the bedroom, so we dashed to the door, and the door miraculously opened and there was a big Christmas tree, up to the ceiling, packed with all sorts of beautiful things. It had lovely glitters and glass balls, as well as candles and many parcels underneath it.

Well, we never quite figured out how my parents did it. Obviously the Christmas tree was decorated and done up while we were out walking. When the bell went, it must have been the old chap next door who rang the bell, but anyway there was lots of excitement. We had lots of toys because my uncle, (my father's brother) had a toy factory. Just after he finished his engineering degree during the war, he started a little toy factory. We received some of the slightly imperfect toys for Christmas. I got the most wonderful doll, (that had a porcelain head, hands and legs) which was dressed beautifully. It was absolutely marvellous, and I was thrilled to bits. That's when I first saw oranges on that Christmas tree. It was one of the happiest Christmases of my life that I can remember. It was just magnificent. Everybody was happy, the house smelled of Christmas tree, the cakes, the candles, it was just magic, absolutely magic.

Some months later, Mum went to visit grandma for a couple of days and with Apuka I cooked my first meal. In the kitchen next to the stove, was a stool and then the table. My father said how about we cook lunch? So, he put a small stool in front of the stove and the table, sat himself on the stool and told me to get this and that. By him telling me what to do, I was jumping from stool to stool and so we cooked something (can't remember what) for lunch. When Mom got home Apuka proudly said 'You can go any time now, I have my daughter who cooks for me.' So, I have been cooking since I was six years old!

My next memories are not particularly so good. It was everyday life, going on. My mother and father were in the business, working all day. We went to school. I started my second class in 1947 September, and in October I got scarlet fever. Well, that meant that I had to be in isolation. My father wouldn't allow the doctor to take me to the hospital, because he said the hospitals hadn't enough medication, not enough nurses and there wasn't enough care. In isolation, it would be bad for me, so, he said he would be the one who stays with me and looks after me. My mother and brother went and stayed with some friends or relatives, I don't know where they stayed, but a few times I remember them coming to the window and waving at me.

But I was a pretty sick girl, so our young girl Manci stayed on. She did the cooking and looked after us, but of course my mother and brother couldn't come because I was infectious. Luckily for me, by that time, penicillin was invented and my father was in a financial position to be able to secure penicillin for me. Scarlet fever can heal with it pretty quickly, but I didn't get better as quickly as they hoped. Very shortly after, I got what they called a rheumatic heart muscle infection, which meant I was in a very high fever for days on end. I had nightmares, screamed, and yelled. My father could hardly hold me down; he said afterward that he needed all his strength to restrain me.

I remember one of those nightmares, that there was a big, black bird, like a crow. Really big, and this black bird was sitting on the end of my bed. I kept screaming, "He's going to take me away Apuka, he's going to take me away!" I still remember that. I sometimes see it in front of me, as if I was a visitor in the room looking in, I see the bird, me laying in bed and my father holding me down in bed as I struggle in my dreams.

Well, that fever eventually dissipated, but the result was that for 8 weeks I had received twice daily penicillin injections. I was so weak that I could not feed myself. I had to be fed and turned. I couldn't even turn around in bed; I just didn't have the energy to do anything. I couldn't even lift my hand; it was a very, very hard time to overcome. I had a wonderful teacher, and my classmates had written little colour get-well cards for me. I used to get 5-6 of them, every day. My father used to bring me these cards and we kept up the schoolwork every day for weeks on end, until I got better. When I could get back to school, I had missed possibly three-quarters of the year, but because I was already ahead of the class in many ways, (my reading and writing was already advanced,) I got to the next class. If they had done what they do nowadays (when you skip a class), they would have skipped me 1 or 2 at least, but I stayed on. I still managed to get a very good result for that year.

It was just as I was getting better that summer came and we were taken to stay with grandma for a couple of weeks. Back in the village, we played in the fields with my cousins. We had a really fantastic time. I don't think I wore shoes for weeks on end, we just rumbled around in the fields, we climbed the fruit trees and ate what we wanted. So, we had a lovely holiday.

Then the following year, somewhere between late March and early April, my father had a heart attack. He was a very sick man. and this time I was the one that stayed with him most of the time, read him stories and tried to keep his morale up. He was getting better. We had high hopes that all would be well and he would be able to go back to work shortly. We had, a couple of times, walked one block, then two blocks, then we walked as far as the shop. So, he was getting better, and things were looking up.

That's when my life's nightmare started, because his brother turned up at the shop one day. My mother wasn't there unfortunately, so instead of waiting or leaving a message or whatever, he marched back to our home and had a mighty argument with my father. Well I don't know if it was an argument, I was told my uncle screamed at my father and upset him so badly that he had another heart attack that night. He never recovered. 10 days later he passed away.

I believe the argument was about a very small amount of money, that they had received a demand from the tax office and apparently, my grandmother demanded that my father take care of it. In Hungary, at that time, you would get a letter from the tax department, claiming that back-taxes were owed. This happened regularly after 1947, after the communists had taken over Hungary completely. This meant that when the department or the government didn't have enough money, they just made up ideas that anybody who owned or ever owned a business (where Burzuy = rich automatically) could be slugged with back taxes or fines, or whatever they thought off. If you were working, you could get fined and money taken out of your wages. They just did what they wanted and you couldn't argue with it. If you were lucky they let you off, or you made arrangements to pay it off, because you didn't have the money. Then eventually it would disappear, but it was a very unlawful time,

My father told his brother, "Look I have all the documentation. Everything was taken care of. Not a penny was owed anywhere, that is not correct, that can't be. We both worked over a year for nothing. We didn't even take extra wages out, only the bare minimum for living. We can't do anymore, you guys can either pay it off or do whatever you like, but just leave me out of it."

Anyway, my father got so upset that night, after his brother's visit, he had the second heart attack. And unfortunately, 10 days later on the 6th of May 1948, he passed away, around 6 o'clock in the morning. We had two big single beds, side by side, where my mother and father slept and my brother and I had a couch in the other corner of the room. But because he was in the big bed, my mother was sitting up with him. I was lying in the other bed beside him holding his hand. He asked my mother for a cigarette and my mother started to say, "You can't, you shouldn't be smoking, you're not supposed to be smoking."

But she lit a cigarette, he took one puff, squeezed my hands and then he was gone. That's how I lost my father!

My beloved father was the only man who ever really loved me. The only person in my family that ever truly cared about me. That was the hardest time in my life and even now, 70 years later it's still unbearable. The loss of him is still heart breaking. He was my all. He was the biggest blessing in my life.

The funeral came, and at the funeral parlour, when my uncle and grandma arrived, I'd become hysterical. I screamed, I ran at them grabbing at my uncle: "Get away from here, you killed my father, you murderers, you killed my father!" They just couldn't hold me back. I would not stop screaming until my grandmother and my uncle left.

We buried my father and that was the last time I saw either one of them. I haven't heard from them, I haven't spoken to them and don't know anything about them. As far as I am concerned they were buried that day for me, because they were the reason, their greed and their selfishness, was the reason I lost my father. My mother, of course, was absolutely shattered, understandably, and really didn't function terribly well for a little while. My aunty, (her sister) had virtually taken over and had to tell her what to do.

(I have to stop for a moment this is still a very painful memory.)

A few months before my father got sick, very early in 1947, my uncle, (Mom's sister's husband, Uncle Stephen), came back from the prisoner of war camp in Siberia. He was captured in Germany in 1943 and had spent 5 years there. Because of some soldier exchange, he was lucky enough to get back home.

We were there when he came back. We travelled to Kiskunfélegyháza to greet him with the whole family. My aunty had prepared a great big feast for everyone because it was such a big thing that my uncle came back. His 14-year-old daughter hadn't seen him for 5 years so it was really a big family occasion. He got off the train; a broken down, skin and bone, old man. He used to be a very handsome man, (which he became later on again.) We took him home from the train, but my aunty was warned by the Red Cross doctors that he cannot be fed more than a couple of potatoes and a bit of rice for a considerable time. If we fed him proper food, normal food, that everybody ate he would die, because he was starved for so long, living on virtually nothing. So, we had to pack away all the food and we all sat down with boiled potatoes at the table. No butter, no lard, nothing with it, just plain boiled potatoes, everybody got a potato to welcome him home. He started to cry saying: "I thought if I came home you would love me. Now you're going to starve me as well!"

It was a hearth breaking thing for a 7-year-old to see her uncle crying that he is hungry and we were starving him, not giving him food. We had to eat in secret away from him. It was a very hard time for them I'm sure. My uncle and aunty had a business before the war, transporting goods with horses on big open wagons. All sorts of goods all over the country. They had quite a few wagons. Most of it was sold off or taken by the army or whatever, so there wasn't much left for my aunty to live on. My uncle, of course, couldn't work for quite some time. My mother and father naturally stayed by them. Financially we were quite well-off; the business was going well, so we were able to help them financially, to maintain their living standard.

In May 1948, after my father died, school finished in June and we went for a holiday again. This time to my auntie's, instead of my grandma's, for a couple of weeks. Then we went back to Budapest and my aunty came to and explained to my mother that there was no way she could look after us if she had to look after the business full time as well. My aunty decided we had to live with her and that we would go to school at her place. Convinced Mum, she need not pay the house girl, she would pay my aunty instead, to look after us. Then she wouldn't have to worry about the housework and everything else. She would come every few weeks by train to visit us and then, in summer holidays, we could go back home and try to manage on our own. Anyway, she talked my mother into it and we were shipped back to live with her in Kiskunfélegyháza.

Well, it wasn't exactly a Christmas holiday living with my aunty. My mother paid well for our keep, (about double what my uncle earned). She now had the money, but still, she could not get certain things, supplies where rationed (even if you had the money) because they were all on the black-market food specialties; like flour, rice and butter. Things that were really everyday items, but when the country is in dire need, they're not available.

Australians may not know it very well, but in

England they would understand, because everything was on rations. Wages were never certain to get paid, money was scarce, life was uncertain.

As my mother had a well-running business and plenty of money, she could afford things that my aunty couldn't. So, she bought everything that the world could offer, or the family could need, to my aunt's house. They and we had the best of materials for clothes and we had the best handmade shoes. That was mother's business, so we got the shoes no problem, but the material was hard to get. We had all tailor-made clothes and we were beautifully dressed, everyone was. When nobody had seen rice anywhere, my mother bought a big 10 kilo bag and things like that, which was absolutely out of this world. So, my aunty and her family lived jolly well on that. My cousin, who at 14 was 6 years older than me, was just going into high school and so she had the latest fashion. She was "Miss Mack", when nobody in town had nylon stockings, she had American nylon stockings for everyday wear and she lived very well. She totally played up as the princess.

They had a house with two rooms, a kitchen and an extra room, which was supposed to be used as a pantry but they used it as kitchenette for cooking and general use. Because my aunty was a manic cleaner, everything had to be always spic and span. Spring-cleaning was a nightmare, she had polished ordinary floors and we could only walk in socks into the rooms, because the polish would be ruined otherwise. Every week we had to put the brushes on our feet and brush and polish the floors, and then polish the brass pots and stuff hanging in the kitchen, yet the kitchen was never used. The stove was polished, the brass pots were polished, we had pots and pans in the pantry where we cooked and ate and virtually lived in, but we weren't allowed to go in to the main rooms because you couldn't get anything dirty. We were only allowed in to sleep and on special occasions, or when my mother or visitors came.

The first room was off the kitchen, which then opened into the second room. The first room was my cousin Martha's. She had her own bed with some white girly furniture. In the big rooms, my uncle and aunty had twin beds which were pushed together. At the end of the beds was a couch, where my brother and I slept. My head was one end, his head was the other end and that was our place.

It was my job before school to make everybody's breakfast, do the school lunches and pack the school bags with books, according to the time-table then, get everybody off in the morning to go to school. When we came back from school there was lunch, which my aunty cooked. I had to wash the dishes and clean up after everyone. In Hungary, you mainly had a cooked lunch and then a light dinner. After I cleaned the kitchen, (actually the pantry) washed the dishes and packed everything away, I then had to prepare things for dinner, (if necessary) and wash the floors. If there was washing to be done, I did it and then I helped with the ironing. Sometimes late in the afternoon, I was allowed to sit down and do my homework. There would be a problem if I didn't get top marks at school. If I just got the second-best mark, I was screamed and yelled at and told that I'm a "stupid, useless, girl" I had to be the top of the class so as to not to bring shame on the family.

Generally, it wasn't a problem, but about when I was 10, my eyesight started to go really bad. It became so bad that within a year or so, I couldn't read the blackboard. I was sitting in the first row and I still couldn't read it and the teacher said, "You can get up and go to the blackboard to read it."

So, I was allowed to go especially to the board and read the writing if I couldn't see it. I kept telling aunty that my eyes were bad. I couldn't see and I was virtually writing with my nose on the paper. I was just told that I was being "hysterical, because I always want to be difficult and different than anybody else." She said I was making it up and I didn't need glasses. "Nobody in our family had glasses and here is my grandmother in her 80s and she doesn't wear glasses. If she doesn't need glasses, then you don't need glasses either!"

My chores included washing-up every day, helping with the small hand-washing that I could do and then at the big wash (which happened every two-three weeks.) I had to carry water from another well, because the well that we had in the backyard wasn't for drinking. There was no tap water in country towns, (to do the washing) as the water was too 'hard' to wash the fine things that my cousin had to wear, like silks, nylon and so forth. I brought home two ten-litre cans of water every morning. I had to bring another two at lunchtime. At that stage I was still not supposed to do any exercises, I was still recovering from my inflamed heart but that didn't make any difference to Aunty, that was my job. My brother had to do the water carrying as well, but most of the other jobs he couldn't be bothered doing, so he just disappeared. The chaffing he got afterward didn't worry him, as he really didn't care. But what he didn't do, I had to do.

One of the jobs, which I absolutely hated, was washing monthly-rags, because at that time we didn't have sanitary napkins, they were linen pieces that the girls used. These had to be soaked, boiled, washed and cleansed for the next time they needed it, so every time menstruation came along, there was a bucket of dirty rags which I had to wash for my 16-year-old cousin. This didn't go down very well in my mind. My Uncle's health improved, he got a better job, and so he went to work in a shop. He finished up working as the manager of a clothing shop.

Then, aunty got pregnant again and there was a baby on the way. I was 10, my cousin 16 and then along came a baby boy. My cousin was absolutely mad, how could her mother bring such shame on her, getting pregnant when she is a grown-up woman already? What a thing to do? She was hysterical; she carried on that way for months. The result was that she got many presents, in fact, anything she wanted. Just to pacify my cousin, my mother would buy her extravagant stuff that nobody in town had seen, Aunty was 'an influential' person, in a small town. She believed she was a 'leading' personality', so therefore her family had to have things that others could not get, be it the latest fashion, or the best of everything. She was always trying to be better than others. She made an awful scene with a tailor one year. My mother got a pattern from an American magazine for a coat, (for my cousin), which she'd had made up with the tailor. He however had the audacity to make a similar one, not exactly the same, but a similar one for his own daughter. My aunt virtually wanted to tear it off the poor girl. She made a terrible scene: "How dare they have something that only our daughter should have!" So that was a type of thing she would do, always having to be the best in every possible way. She was keeping up with the Jones's, however she was the 'Jones' of this medium sized town. She was 'Mrs Bucket'.

My mother made sure that there was always a couple of pigs to be slaughtered in the wintertime, so we had meat all the time. We had the best (even when you could not get it in the official market). We never went short of anything at that time, we had all the sausages, plus hams, anything that was from the slaughtering, which was then taken into the loft to dry.

One summer Aunty decided to make some plum jam. Somehow, she got maybe a ton of plums and we made plum jam. It was stored in big wooden, industrial-type boxes. You could slice it, it was thick and jellied, because it had a lot of sugar in it. We had lots and lots of plum jam. My brother and I had to take plum jam sandwiches for school lunches every single day, all year round. But my cousin had salami, sausage, liverwurst, and all sorts of goodies from the larder. So, a couple of times I had gone to the loft to get some sausages or liverwurst or something for her and I would get an extra piece; I put an extra piece of sausage into my brother's and my lunches. Now and again Aunty went up to the loft too and screamed and yelled, "What happened, somebody's stealing the sausages!" Well, it wasn't stealing, I was taking mine because my mother paid for it, but that's not how she saw it. From that day till today, I really cannot stomach plum jam. For two years I had plum jam sandwiches for every school lunch, so one can not forget those things easily, as they were not really happy memories from that time in my life.

Every 3-4 weeks, my mother came for a visit and I would tell her about the things that happened. She was made a big fuss of, Marta knew how to run around after her and butter her up, because my mother was the source of all her goodies. So of course aunty was always nice to her to. My uncle was a nice man all the time; he was always very kind to us. And every now and again, I tried to get my mother on my own, to tell her that I really shouldn't have to carry the water cans, as they were too heavy for me. I shouldn't have to get up in the morning to get everybody's lunches ready, an hour earlier. I shouldn't need to be a servant. When the baby was born, if he cried during the night, who got up to it? I had to get up to it. As soon as I came home from school, I had to take on the babysitting, look after the baby, take the baby for airing and what have you, change the nappy, wash the baby's clothes. These were all my jobs. I was virtually the one who brought up my cousin for the first two years of his life. His sister wouldn't even look at him, let alone, change him. His mother did it, if she had to, but if I was on hand, it was, "Go look after the baby".

So, when I said anything, it was always explained away by my aunty as: "I'm trying to make trouble, I am lying, I'm doing this, I,m doing that," My mother never believed or supported me against my aunty.

Another memory that stands out was; for one Christmas I asked for a sled. Wintertime has a lot of snow in Hungary and I would have really loved to have a nice, sleek, modern sled. At Christmas, a big fanfare was made and Aunty made everybody come out to the porch to have a look, "This is your Christmas present,"

In the passage was a big, clumpy wooden sleigh that looked like it was made 100 years ago. It was heavy, big, clumsy looking and old- fashioned. It was absolutely nothing like the new sleds that were around at the time. Being told, "This is very special, it's handmade no-one has anything like it," didn't help. I was so very upset; I didn't want to say anything at Christmas. I wanted to crawl into the corner; I didn't want to talk to anybody. I was so disappointed that my mother allowed herself to be talked into having this made and buying this monster behemoth of a thing. I don't know what her reasoning was because she could have got one possibly half the price. But now I'd been given what aunty decided I should have. To say I was disappointed is an understatement.

I was looking forward to the summer, because on summer holidays for 6- 8-weeks, we spent the time with Mum in Budapest, which was fantastic. I did the washing, the cooking, and the cleaning for the three of us. My mother gave me a certain amount of money, so I did the shopping, I went to the market, I did all the housework and after that I could sit around, read or go to the bath, just be myself. It was wonderful. The summers were absolutely wonderful and I thought. "Why can't we do this all the time?"

So, I think that is when my mind started to conceive the plan about how to end the time with my aunty.

(L-R) Maca Márta Jancsó Mum with me
in the back standing Granma
Kiskun-

Maca, Márta, Mum
Jancsó & me

My Farther (L) with his new
enterprise 1943-44

1 Million Pengő Value = 1 Egg
Inflation Currenci in 1946

Starting school
Joska 1st me 2nd Class
September 1946

My Mother (centre) with staff at our shop 1952 (could still see the bullet holes on the walls)

My pretty young Mother 1952   Holiday with best friend & family at Balaton 1955

3

Following on from my childhood memories of the life with my aunty, (which wasn't a very happy time), my brother and I both had to excel in school. My brother was always smart, but terribly lazy and he always just wanted to play. Even when he started first class, he used to just go out and play and not worry about homework. Then late in the evening, after dinner, homework came out. He cried and carried on, screamed, yelled "I can't do it" and finished up in fits. Both of my parents lost their patience: Mum would say, "Come on Ica, just do his homework, as he needs to go to bed." So I did most of his homework in the first year, but then my father put his foot down and said, "No. He has to do his own work, whatever he gets, otherwise he'll never learn to read and write."

But with my aunty when we were there, homework for him was the first thing he had to do, otherwise, he couldn't go out to play, so he was a good student. Without really very much effort on my part, I managed to be top of the class.

I said I had problems with my eyes when I reached about 9-10 years of age, which became a serious by the time I was 11.

There was no mention about taking me to have my eyes checked. My aunty refused and convinced mother that it was just a phase with me, so I wasn't believed. So in the summer of 1951, when we went to Budapest to stay with Mum for our summer holiday, I was really just about blind. I could hardly see, right up close, in front of me, half a meter from my face, I just saw blurry things. As it happened, I was on the tram going to the shop to be with my mother and prepare the lunch or whatever. The tram slowed down a bit (if you don't see, it feels like it stops) and I thought if it slows down, this is the stop. So as it slowed, I stepped off the tram and right in front of a great big truck. Next thing I knew, there were screeching brakes and everybody had a nervous breakdown. This burly truck driver rushed up to me and started screaming and shaking me: "You stupid kid, you stupid kid, you nearly got yourself killed and I would be in trouble and my family would lose their father," and so forth. "Do you realize that I could be in jail if I hurt you? Didn't you see the car?"

And I said, "What car?"

It was about a meter away from my face. He said, "Do you see this?" And he held up something.

I said, "No, I can't really say I can see it, it's a blur."

He said, "Oh my God this kid is blind! Where do you live? Where are your parents?"

I told him where my mother's shop was. So he bundled me into the truck and drove me there (it was only a couple of streets away). He made an awful fuss and screamed and yelled at my mother. What an irresponsible parent she was. How on earth could she let a blind kid wander around the street without any assistance, and so forth...

My mother actually got quite a shock. She hadn't taken any notice before, she had just accepted my auntie's assurance that I wanted to be fancy and different, and not like anybody else in the family. So the result was that I was taken to an eye specialist (actually to the eye and ear hospital), where I had a thorough check-up. The specialist declared that if they had waited 6 months more, I would have definitely been blind. The nerves in my eyes had been really badly damaged because of scarlet fever and the rheumatic fever. I had glasses virtually within half an hour after the examination.

That was brilliant, because from then on I was able to see normally. I could read again, as by this time I was very distressed, as I didn't have the energy to read very much because it hurt. I had to have the book right in front of my eyes. So, I got my glasses and when we went back to aunty, and my mother told my aunty what had happened, she said: "Oh well, now she can be special, as no one in the family has glasses, even Grandma doesn't need any"

All these things play on my mind at different times.

I was in Grade 6 and my cousin was in Matriculation. When we were close to finishing the year, I heard big lectures about, "You got yourself fancy glasses now, there's absolutely no reason for you to have one black mark or even a greyish mark on your exam papers, because you have to be the top of the class!"

Because of the occupation, we had to learn Russian as a second language. For two years, I'd been learning Russian, and it just wasn't working for me. I couldn't for the life of me grasp the Russian language. As it turned out, I learned Russian for 5 years, but I don't understand two words, possibly thank you and a couple of words that might come back to me, I couldn't remember the alphabet, I was absolutely useless, I just didn't want to know.

Anyway, for Russian, I got the second best mark because the teacher just didn't want to ruin my report. She said, "By rights I shouldn't let you pass into the next class, but everything else is on the top so you just go ahead. But please don't tell anybody who taught you Russian!"

So I took home the end of the year report and there was this second-best mark, and my aunty went absolutely berserk. She called me all sorts of names, how I was a lazy so and so, blah, blah, blah. Anyway, that was OK I didn't really care what she said. My cousin Martha then finished her matriculation. There wasn't much talk about how she did, as nobody had seen a report card or book. We had a small book like a passport that had every year's results written in. I was determined to find out what her marks were, because of the carrying on about how I got a bad mark in Russian. And somehow or other, I heard on the grapevine from other kids, that my cousin was registered for the end of summer, for a second examination for her matriculation. As it happened, she had flunked three very big subjects. I managed to find her report book, which was hidden on the top of the wardrobe in a box, that had confirmed her results as 'not satisfactory'.

When my mother came to take us to Budapest for a holiday, I made up my mind that I'd make my big announcement that I knew Martha had flunked her matriculation and that she had to do this second set of exams. I refused to be treated badly by aunty any more. I'd had enough of that kind of life. When we'd been back in Budapest for a couple of weeks I just told my mother that I wasn't going back to my aunty. The alternative was if I didn't go to my aunty, I'd have to go to an orphanage. The orphanage always had such a bad reputation.

I said to my mother. "I don't care. I rather go to an orphanage than go back there. I don't see why I should go back, be the maid to my auntie and her daughter, a babysitter for her son when I can do the same work here instead. I can do the cooking, the cleaning, and shopping, the washing, the ironing. We don't need anybody else, the very small amount of work around the house I can do. I have the abilities, I can manage the house, we can be perfectly good and you can even save money. I'm not going back!"

My mother virtually was put on the spot, because my aunty demanded that we go back and I refused to. It was a hassle, I had to fight hard, and at the finish of it, there was a big argument and I was blamed for it all. My mother and aunty stopped talking to one another. It was my fault, because I brought the argument into the family. Well for my aunty it was a terrible blow, because by then (1952) many more restrictions had come in. It was harder to get things and to have my mother's support and money withdrawn made a big difference. My uncle's wages weren't that brilliant, so they had to tighten the belt a little bit more and with that. It also meant my cousin couldn't go to university. At least that was the excuse, however, she didn't have a brains for it, or the marks, so she couldn't get in. But with connections, my mother organized that she was taken into the bank as some kind of administrative staff, where she remained for the rest of her life.

Anyway, we stayed at home with my mother. We enrolled in school in Budapest and I was doing what I always did, just stayed at the shop, went to school, came home, prepared lunch and then I did my homework. Then I did the housework or whatever needed to be done. We spent our lives at my mother's business, in the shop. Our flat, (one room and kitchen apartment) were about 3.5kms away from the workshop. However, the school was closer to the shop and my mother wanted us to be under her eyes. So we got up in the morning, got dressed, went into the shop where we had virtually everything kept as far as food was concerned. We had our breakfast there, went to school from the shop, come back to the shop, had our lunch there. At the back of the shop was a little section divided off that we used as a kitchenette. We did our homework there and we went out to play afterwards. When my mother finished work, we packed up, went home and went to bed. We did this from Monday to Saturday, because my mother worked six days. Only on the Sunday were we home all day in the flat; otherwise, we spent our time in the shop.

In the winter-time, that was a blessing, because in the shop it was always warm. The shop needed to be well-heated in the winter, because my mother was sitting down working, repairing shoes, so the best way to heat a big shop or a big area, was using a special kind of heater, which was like a combustion heater. We used sawdust in 44-gallon drums, that were filled in, lit in the morning and that burned over 24 hours. By the time we came back to the shop in the morning, the place was warm. The fire in the drum would be just finished and we started it over for the new day. So that heater provided magnificent warmth. We cooked on it too, but for other times we used a little kerosene cooker. In the summertime especially, we used the kerosene cooker, but in the wintertime, we cooked anything that needed slow cooking, (like making a goulash or soup) on the stove. We would put it on in the morning and by the time we came home from school, it was ready and cooked and tasted great.

But the wintertime was pretty miserable, because our little flat only had a little wood stove that didn't hold the heat very well. By the time we got home at night, usually about 8 or 9 o'clock, there wasn't any point lighting a fire, so we just crawled into bed and got up in the morning. If it wasn't too cold then we could have a quick wash, but sometimes we just had to break the ice on the bucket the water was kept in. The water tap was outside in the yard and we had no electricity until 1956. (A few months before I left Hungary, I finally arranged and paid to have electricity in our flat). Until then we used kerosene lamps and the wood fire, plus the coal stove.

So the light was a kerosene lamp and usually I had it by my bed, because my mother liked being read to. She was too tired to read herself, but I loved reading, so we used to start a book and I would read aloud until she fell asleep. If it was a good book I kept on reading, until maybe she woke up in the middle of the night and told me to turn the light out. But sometimes I read until 2 or 3 o'clock in the morning, then had a bit of a sleep and went to school. Even so, I had no problems with my studies.

Of course, when the weather is minus 5-10 degrees, with snow everywhere, it's not very pleasant to go from the warm room, (which was the shop) to put your coat on and trudge home 3.5 km, to an icy cold house. Crawling into an icy cold bed as I used to, means I cannot stand a cold bed now, sometimes I have trouble warming it up, even today. They say your body warms up the sheets in no time. However, I was rolled up sometimes so tightly, that in the morning I could hardly stand up, because I wasn't able to stretch my feet out on the cold sheets. It was so cold; it was a very unpleasant time of the year in winter. Even so, with these uncomfortable things, I was still so much happier and life was so much better, because I didn't feel I was being used as a drudge for somebody else's benefit. What I did, it was for the 3 of us. The 3 of us were family.

Mind you, my little brother, by that time, became

very self-assured and the man of the house. He got into a lot of trouble and my mother used to grab him and beat him with the wooden spoon. But it didn't make any difference; he just ignored everybody and did what he wanted. In the long run, he could get away with murder. Mum always thought the sun shone out of his backside, so he was her boy and nothing he could do was wrong. And at that time, if we had an argument or something went wrong, a few times she turned around and said: "I don't know why I've been saddled with you, or what God meant by this. If your brother had been born first, you would never be here. I never wanted a daughter."

But that is something that you just take in your stride and carry on with, regardless. Not a good feeling but it's one of those things in life that you got used to.

In year 1953/54, things were terribly tight and difficult for everyone. There were no more export jobs. The government stopped any business with the West. So my mother's business virtually dried up. After my father's death, she carried on the business for the following 3-4 years and it went very well. But then, government regulations, plus a lack of materials, made it nearly impossible to keep going. Nearly all business was taken over by the government and little ones like ours just couldn't survive.

The local market wasn't lucrative for the specially embroidered slippers. She could sell some, but it wasn't that many. She couldn't make shoes for order because nobody could afford to pay for them. My mother couldn't get the leather or proper material for it anyway. So, life in the business was pretty difficult.

The Communists were in full steam, via Russian rules and regulations, for everything. The government was tightening everything. They were against all sorts of private enterprise. Everything had to be nationalised. All the factories were nationalised, all the big apartment houses were nationalised. They'd just take away ownership of whatever it was that you had, be it land, houses, business, etc. It all now belonged to "the people".

The farms were acquired and put into communal farming, and if the farmer was lucky he could join the commune. Everybody was doing what he or she was told. Anybody who had any kind of property, or some higher ranking office, ministers from the previous government, as well as priests, teachers, (good teachers) were not allowed to work anymore. They were sent to work in factories or farms, but they had no idea what they were doing. The owners of factories were thrown out and a government manager was put in charge. In the larger flats the owners, if they were lucky, could stay in one room of the flats. Because so many houses were bombed, accommodation was very difficult to find. The bigger flats of well-to-do people, who had 3-4 room flats, were divided up. They had to share with other people, (if they were not sent to the countryside) who were given a room in there as well. So they had to share the kitchen and all the facilities, sometimes between three or four families. All these previously high-ranking people or officers were put into work in the country or in mines and farms. Ministers and people with education, who had no idea what it meant to be digging trenches, were put into these kinds of jobs. You weren't sure how long you could be in your position, everything was secret and nothing was true. Everything and everybody had to be under surveillance and the secret police had absolute power.

The whole of our country was in the grip of absolute fear, everybody feared everything. Everybody talked very quietly. Hush-hush. You just couldn't say what you thought, because if you said anything you were in jail in no time.

It happened to my family, my favourite cousin, my mother's eldest brother's son Jancso. (Who had two sons, the elder one died in a bomb attack during the war. He was at university, in Budapest. The tram he was traveling in got hit with a bomb, consequently he died). It was 1952 and he was doing his matriculation. Just before they had the final closing off for the year (the exams were all done) they were having a big ceremony. However, this fell on the "official" day called "freedom day" declared as such because that was the date we were given to Russia, (4th of April). On that day, all the schools had to be decorated with the Russian flags and the new Hungarian flag with pictures of esteemed leaders including Stalin, Lenin and the Hungarian president Rakosi. All of Hungary had to get ready for the big march and ceremony on that day. My cousin and three of his classmates, (two more boys and a girl the cream of the class) decided to sabotage the proceedings for the 4th of April. The night before, they went back to school and burned down the decoration flags and pictures of Stalin and so forth.

Apparently, my uncle was listening to what they called "The Voice of America", the Hungarian language news reports from USA. Of course, he wasn't allowed to listen to that. Very secretly, people would have radios and listen to the news and learn about what was happening in the world. Four o'clock in the morning, my uncle got up to listen to a Voice of America news broadcast and heard that the secret police and the authorities were looking for 4 young people from the school that my cousin went to. The names were read out and one of the names was of course his son. He nearly died from shock. They were already in big upheaval and worry because, he didn't come home from school. Then my uncle heard that the police were looking for him.

Anyway, the four of them were apprehended a couple of hours later and taken to jail. They had some very horrific experiences of being interrogated, however he never talked about it. As luck would have it at the time, my mother still had a lot of money, a good reputation and a lot of high-class connections. These kids were taken to Budapest, to jail, then to court. However, my mother managed to bribe the jailers and managed to get better treatment for her nephew. After the trial, the boys were put into various mines and the girl was placed somewhere else. He was given a 6-year jail sentence. He had to go to work in a coal mine in the south of Hungary. For 8 months my uncle and aunty couldn't see him. My mother got information through her friends and was able to bribe the other guards and ease his time. He worked very hard and part of his punishment was that he couldn't get his matriculation certificate and therefore wasn't allowed to get into any university in Hungary, so he spent three years in the mines.

He was a hard worker and also a very good footballer. That was his lifesaver, because he got into the mines' football team. And while he was there, they won three premierships. So his 6 years was reduced to 3. He was let out after 3 years but had to redo his last year of matriculation. He stayed on working in the mines, but not doing manual labour anymore. Because of his football skills, he was in a better position. Eventually he got into university and in 1955, he managed to complete his doctorate, which he'd always wanted. This was about four years after he should have finished it.

So that was the scary experience in our family. You heard about such things, like people disappearing and families losing everything, or being thrown out of their home or off their land. They were very, very sad times.

In early 1955 the situation was so bad, that at the time my mother would say. "I hope somebody needs a heel on their shoes because we won't have money for bread!

We, and the whole of the country, really had a hard time but you got used to it. You adapt to anything. A family that lived in the next block of flats, they had three young girls, (much younger than us) and one night the secret police came, knocked on the door and told him to put on his shoes and coat. They took him away and nobody ever saw him again. Nobody knew where they took him, why or what happened. The wife was left there, with three children, no husband, and no income. She eventually packed up and went to live with her parents as I presume there was nothing she could do, he just disappeared. I asked my mother once if they ever found out what happened to him and nobody ever did.

Life became, "Watch what you say, and watch what you do." Don't look at officials in the face, don't make any noises. That was the way we all lived for many years.

The Government took over everything, so the small business people like my mother were forced to go into a government managed corporate arrangement. They would pool all their stock and machinery and work as a community, but that was just like the factory boss telling you what to do, where you go and you get paid every month. However, my mother could not join a co-operative because by law the business officially belonged to my brother and myself. My father had died without leaving a will, so officially my brother and I were the owners of the shop and my mother was only managing it, looking after it for us.

As we were underage, we couldn't sign for her and this meant that she couldn't join the community group. She couldn't hand in the business registration because it was ours, she had no rights, so therefore she couldn't get a job. She had to stay on in the business and just hope for the best. She made a few slippers, which she tried to sell in various markets and things. Sometimes we went to the different markets with her. She tried to sell them to official, government-owned shops, to get a sympathetic buyer, who may have bought some from her. But mainly she worked on repairs. She struggled to get leather and every now and again if she managed to find some, then she could make one or two pairs of shoes for sale.

Everyone was living on virtually "the smell of an oily rag". The wages were so low and the supplies were bad, so you were lucky to get some of the essentials. There was nothing in the shops. You go into the shops for the basics, but you had to make sure that you got to the shop when the delivery came, so you could get the bread or the flour or lard or whatever for the cooking.

A lot of people had little gardens and grew vegetables. If they had too many, they sold it to their neighbours and that's how we had vegetables. While things were good, my mother collected some nice things, which she later sold off, like her nice linen, to buy the essentials. She sold off some good clothes and jewellery to buy food, like sausages, so we could have it later on. It was a pretty tough time

The butcher shops didn't have anything. They had a couple of tins of sauerkraut but nothing else on the shelves. We used to go out at 2 o'clock in the morning (or even before) to stand in line in front of the shop. If you went after 2 am, you probably were the 50th in the line. Some people went straight from work and stood at the shop in line, when the delivery was expected in the morning. Everyone was given half a kilo max of this or that as it came. It was rationed. If you were not so lucky you just got the bones.

It was the routine that one of us spent half the night standing in line at the bread shop, the butcher's, or at the grocery shop to see if we could get some rice or any other food. It's just what we had to do.

There wasn't any other way to manage, and at this time if somebody had something against you and they told the secret police that you were talking against the government, your days were numbered. They might come and beat you up for it, or just make some sort of a stupid excuse and lock you up for a time.

I came home from school one day and was doing my homework in the shop. All of a sudden, a big black car stopped outside and three men, all dressed in black, marched into the shop and started interrogating my mother. They were looking for a shortwave radio, because apparently somebody said that my mother had a shortwave radio and she was listening to the Voice of America. People apparently came to the shop to listen with her, to the forbidden radio Voice of America.

Well, we did have a radio, but it wasn't the shortwave kind; it was a Crystal set my father had made himself. It was in the shop and sometimes my mother put the radio on to listen to some music. They rumbled through the shop, went through everything and told my mother to get in the car with them. She was shaking from fright and nerves: I was worried she may collapse.

I said, "I'm coming too!"

They said, "No, no you can't."

I said, "I'm not leaving my mother." And hung on to her.

So, they drove us to our flat and got us to open the door. In they went, looking for the shortwave radio. They threw things out of the cupboards; clothes were thrown onto the floor, as well as the bedding. They made an awful mess of the flat. Of course, they couldn't find anything. I asked, when they were sort of halfway through the rampage, "What you are looking for?"

He said, "Your radio."

I said, "How can we have a radio when we don't even have electricity?"

They stayed for a little while and then just turned around and walked out, didn't say "boo" or "sorry" or anything. They just walked out, got in the car and drove off and Mum and I were left there standing in that horrible mess.

I said, "OK, let's tidy up."

She was a bundle of nerves, she was shaking and crying and couldn't do much. I went next door and got the old chap that lived in the house, (his wife had died by then) and I said, "Please talk to my mother, get her settled down, while I tidy up a bit."

Of course, he'd seen the men come in, but he couldn't work out what happened. He took my mother into his place and made her a cup of coffee and I tidied up the best as I could. Then we went back to the shop, because my brother was coming back from sport.

From that day onwards, my mother, virtually to her dying days, started shaking if she saw a big black car. Wouldn't you? There is no excuse for a lie! Somebody, somehow, got some stupid thing in his/her head or whatever. We don't know who it was, or why it was, but just that it happened. Someone decided to "inform" on my mother, saying she was listening to the Voice of America, which was a very low act. It could and did happen to anyone at anytime

We, and everyone else, always wanted news, wanted to know what was happening in the world. But we were very let down by America and England, the western world. They kept on saying, "Keep your fight up, keep your fight up, we will be with you, we're coming to help you."

It was just empty, empty talk.

In 1955 the winter was pretty heavy, there was quite a lot of snow and there wasn't very much work to be had. My mother decided to go and shovel snow at night. You could get a job shovelling snow off the main roads and the tramlines, so the trams and cars could function in the morning. It was reasonably well paid. So, my mother would take on the job and then I would stay with her until it started about 8 or 9 o'clock at night. I would then go and help her. I had my own shovel and we would shovel snow until about 11 o'clock, then my brother would come and I'd go home. He'd help my mother till 3 or 4 o'clock in the morning, then they'd come home for a couple of hours sleep, and then we went to school.

We'd done quite a few nights of snow shovelling and that had helped keep us in food, clothes and shoes. We were not hungry or without the necessities, we had enough, but it was still very, very hard to manage. During the day we were always warm, because of the sawdust heater in the shop. That provided fantastic warmth, not just for us but for others as well. We would usually, have five or six people from the block of flats, the ladies would come with their knitting or sewing, or whatever they had to do, and the kids would be doing their homework with us.

Our shop wasn't very big, but sometimes we'd have fifteen people there, just to keep warm, because there was no heating elsewhere. Heating was so expensive, while sawdust was reasonably cheap. In the summertime, my mother used to get sawdust from the furniture factories. They'd deliver it into the cellar and our cellar was full of it. All summer long, we had it brought in and then in the wintertime, it was comfortable and warm. It wasn't heavy work to fill the drum with the sawdust and stamp it down. Then we'd get twenty-four hours heat from it.

In Hungary, the compulsory schooling was eight classes by the time you're fourteen, then you could go to high school or become an apprentice. I wanted to go into technical school because I had it in my head that I wanted to become an engineer. I knew I was good with my hands and with maths. But my teachers decided that I had achieved high marks and therefore I should be going into humanities, to higher education, so I was put in what was called in Hungary a 'Gimnasium'. It's not a physical gym, it's a high school and I was enrolled into the best in the area. I loved it. I always loved going to school. Schools and books were the absolute top pleasure of my life. I always loved learning. I thought I was in high heaven if I could have my books. Summer holidays were the best time for me, after I finished all the housework, the shopping and so forth.

Our shop was in a three-story apartment house. Downstairs we had four shops. One was actually a flat because by this time, so many houses had been bombed. There was a shortage of accommodation. There was a milk bar, which was an actual 'milk bar' that only sold milk, butter, yoghurt and rolls, things like that. Then for a while there was another shop, a Greengrocer. That later became a tailor shop and then it became a hairdresser. The hairdresser made it partly into a flat and lived there as well as running her hairdressing business.

Behind the apartment there was quite a nice garden with green bushes and a bit of grass, so it was a nice little garden area at the back. During the school holiday times, I would take my little stool, go out to the garden, sit down, grab my book and I was in heaven. I would spend most of my holidays there. I didn't want to go very often to the baths, sometimes I did with my friends and my brother and we had a good time. But mostly I spent my afternoons sitting in the garden reading. I was constantly back and forth to the library for books. Given they were the best times I had, it was probably the reason why they thought I should be studying something more academic, rather than technical stuff.

So, I did my first year and it went off well. Just as I got into the first year of high school, my mother become friendly with a lady who was originally born in America. Her parents went to America sometime in the 1920s. She was thirty-something by the time we met her. It happened that her parents brought her back to Hungary for a holiday, then the war broke out and they couldn't go back. Her parents died in a bombing and she was stuck in Hungary with some relatives. She spoke Hungarian and had been quite well educated, but she couldn't go back to America.

She couldn't get an exit visa, didn't have money for bribes, so they wouldn't let her leave. She worked in some kind of an office. By the time we met her in 1953-54, she was teaching English privately to get a bit of extra money. Some people had their kids study other languages after school, as only Russian was taught in the education system.

My mother had this friend who was telling her that her cousin (or some relation) had married her daughter off to an Englishman, as some sort of mail order bride. The girl moved to England and regularly sent home parcels of all sorts of goodies. So this friend told my mother that if I was so good at studying, why coulnd't I learn English? Then she would get in touch with these English people and organise for me to go to England and marry someone there.

I was fourteen!

So, I was sent to an English class. I went religiously for about six months and did everything I could, but it just didn't stick. That poor teacher said to my mother, "I am sorry to say this, but don't waste your money, Ica will never learn a language; she just has absolutely no talent for languages. I cant take your money for it (even though I need it) she is not improving, she can't do it, and she won't be able to speak English or any other language ever."

But while I was studying English, I also had some professional photographs done. I was dressed up, had my hair done and makeup put on, to produce very glamorous professional photos. I looked more like a twenty-year-old. Those photos were supposed to be sent to England to secure me a potential husband.

I was terrified! Secretly, I prayed that no one would want me. I was so frightened, I used to lie in bed and shake like a leaf from the thought of what may happen. I would be sent to England, to a country where I didn't know anybody. I wouldn't be able to speak the language, and nobody would be able to understand me. How were they going to treat me, what was going to happen to me and what kind of a man would marry me? They'd probably marry me to some old badger. All this so I could go to England to provide good things for my mother and brother back in Hungary!

I lived in fear for about eight to ten months, with the constant thought that this was going to happen to me. I don't think my mother ever really gave up the idea, but she eventually said, "Oh no, those people didn't respond."

It wasn't that she had given up the idea, she was always secretly hoping there might, at some point, be an offer.

So, by now, I was fifteen. One of our dear friends was the lady of one of my mother's fledglings. She had lived with my parents when I was born. My mother and father had looked after her like a daughter and even paid for her wedding. They were lovely people, Annus and Pista. They called my mother Mama and we were very, very close friends. They had a daughter about seven or eight years younger than I was. Annus and Pista were working in the factory where they were making aluminium gutters, and plumbing materials. He was doing some office work and his wife was working there also. His second job was as a projectionist at the picture theatre. I was able to go in and get discount tickets, I didn't have to pay for the last movie of the day because there used to be two or three projections a night. One finished and then another started again fifteen minutes later, at six o'clock, eight o'clock and ten o'clock and so on. Annus and I would go to the last screening and if we didn't want to watch the film, we'd wait till Pista finished and had closed up, then, we would go out dancing, mostly on weekends.

He loved dancing, and he was a fantastic dancer. We would go for coffee and would dance until 2-3 am, on Friday or Saturday night, mostly Saturday night, because Annus and Pista still had to work on Saturday and I had to be in school. But Saturday night we would often dance until 4-5 am, until every coffee shop was closed. In Hungary, the coffee shops usually had someone playing the piano, or a piano and violin, providing music for a bit of dancing. There weren't such things as pubs. There were private bars, things like that. We would go to concerts, we would go dancing and then go back to their flat, sleep a couple of hours and on Sunday afternoon at three o'clock the coffee shops started again, with more dancing. So by one o'clock, we would get together and get ready and go dancing again.

I had this "high life" for about ten months. It was

absolutely fantastic, as every weekend I was out. That was my youth, short lived, but thoroughly enjoyable.

By the time September 1955 came, I was due to go back to the second year of school. However, my mother announced that I wouldn't be going back to school. I had to get a job and earn money so we could manage, because her earnings were not enough. My brother had one more year in school – then he would need to study, because he was a boy, so he had to have a trade and proper education.

I was devastated. We went to school and my mother told my class teacher that she was taking me out of school, to go to work. My teacher said, "No, no, no, no. We can get her a scholarship, you don't have to pay for anything, and she will get all her books, all her things provided."

Mum said, "I still can't afford it, because she needs uniforms and other clothes and everything else and I have another child and I can't afford to pay for it."

The teacher said, "I can arrange that she gets a clothes allowance, as well as her uniform, just keep her in, let her stay in school."

My mother was adamant. "No, she cannot stay, she has to go to work."

The teachers enrolled me for evening classes, as a compromise. Then my mother found me a job cleaning offices at the army headquarters.

It was hard work and awful. Worse still, it was boring. I didn't know what to do with my head, so I decided that it's not for me I'm going to find something else. Somebody mentioned that there was a job in the 'button' factory. It was a little factory that made shirt buttons from mother of pearl. I got a job there working on a little drill. This meant I had a double-headed drill and I had to push the button into a holder, put that drill on it and drill the two holes in the button to make a shirt button.

But the problem was I was absolutely unco-ordinated. We had a very thick metal shield like a thimble, put on our left thumb for protection, so when we put the button in and you pulled the drill quickly, you could drill your fingers through. Well, I ruined half a dozen thimbles in the first day. I think I drilled even through that. I managed to work there for about three or four months. I tried to keep up with the other women. However, there was a quota you had to fulfil and because we were in a group, if everyone didn't fill the quota, then everyone in the group was paid less. So I was really holding back about six women, who worked like slaves, but I just couldn't keep up with it, so I was let go.

Then, I did a couple of odd jobs, though I can't even remember where I helped out, here and there. A lady, two doors down, was doing a 'photo reconstructing' job. What she did was take an old photo, enlarge it, and then put it on to a thicker paper. I don't know how they did it at the time. She would have the photo in her hands and to make it look nice, she took out all the creases or the blemishes on the old photo and made it look like a portrait. Some of them were coloured. She was doing this process for orders and actually earning quite good money with it. She said to me, "You've got such a good hand, you'd be able to do this."

Well, I didn't do very well. You needed to have

some flair, but I wasn't very good at it, definitely not a painter or artist by any means.

But in the meantime, I could still go dancing. I went out with a young group that worked in the factory with Pista and Annus. It was like a youth group and we went for picnics, hikes and so forth, as well as to the baths in the summertime. I met this guy, Frank. He was quite good looking, very friendly and we got on quite well. He was a plumber by trade, but he was working as a teacher in the trade school. It was a co-ordinated trade school for bricklayers, plumbers, electricians, roofers, all of the building industry trades that you needed. They created the school that had all the trades in it, as a 'Building Industry School'. Most of their teachers were actual tradesmen.

Frank was teaching in the plumbing department, and with the students, they built an apartment house. At that time there was a big shortage of housing and the need and drive to rebuild from the damages of the war was great. It was ten years after the war, so we needed to be having a bit more oomph in building production. To get an apartment was just about impossible, as the waiting was years and years.

Anyway, he told me that soon the eight apartments in the house they were building would be ready. They were all one-room, kitchen, toilet, bathroom sort of thing. Nothing fancy, but they would be ready in September and he was in line to get one of these flats. So, I took him a bit more seriously.

By that time, things weren't very friendly at home. My brother was obnoxious. He was very difficult to get along with. I was unhappy, I couldn't go to school, I didn't have the motivation anymore to do my night studies, I didn't have a proper job, so I thought. "I have to get out of here." Plus they were still coming up with that talk that it would be a good idea if I went to England and marry a stranger to support my family.

4

So, I met my future husband, Frank, at the youth group, as already mentioned. We started going out and he mentioned to me that he lived with his mother, which was very far away. His sister had married an army officer and they had flat in an apartment house, which was reserved for the army. They had two children, a young boy and a girl about 2, 3 or 4 years old. We had done quite a few things together and got on very well. He was very clear he wanted to be a pilot, but for some reason or other, he didn't make the cut. However, he was a hobby pilot in a club with Glider planes. He had taken me a couple of times, for a glider-flight, which I thought was fantastic.

His family was fairly poor, his grandfather had four or five daughters, three of them were unmarried and lived at home with him and the children. I didn't know where his father was, he never talked much about him. His grandparents weren't alive. His mother was alone and on a small pension.

They believed in Communism, but politics didn't interest me in any way, so it didn't worry me. I was thinking very strongly of what I was going to do with my life. How would I manage my life? I couldn't work the way I wanted. There weren't any decent jobs. My mother was still playing on this idea of sending me off to England, which I didn't want to do.

Frank had mentioned that he would be eligible for a flat in September 1956, through the school's building project, but he had to be married in order to get the flat.

He was saying he would like to get married, so he could get the flat and he suggested that we do that. It was very important for him, and I thought it wasn't a bad idea, and it would help me get away from home. Why not get married? So we decided to get married in August 1956. My mother wasn't happy about it.

I said, "Well, I want to get married and I'm past sixteen (just) now and you can't stop me. (Under sixteen you had to have your parent's permission, but after sixteen you didn't.) With that idea, I would be the first in the family to get married, because all my cousins were older, but hadn't married yet. My aunty somehow had made up with my mother, and they plotted about how I had to have a big Catholic Church wedding.

Frank said he couldn't have a Catholic wedding as he was a communist and with family in the army, they wouldn't be able to come. One way or another, my aunty managed to overpower them all. She was organizing a church wedding; with everything the way she wanted it. It was a very difficult time because we didn't have much money for these kinds of things. They found a dress that I borrowed and the only thing I had that was mine was the veil I bought for myself.

Before that white wedding in a church, we had some problems because when we went to the church to register for the wedding, the priest said, "You have to come for three pre-marriage lectures."

So, we fronted up. They were conducted by the priest, and designed to lecture us about how to behave in marriage, plus our children had to be Catholic and so forth and so on. A celibate priest lecturing us about marriage?

Frank was reluctant, but I told him to agree to it, it didn't matter, once we were married, we didn't have to do what they said.

The priest said that three days before the wedding, we had to go to confession. If we didn't do confession, he wouldn't marry us. I said OK we should just marry in the registry office, which we were planning anyway.

I was not going to confession. I didn't have anything to confess and I was holding to what my father always said: "There is no sin that I and God between us cannot reconcile and there is not another person, (man or woman) in the world, that could forgive me for what I can't forgive myself."

I said there was no way I would go to confession, and I didn't.

My aunty came and made a big fuss with the priest, so we were married on the 11th August 1956, in front of a few friends and the family. My cousin Jancso came and gave me away. My mother made lunch at home, in the back yard of our place. Because it was August and in good weather, we had a big table put up outside and that's how we celebrated. We had photos taken. Frank produced a uniform for a flight officer. I don't know where he hired it, borrowed it or where he got it from, but he wanted a wedding photo with him as a pilot, in a pilot uniform. So that was quite a strange thing to do. He had some weird ideas. Anyway, the arrangement was that we were going to stay with my mother until the flat was ready a month later.

So, we had the room to sleep in and my mother and brother slept in the kitchen. For our honeymoon, some of Annus's friends had the use of a boathouse (from a group he knew that was doing a lot of rowing.) They had sort of a holiday camp by the Danube, where the rowing squad usually stayed if they had competitions, so we stayed in that holiday camp for about 3 or 4 days. It wasn't very pleasant. He was very strange, very strange indeed! He was entertaining me on our honeymoon with the histories of the girls he'd slept with, including one of his cousins! She was younger than I was, so it didn't come out very well from my point of view, but anyway the deed was done and we settled into married life.

Then two weeks after the wedding he came home and said. "The flat is not available." We wouldn't be able to get one because someone else got in before him, so it will be another fourteen months until another one became available. I thought, "Oh my God! How are we going to manage here?"

I wasn't very happy, living with my mother and brother, in this small place. Frank wasn't exactly the most welcomed part of the family. My mother wasn't happy with him and my brother couldn't care less, it was very crowded and very uncomfortable.

At least I got a job in the factory to do some packaging.

The next thing that happened, six weeks later, on October 23, 1956, was the most heart-breaking thing that could happen to Hungary.

The revolution – the uprising – started. This was, of course, a terrible time for the whole country and us. It was quite frightening, because the radio stopped broadcasting and all sorts of stories were going around about what was happening. It became clear, very quickly, that it was definitely a revolution. We heard about the students being killed during a peaceful demonstration near the parliament. The army started shooting, the people grabbed guns from the soldiers and started shooting back, and it was a very frightening time.

My mother said, "The retribution after this will be much worse than what we had before. If there is any way, you'd better get out of the country!"

She'd already had the idea before to send me off to England to marry, but seeing that I was already married, she suggested we leave the country, and find a new life. Then when we were settled, I could get my mother and brother also out of the country as well, because it wasn't going to be a very nice place to live after the revolution. It was quite obvious that the Russians wouldn't allow Hungarian independence to happen.

Within days, the Russian army started to bring in extra troops. Most of the Hungarian army refused command, so there was quite a lot of uncertainty. Then about a week later we heard that the Russians were coming through the borders but already there were a lot of Russian soldiers stationed in Hungary, they were getting orders to get out there and fight the people. I did not get involved very much, I stayed at home with my mother. My husband was always out and about, I didn't know what he was doing or where he was. I have to laugh now, but I really didn't inquire very much, I was far too scared to worry about it. Of course, the shops hadn't had much in them before, but very quickly, they ran out of everything. We had to stand in line again for long periods of time, for bread, milk and so forth. Quite a few times there was news about people getting shot while standing in line.

It was a harrowing time really, we didn't know what was going to happen. The looting began, as the fight for survival unfolded. Then my 15-year-old brother arrived home one day with a machine gun and a great big bag of ammunition. Where on earth had he got them?

There was an army depot not far from where we lived and apparently somebody broke into it. They were handing out the guns to everybody going past.

My mother really told him off, gave the gun to my husband and said, "Just take it and get rid of it. I don't want any kind of thing like that around the house."

Teenage kids, some as young as twelve, were on

the streets with machine guns. My brother had to be virtually put on a leash, to make sure that he stayed home. The kids out there were getting killed. We'd walk through the post-skirmish streets, where people had been hung on trees (maybe they were informers? Nobody knew). We'd see burnt out cars and burnt out tanks with the bodies in them. The streets were littered with bodies. It was horrendous things and it was going on everywhere. Even along the back streets, the tanks just went and started shooting indiscriminately at anything, even into flats. Two and a half weeks into the fighting, the Russians really retaliated. Apparently my brother-in-law (in the Hungarian army) was ordered to go out on the street and shoot at people. I don't know if he ever did or not, but most soldiers refused.

I didn't see any of my husband's family at that time. My husband went to visit his mother and his sister. His sister was terribly worried, so she packed up the children and went to stay with her mother, because she was too afraid to stay in the army house. Anyway, my mother managed to talk my husband into leaving the country. To tell the truth, I was quite happy to do it, because what we had was not a life! Living in cramped conditions, out of work, chaos outside, guns and tanks. I'd married to leave home, to get away, but instead of getting away, my husband had moved in with my family. That wasn't what I'd hoped and planned for my life to be.

I suppose I was not really in love with my husband. I liked him quite well but I wasn't that ... well, I didn't know about love. Love is something that means you don't think of anything else except that person. Well, I'm sorry I never had that kind of love for him or for any man really (except for my children and my father). I always had to think about what today or tomorrow would bring. Maybe I am not capable of that kind of love I don't know.

But we had to leave. My husband went to visit his mother to say goodbye to her. She told him his old school friend was now living in Australia. The school friend's widowed mother and younger brother (her neighbours) were still living next door. This friend's mother begged my husband to take her young son and let him come with us, to get to his brother in Australia. Well, I think he must have been 18 or 19, so not much older than I was. He had his own bicycle. We had one bicycle between the two of us. So now we had three people and two bicycles to take on the world.

The border was about 280 kilometres away from Budapest. We had a change of clothes in a small bag, with a change of underwear and extra jumper and whatever money we could get together. It wasn't very much. My mother had given me a gold necklace, which was of reasonable value. We set off on the 3rd of November from Budapest to get to the border.

We weren't game enough to get on the train because the Russians patrolled the trains. By that time, the Russians were everywhere and the main highways were patrolled by Russian troops too. We had a map and we were sticking to the small roads between the small villages, but this made the distance much longer.

Between the two boys I was mostly sitting on the cross bar of the bicycle with a small pillow, I'd be with one of the boys for a while, and then I'd change over. Sometimes I was on the bike and my husband sat on the cross bar, which was very difficult, because he was much bigger than I and it was much harder for me to peddle, so I slowed us down.

It took us six and a half days to get close to the border. In the mean time, we had some food with us and we stopped to sleep in haystacks, in sheds with the animals, and on farms. A couple of times we were lucky and the farmers allowed us to go inside and sell us some food. It was starting to get cold. November is autumn and it could get quite cold, so it wasn't a very comfortable trip. But, in 5-6 days, we arrived in a small village near Mosonmogyorovar, a small town close to the border. From there, the village 'Janos Somorja', was 8 kilometres from the border.

Thirty kilometres from the border was the border control zone and you could only get into those villages with a special pass. At that time, the Hungarian-Austrian border zone was filled with booby traps, grenades and explosives in the ground. The Russian army controlled the border all the time. So, late one evening, we managed to secretly cycle into that village, which was closer to the border. Somebody told us that a certain farmer would take people across the border, during the night. We finally managed to find this person and gave him all the money we had. Watches, necklace, everything that would be valuable, as well as the bicycles of course. He promised to take us across the border that night. We had to trust him.

We waited until it was dark and about fourteen people gathered there.

Amongst the people, some of them had children. They were given sleeping pills so they didn't cry and were carried in back packs. We had with us two babies, very young ones and three or four other little children in that group. We set off at 10 o'clock at night, to walk eight kilometres across the field: it had been ploughed, already frozen and hard to walk on. The farmer knew where the grenades and land mines were. When the army patrol came, we'd lie down on the ground and keep as quiet as possible. I don't know how long it took us, but it wasn't easy. We carried the babies between us, everybody, carried them for a little while and when you got too tired, you handed the baby to someone else. The younger children were put into backpacks, on their fathers' and mothers' backs. It was getting near daybreak, getting lighter, and the farmer said to us: "Now you don't have very much further to go, just go straight. If somebody calls, keep running straight ahead, because you are very close to the border. You are on 'No man's land' and soon you'll be in Austria. Keep running. If anybody says anything, just keep running."

Well, we made a final effort to rush through the last section. We ran, even though no one was after us. Everybody was holding their breath, praying and running, trying to get through this last section of the field.

Then we saw lights and people standing in front of us. All of a sudden there we were, all these people saying: "Welcome! Welcome! Welcome!" and wrapping us up in lovely fresh new blankets and giving us hot drinks.

We were taken to the school in 'Andau', (the first Austrian village) and in the big school hall we were given brand-new blankets. We just all lay down on fresh straw that was spread out on the floor. One after another, couples, families, we all slept here for about ten hours I think. It was late in the afternoon when I woke up. There was my husband and his friend who was with us. He was a nuisance of a spoiled brat, but we managed to get through the border with him and now we were in Austria.

Later that afternoon, when we woke up, we were given fresh fruit and a hot meal. Then some buses came and started transporting us that evening to a nearby town called Traiskirchen. It was about twelve or fifteen kilometres from the Hungarian border. We were taken to a big, three-storey army barracks, where only 12 months before, Russian soldiers had lived while occupying Austria.

After the war, Austria was under occupation by the four powers English, American, French and Russian. Only a year before, Austria had become 'neutral' and all occupational armies left. This south section of Austria was under the Soviets.

The army complex was a square block and we were put into a room with eighteen couples and six single people. So, around 42 people to a huge room. We were in that camp until the end of January, early February. There were people from all over Hungary. People we knew, people we didn't know and the young single boys and girls were put in with couples, to be looked after. Those who had relations anywhere in the world, were very quickly processed. My husband's friend John was processed within a few weeks time and sent off in a ship to Australia. I was quite worried about him; he was very irresponsible and spoiled. I didn't want to have the responsibility of him doing something stupid, so I made sure he got on the first ship for family reunification.

While we were in that camp, Frank got work a few days after we arrived. The barracks were in pretty bad condition. The Russians left them in a desolate state and where we were put up, it had already been renovated and cleaned up, but there were sections that needed repairing badly. Being a plumber, he got a job straight away working on the renovations.

""Kirayhida –utca 32" (as it is today)
the house we lived in when I left

Mum and my brother, just before I left Hungary.

5

Frank's work meant we had a little money, with a chance to buy a little extra food, or anything else we needed. He got very little pay (I can't really remember), but it did help us to improve our conditions. In the same room, where we stayed, (with all those people) I specially become friends with a young couple, Panni and Bill, who were just married. Panni was pregnant and suffered very badly with morning sickness.

The food at the camp wasn't what we were used to, so everything was very strange. The camp was under the management of the Swedish Red Cross. Unfortunately, the way Swedish people prepare food was very different to the Hungarians. Some of the things were unpalatable for us, and Panni being so sick, couldn't eat many things.

What she ate didn't last long. I tried to help her as much as I possibly could. For weeks, the only thing I could eat was the babies' porridge, which was in a big pot for anybody to help themselves. I couldn't eat the food either, it was quite a challenge, but because I liked the porridge, a plate of that would satisfy me for the day.

Our main occupation there was trying to find information about different places, and what we could do with our future, where we could go and what possibility there was to earn a living. My wardrobe was like everybody else's, quite limited. I had high boots and breeches, which was fashionable at the time. Three-quarter pants tied under your knees, (some sports people wear it nowadays) a couple of jumpers and only a couple of changes of underwear. We had a great time sorting through the Red Cross 'clothes bins'. There was a big room with donated clothes and shoes and all sorts of things that could be useful for our needs.

    Luckily, I found a box of needles and threads and a little pair of scissors. This was helpful to adjust and remake the clothes we found, if they were of good quality but didn't quite fit. I am quite good at doing that. Panni could crochet, but she wasn't very productive at the time. Anyway, I started crocheting with some ordinary sewing cotton, (which is fairly thin,) during those months in the camps. I made a reasonable-sized, (nearly a meter-by-meter) tablecloth that I crocheted. I used it for many years. Now it's in tatters, as obviously, the cotton has disintegrated, but I haven't got the heart to throw it out, so it's still in my cupboard.

I adjusted clothes to fit me, and helped do this for the others as well, if it was too big or tight, to let it out or pulled it in. We did the best we could, to keep us occupied and of course to have a change of clothes, as we only could take the bare minimum with us. Reading materials were very limited. Whatever little magazines or books we could get was read and passed from hand to hand, until it fell to shreds.

Because Frank earned money, we bought some food in the town that was more like Hungarian's stuff, being so close to the border, they had a fairly close connection to Hungary over hundreds of years. Austria and Hungary were virtually one country in the time of the Empire.

To go into the town, you needed to have a special permit because soldiers were guarding the camp. You couldn't just walk out. There were thousands of people in the camp and as the town was small, we would have overrun it. So, we were actually under army guard. We were in a camp, a refugee camp and that was normal and accepted, but with special passes you could go for a couple of hours to the town. A few people every day could go out into the town to walk, look around and so forth. So, because Frank was working we had more passes to go out. We would buy some special foods, which we shared with the people in the room to try to make our life a bit better. We provided Panni with some stuff that she could digest and this made her a little bit happier.

She wasn't a very happy girl at that time, I understood she was feeling sick, she was lonely and worried. Anyway, we spent our days just sitting around, doing virtually nothing, trying to sew or crochet or just talk or play cards. My God the number of cardgames we played: 'Gin Rummy' nonstop, day and night, until lights out at ten o'clock. It wasn't the most comfortable environment with so many people in a room. There was always some kind of a scuffle or extra noises and so forth.

But you get used to it and that was part of life I suppose. The bathroom facilities were like an army camp's, labelled Mens and Ladies. A great big room with twenty or so toilets and twenty or so showers. There were just some wash basins, all in a line and so everybody just went in. But when you have about five hundred people sharing two or three bathrooms, it can get fairly crowded at times. I tried to get to the showers early in the morning, sometimes three or four o'clock in the morning, which was a blessing. Because of the unusual food and without enough exercise and so forth, I suffered terrible constipation. The fact of the matter is that I just could not function when people were in the bathroom. So, I would have to go to the bathroom in the middle of the night, when very few people would get up to go to the bathroom and to go to the toilet. It was quite a challenge to manage the bodily functions.

We had rigged up in the room a little corner with blankets, for cooking extra coffee or such – the blankets also allowed the girls to have a hot water wash in private. We had a wood and coal fired stove in the room that kept us cosy. There was no central heating working yet. Because, Frank worked and he knew where things were, he got leftover wood and coal from work, so we always had very nice warm rooms, and therefore a lot of people would come visiting.

I realised Christmas was coming up. Frank and I decided that we were going to provide a Christmas meal for everybody, for Christmas Eve. What could we cook? We bought some meat from the town and one of the guys had borrowed some knives and a board from the kitchen. We had some big conserve-tins, (they were about five-litre tins that originally had jams and vegetables in them). We used those tins for cooking pots and Frank made sure that they were properly turned around the edges so they wouldn't cut us. We decided to make Hungarian goulash 'paprikas' with pork and made some 'nokedli' (noodles, like very small dumplings) to go with it. So, 3-4 of us girls worked like anything. We bought the onions and we managed to get some lard, flour, eggs and everything for the meal. We even managed some cakes from the shops and two bottles of wine. It wasn't very much for twenty people, just for a sip for everybody.

We cooked behind the curtains, because the stove had to be running really hot to boil water and cook the meat and the nokedli. We had to change places every few minutes, as the heat from cutting the nokedli dough into the boiling water, was so intense. We were standing there in knickers and bras! We couldn't stand it for longer than five minutes in front of that stove.

Frank cut holes in the bottom of one of the tins to use as a strainer. It was a hilarious way to go about cooking for Christmas Eve, but everybody had proper Hungarian goulash or 'porkolt' (stew) and nokedli. We managed to get some sour cucumbers to go with it and we also had a piece of cake for everybody and a sip of wine. We had a fantastic Christmas in unbelievable circumstances. It was happy time, everybody was really helpful and we had a really good day. You wouldn't have noticed that we were virtually country-less, moneyless, family-less, everybody was family and it's remained in my mind that we had a real community-spirit happening that day. It kept us going, for a long time to come, even today, for some of those people.

Very shortly after Christmas, I think early January or mid-January or so, Panni and Bill left because Bill had an uncle in Australia. They were the first lot to leave the camp. And they were taken to Italy to be put on a boat to travel to Australia. I don't think that was the best way for them to travel, as I heard afterward Panni was sick the entire boat trip. It was too long. I think it was four weeks or something before they got to Melbourne, where they were reunited with Bill's uncle: they lived with them for quite a while.

We put in our papers choosing Australia. First of all the idea was for us to go to Australia, as far away from the Russians as you could get. Also, Frank wanted to be where his old schoolmate was, and of course because John, his friend's brother was there as well (he had travelled with us to the border.) They started processing the application in the Australian consulate.

At times there were chances to go else where;

there would be five or six buses coming to the camp ground, with loudspeakers announcing; 'Anybody who wants to go to Sweden get into a bus number one anybody who wants to go to France go to bus two, to go to England three,' and so forth. So, you could virtually be on the bus, full of people and be taken once or twice a week to various countries. I suppose if we wanted to we could have settled in one of those countries close by.

But we decided on Australia, so we had to wait. Then we were taken to Vienna to the Australian consulate, to have a medical, and provide all our papers for scrutiny and tell our history. We were interviewed about three times. They were questioning that I wore glasses. Some people were knocked back because they had bad teeth, so they had to try to get their teeth fixed if they wanted to reapply. We didn't really have that kind of problem, as the only thing they were questioning was that I always wore glasses. I am shortsighted, so, that's it. Because Frank had a trade as a plumber, it was easier to be accepted, because Australia wanted tradespeople, not so much university degrees, doctors and lawyers. Trades were very popular.

There was a couple in our room, he was a lawyer, and they finished up going to South Africa because Australia wouldn't accept him. He was in his late forties. Australia wanted young healthy people, preferably with some physical trade that would be useful for the country. So, we were lucky in that respect that Frank was a plumber. We passed our interviews and medicals, and I was told that eventually, we'd all get to Australia and then in February or so, we were told to get ready to leave.

Unfortunately what happened next was that we were taken to another refugee camp, this time on the other end of Austria, far away from the Hungarian border, which truly didn't worry me much. We were taken to Salzburg, closer to Germany, to another big army camp but, this one was an American camp and the rooms had sixty cubicles. They were concrete walled cubicles with two bunk beds in each cubicle.

A family with a child or two children, got one cubicle to themselves, but two married couples got into one cubicle. There were so many cubicles, thirty on each side, it was huge long room and there were babies crying or children screaming at night, as well as men speaking in their sleep or families arguing. I laugh, but it was less public than what we had in Traiskirchen, where there were no dividers between the beds at all.

In Salzburg, Frank straight away went and offered his services, he started working with the plumbers in maintenance, doing whatever needed to be done. I offered my services in the kitchen, which was okay. For a little while I was helping prepare vegetables and so forth, but I was soon put to work looking after the children. They collected the children, usually into a kindergarten type of arrangement, where they had to be entertained and kept busy. So, I was employed there.

There was less possibility of going to town because this camp was about five kilometres out of Salzburg so, we never managed to get into town: the camp was located between fields and hills. That didn't worry me, and while we worked, we were able to save some money and buy ten American dollars. That was the full extent of our wealth, ten American dollars by the end of March.

Then we were told that we were going to Australia. We would be going by plane. That was fine for me, I couldn't care less how we got there, just let's go. Secretly I was glad it wasn't a ship.

We were taken by bus to Linz airport, another big town in Austria. We had to wait there, in the same type of barracks that we'd been in, for two nights before the plane arrived. They were big American troop transport planes. They didn't have very comfortable seats. Very small and very close seats, like today's economy probably. We got on the plane, left Linz and flew to Greece. We stopped in Greece for refuelling.

Then I believe we had three more stops and one was definitely in Abu Dhabi, which, at that time, was still fairly primitive. We were allowed to get out of the plane and have a meal at the airport. When we had to go to the toilet - that was an experience! They were showing the other girl and myself, that to go to the toilet we had to go outside, between mud huts, in a very narrow passageway. Left, right, round this way. Anyway, we got to the toilet and at that time it was evening, so quite dark. There was only a small electric light shining and as we left to go back, there was an Arab whom I believe must have been a soldier (I'm laughing whenever I remember it). He was standing, black as the night, dressed in the tradition of loose fitting, black clothing with a great big sabre on his belt. And he just stood there like a statue! I think we both nearly died of fright and didn't know how to get back. We nearly needed to go back to the toilet again, and I'm laughing now, but we were so frightened then!

We made it back to the plane and the next stop was Delhi, India. Well, we'd left in March, which was still cold, wet and snowy in Austria. Abu Dhabi was hot and humid, but it was night so it wasn't as bad. But in India, we arrived in the morning and the humid heat and smell of spices and humanity - it was overwhelming. Absolutely overwhelming. We were put onto quite rickety buses, which stopped for cows (but not for people). Cows were everywhere. The buses took us to one of the major hotels in Delhi. It was a beautiful building, absolutely beautiful. On the trip to the hotel, some of the guys were just standing on the platform, because the bus was rickety and had no windows, no doors, so they were just standing on a platform. There were millions of people everywhere, quite overwhelming.

We thought a thousand and one times that the driver would probably kill half a dozen people before we arrived. It was a fairly harrowing experience, the trip from the airport to the hotel. I don't know the name of the hotel, but it was a high-class hotel. We were put into rooms and were told that because the plane that came before us had motor trouble, the people that stayed in there had left with our plane and we had to wait for the next one.

So, we didn't know how long we'd be in Delhi. We got a room on the fourth floor, which was a very economical type of hotel room, but for us it was absolute paradise because we had our own room. We were served meals in the hotel dining room, which had the most opulent surroundings of baroque carvings, with silk and velvet covers. There were curtains and carpets, gleaming silver and white tablecloths. I think there were one hundred forty of us from the plane who sat down to a meal.

There were more people standing around by the walls, to serve us, than diners. Virtually two servants for one guest. They were all beautifully uniformed with Indian turbans and clothing. All in red with gold embroidery and tassels and what have you. The interesting thing was, that the person that would bring you a glass of water would not take any notice of you if you asked for anything else. The one who brought the food brought the food, the one who gave you a glass of water gave a glass of water. Everybody had just one job. They wouldn't do anything else. The waiters wore these beautiful uniforms, but they were all barefoot. Nobody had shoes except the overseers. They had their embroidered Indian shoes. They also had a whip in their hand and anybody who was sluggish or didn't do exactly what they should had their feet whipped! I could not eat my first meal because I was so upset about seeing people being whipped.

That was something absolutely barbaric as far as I was concerned. Nobody took any notice of it, but that was the routine of their lives.

Anyway, we went out on the street and nearly got killed, because the beggars and the kids swamped us. We were told not to go far away from the hotel. Anyway, the first day we didn't go very far. We more or less ventured around the hotel to see all the rooms. One of the couples, (actually one of the footballers that had competed at the Olympics in Australia) had gone back to get his whole family. They had a big suite on the first floor of the hotel for the whole family, mother, father, two children and grandparents. It was absolutely magnificent! Marble bathroom fittings with gold taps and a huge king size bed. I'd never seen anything like it in my life, not even in films. The room was opulent, it wasn't just one room; they had four rooms and the bathroom. I know now it was a Suite. We sat and marvelled at the luxury in that hotel.

The second day we went out a little bit to walk around, but it was frightening, the masses of people everywhere. There was a very nice palace nearby and outside were soldiers, with guns, standing guard. So, there must have been some very important person who lived in that palace.

I found it heart breaking, when you looked out the window, first thing in the early morning. There were people virtually covering the footpath, sleeping all around the hotel. They'd move, about 7 o'clock in the morning. Fresh water was pumped through the gutters, which were normally full of rubbish. But first thing in the morning the people would squat and wash from the gutters and then get up, and go about their business.

We saw some people spitting red; we thought it

was blood! The people who could speak English (we had a couple with us) found out it was from some pods that everybody chews: it is an appetite-reducing berry, so they don't get hungry. They chew it, but it's got this red, very red juice and when they spit (and they spit everywhere) it's like having blood spread around.

Another experience was around getting to lunch. Because we were on the fourth floor you could only go down by lift. We couldn't see any stairs, so we waited by the lift but the lift didn't come. The lift wasn't automatic, there was always somebody driving the lifts up and down. Finally, Frank said: "Let's find a way down." So, we saw some people like cleaners coming out of one of the doors; so, we went around the corridor and found a door, which opened onto stairs. So, we walked down the stairs and came out into sort of a back corridor. We ran into one of the overseers who was absolutely incensed! They found an interpreter to explain to us that we had used the stairs that were only for 'untouchables' and we were not allowed to use it. We explained that we'd waited for ten minutes for the lift, knew we had to come for lunch and didn't want to be late. It turned out that the lift operator wouldn't come to get us because we didn't give him any tips. They couldn't understand that there would be white people in that hotel with no money. For them, this idea was unbelievable and therefore unacceptable. We would have loved to give them tips but we didn't have any money. The only money we had was a single, tell dollar American note, which was our 'life savings'. I couldn't possibly give that as a tip! I suppose it was a misunderstanding and I apologised. I was very sorry, at the time, that this person must have got into big trouble because of our ignorance about their culture.

To this day I still don't understand how there's such a thing as an 'untouchable'. I can't walk on the stairs where some other people walk because they're 'untouchable'? I accept that this is their culture but I could not personally condone it.

On the third day, our plane arrived. The next step was Singapore, where we also stayed for a night, in lovely rooms, in a very nice hotel. It was a total contrast to India, because it was so clean and courteous and there was none of that servant type behaviour. We slept overnight and the next afternoon we were put on a plane, for the longest stretch of our flight. This was a fourteen-hour flight to Darwin. We arrived to an absolute heat wave. India was hot and smelly; Singapore humid and hot, but Darwin topped it.

It hit us like a ton of bricks as we got out of the plane. We were shown upstairs to the airport lounge and they showed us to the restrooms, which had hot showers and clean towels. Beautiful! It was wonderful to refresh ourselves. I think we had a few hours' stay in Darwin. But, as soon as we got out of the plane, a big storm came. Our entire luggage was on the trolleys, which we could see from the window above. Even though the porters pushed the trolleys under the plane, all the water was running onto it so, when we got our bags, everything was soaking wet! All our 'beautiful' clothes that we'd collected from the Red Cross! So, we just closed the bags and hoped for the best.

After having a meal in Darwin we were put back on the plane and flown to Melbourne. We hit Melbourne's Essendon airport on the 4th of April 1957. Well, the 4th of April in Hungary is called "Freedom Day", so what I did when I got out of the plane, was to jump up and down and say, "Oh, Freedom Day. Freedom Day. Freedom Day!"

We were taken into some kind of camp where apparently the English "ten pound Poms" had lived. They were bungalows, dozens of them. Like you would have now at a caravan park. We spent a night there, and the next day, we were put into buses that took us to a new place. I must say it was a bit of a shock, coming from Europe, to sit in a bus and drive for miles and miles and see nothing but yellow ground. It wasn't anything; really, there were little hills and rivers and towns we passed. And then we arrived in Bonegilla, an army camp filled with fibro cement cabins. I think it was three rooms with one side and three rooms on the other side. Every couple got a room and families got two rooms. Well, this was something beautiful for me, our own room! Plus a communal kitchen again, with good-natured cooks who tried to cook 'Hungarian (with lots of dripping) thinking that we liked fatty stuff and off course, lots of mutton.

The food here wasn't anything better. I did not believe the chefs who cooked here were from any European country that's for sure! But they thought that because we were Hungarians, that we like paprika, so everything was red!

All the meat was lamb, or rather, mutton. We had mutton stew and lamb stew and more lamb stew with mashed potatoes, plus pies and pasties and stuff that was totally unrecognizable for us. Of course having lamb, lots of things were cooked in dripping. Another thing we didn't know.

So, it was back on the porridge again for me for quite a few days. Well, most of the times anyway, it was porridge. We were told: "We just have to wait and eventually some jobs will come up. We'd have to apply for them, we're in a depression and things were not going too good in Australia not many jobs were available."

Somebody said we could get a lift by walking to the highway and hitchhiking, the trucks come and go to Melbourne and Sydney and Adelaide, wherever.

So, it was decided that Frank and the husband of another couple that we'd got to know, (he was auto mechanic), plus some other men, would go to the highway one day and try their luck. Most of us women were just waiting around and praying that they were able to get into town and possibly find a job.

Refugee camps Austria
Dec 1956   March 1957

Salzburg lager   Start of the Journey to Australia

Kolkata (India) stop over   Stop over

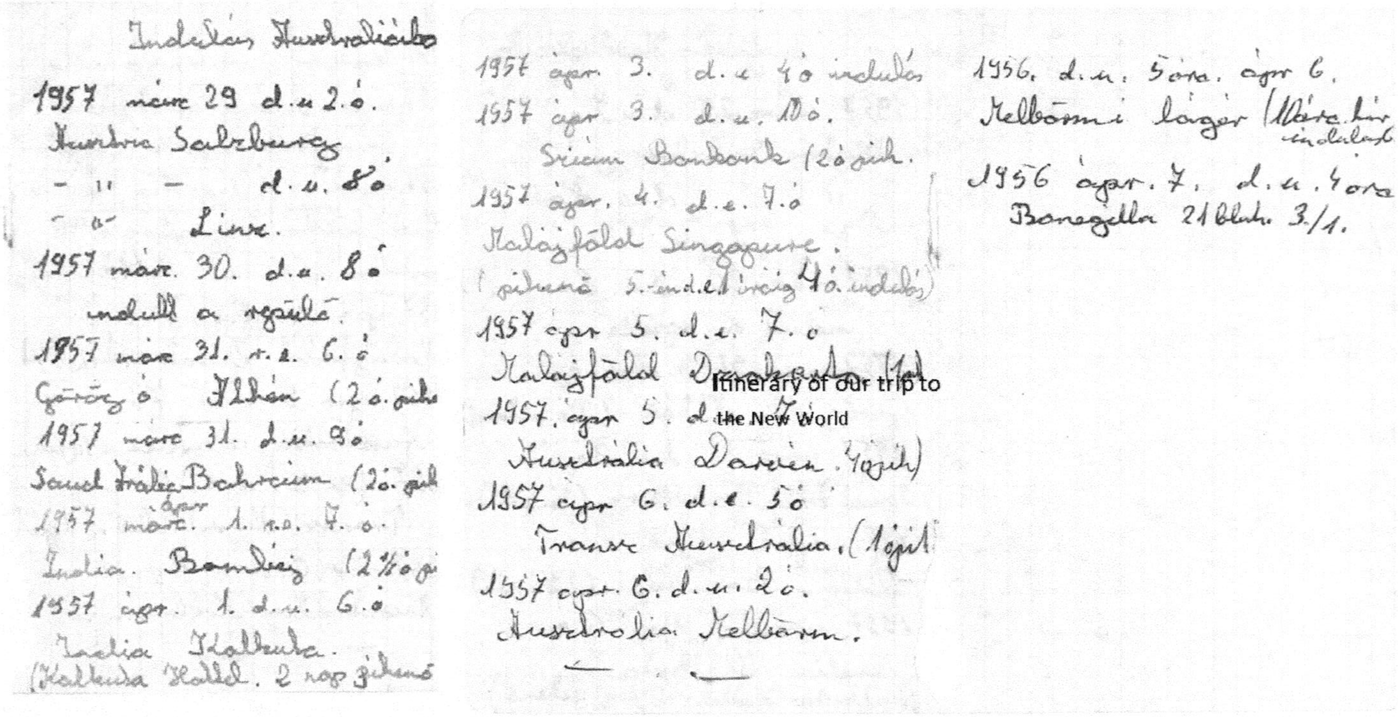
Indulás Ausztráliába

1957 márc 29 d.u 2.ó.
Ausztria Salzburg
– " – d.u. 8.ó
– " – Linz.
1957 márc. 30. d.e. 8.ó
indult a repülő.
1957 márc 31. r.e. 6.ó
Görög o. Athén (2 ó. pihe
1957 márc 31. d.u. 9.ó
Saud Arábia Bahrein (2ó. pih
1957 ápr márc. 1. r.e. 7. ó.
India. Bombáj (2½ ó p
1957 ápr. 1. d.u. 6.ó
India Kalkutta.
(Kalkutta Hotel. 2 nap pihenő

1957 ápr. 3. d.u 4 ó indulás
1957 ápr. 3. d.u. 10 ó.
Sziám Bankonk (2 ó pih.
1957 ápr. 4. d.e. 7.ó
Malájföld Singapure.
(pihenő 5.-ig d.e. 4 ó. indulás)
1957 ápr 5. d.e. 7.ó
Malájföld Darakata (1ó
1957. ápr 5. d. 7.
Ausztrália Darvin. 4 ó pih)
1957 ápr 6. d.e. 5 ó
Transz Ausztrália. (1 ó pih
1957 ápr. 6. d.u. 2 ó.
Ausztrália Melbourn.

1956. d.u. 5 óra. ápr 6.
Melbourni láger (Mára kir indulás
1956 ápr. 7. d.u. 4 óra
Bonegilla 21 blokk. 3/1.

Itinerary of our trip to the New World

Itinerary of our trip to the New World

6

Three or four days later, the men rang up from Melbourne. Two of them had got a lift from a truck driver who was heading to Melbourne. He knew about the Hungarian refugees, so he delivered them to the Hungarian Reformed Church in Fitzroy, which I believe is somewhere near St Georges Road. The pastor in that church organized a big dormitory for the men to stay, and provided meals for them. By this point, quite a few Hungarians had immigrated to Australia after the war, in 1948, '49 and '50.

Already there was a sizable community of Hungarians in Australia, who had been in Melbourne for several years, who already had homes and jobs. So, this Padre organized the Hungarians to help the newcomers and try to find them jobs and accommodation and so forth. It seems that Frank and Stephen (the guy he was with), managed to get a job in a car battery factory in Cheltenham within about 4 days. They stayed in the refuge at the church for another ten days until they got their first-week's pay.

From the first week's pay, somebody organized to rent a furnished house in Northcote. A three-bedroom ordinary weatherboard house. The beauty of it was that it was fully furnished and as it turned out, somebody must have passed on. The house had everything in it, from cutlery to towels, sewing needles and everything that you could wish for. It was a quite lovely little house. And so the two men rented the house for us to share, Stephen stayed in Melbourne and Frank came back to Bonegilla, with another Hungarian, who had a car and had been here for some years, to take us all back to Melbourne.

They paid the first week's rent with their first pay packet and then by the time they came to get us, it was the second week's wage and we really started living. The men were using trams and trains to get to Cheltenham from Northcote. We were living very close to St Georges Road on a side street (the name of which I can no longer remember). We had one bedroom to live in and the family took the other two bedrooms (they had 2 sons) and we shared the kitchen and lounge room.

The wife turned out to be a fairly bossy lady and I was sort of delegated to child minding and helping around. It was difficult to organise, because the men came home together and we cooked separate meals. I was mostly in the background because the kids had to be fed early. Then the husbands had to come first and finally we could sit down in the kitchen to eat. It wasn't a very good arrangement, and, for obvious reasons, I wasn't very happy about it.

I'd come from one lot of servitude with my aunty and cousins then to my brother and mother and now into another situation that was exactly the same. I was being a maid to a total stranger and her two children, people I'd only known for a short time, from the camps. The older one was about 6/7, the younger one about 2 and they were both fairly spoiled. In fact, the older one was a nasty little piece. He always made sure that he did something to annoy me, or he'd go his mother to blame me for whatever he had done.

We were given a Hungarian-English dictionary, which was a Godsend. I was trying to learn a few words, and when we got here I went shopping in St. Georges Road. There was a little shopping strip, with a little grocery shop, vegetables and a butcher. So, I went shopping, as I'd decided I was going to make some goulash and nokedli or noodles to go with it.

I asked, "Can I have a packet of flour?"

The lady in the shop pointed to the shelves and asked, "Which one?" There were about 4 or 5 different coloured boxes of branded flours. I will never forget there was yellow, red, blue, and I think green. So, anyway, all these boxes were there and I said. "I don't know." So she just picked up a box of red flour, handed it to me and said that's the most used. That's how I understood her at the time.

I took it home, made my goulash and I mixed enough dough to last us for two meals so I didn't have to cook every day. I boiled the water and cut the first nokedli into the boiling water and it started to grow … and it grew, and grew and grew until it filled the pot!

What am I to do now?

I fished it out and tried the smaller piece that grew and grew, so we ended up eating goulash with only two nokedli, and even two was far too much! When I remember it, I'm laughing now, but as it turned out it was self-raising flour, which I'd never heard of before!

There was a Hungarian couple that every so often would come by and try to show us where to shop, what to do and how to do things in this country. Like how to use the refrigerator, the washing machine and the oven.

That lady was very helpful, she was laughing like anything that I bought the self-rising flour instead of plain flour. It was a waste because we just couldn't eat it. First of all, it didn't taste great and secondly like I said, one nokedli filled the pot. The other thing that happened was that when I went to the green grocer, I just didn't compute the fact that pound weight and kilos were different. I knew that two pounds was one kilo. But it just didn't compute when I looked at it. I thought, 'If I buy a kilo of potatoes that should be enough for us for a few days'. (Australia was still using pounds and ounces at this time and the money was in Pounds, shillings and pence.)

So, I said to the greengrocer, "I would like one pound of potatoes." He looked at me and said, "One pound?" He just looked confused, went to the back of the shop, where there were 5lb bags of potatoes. Potatoes with the red dirt still on them (unwashed). A 5lb bag (which is two and a half kilos,) was far too much for us.

He came back with a potato that was the size of a melon. I don't even think he charged me for it. He just gave it to me and this huge potato lasted for nearly two weeks. This is how I learned the Australian way of housekeeping. Someone explained to me later that I should have asked for a bag of potatoes instead of pounds.

We'd arrived in Melbourne at the beginning of May and winter wasn't very comfortable because it was cold and wet. We only had one kerosene heater, which was in the living room. The family was in there most of the time, so it was a bit difficult. By that time, we got in contact with Panni and Bill. She was nearly ready to have her baby, so we decided on Sunday to go and visit them. Which was quite a trip! We had to go into the city by train, and then get another train from the city to Brunswick where they lived. Panni and I were talking, she was very unhappy with her uncle's wife, a German lady. She was also expecting any minute with her first baby as well, both of them were pregnant and pretty edgy. She wouldn't let Panni use the house facilities because that was their home. Bill and Panni had one room and they would have been getting the same kind of treatment that I was - so we were both unhappy.

Bill, at that time, already had a job in the railways, via the uncle, who had worked there for many years. Bill had also taken a second job at night to clean in the old exhibition buildings. He was telling us that we could get a small flat, somewhere closer to the city that would be easier for Frank to get to Cheltenham. We would no longer need to share a house. Bill found us a house, in Nicholson Street. An Italian couple owned the house. Actually, the Italian couple owned 6 of these terrace houses. The whole block was theirs. The house was divided in to three flats, in the large downstairs one lived a Hungarian couple who been there for some time. The husband was much older, he was already retired so, he didn't do much, he just sat around at home and read books and enjoyed life. His wife was working in the Royal Women's hospital as a cleaner. The Morrison's had two rooms and a kitchen and bathroom downstairs. Upstairs, the top flat was let to a couple; it had the large front room and a kitchen and the bathroom was shared with us. We had the small back room, our kitchen was in the backyard, there was a bungalow fitted out with stove etc. I was ecstatic about it. It was going to cost 2 pounds 10 shilling, which would be about $5 dollars (as the pound was divided in half when we changed to Dollars). Frank earned 13 pounds a week in the factory. He needed about 5 pounds for his travel and cigarettes and incidentals. That left us with 8 pounds. So, I worked it out, if it's 2 pounds 10 shillings for the rent (which included gas and electricity at the time) we would be able to save. So, that was that, it was really good. They had furniture in it but we didn't have kitchen equipment, cutlery, cups, pots or sheets, nor towels and pillows and so. But there was a bed and cupboard, a stove and table and chairs.

We decided to splurge and so rented this little flat. We moved out from the house, which actually produced quite a lot of bad blood, because the family was devastated. We were paying half of the rent, which was at that time 6 pounds, but only had one third of the house. It was always very difficult sharing the bathroom, the kitchen and so forth. They said they wouldn't be able to manage with the two children and pay the rent, because he was only earning 13 pounds a week, the same as Frank. I said, "I'm terribly sorry but I can't live this way. You can arrange to maybe get a boarder or something and that will help to pay the rent." Young boys would go into boarding with Hungarians families, so they had somewhere to live and therefore paid for board etc.

Anyway, it wasn't a very amicable goodbye with this family but I stood my ground. Frank would have buckled a couple of times and suggested we think about it.

I said, "No. I came away from Hungary because I wanted my own home. I want my own place, my own family. I am not going to be a slave to someone else again. I want a place for myself, so we are moving."

With that, we moved into our new flat on a Saturday. We picked up our stuff (which wasn't much) and moved in. Then we went to Bourke Street, to 'Coles' department store (it was 'the best place to shop') and did a big shop to fit out our home. We used up 10 pounds of our precious savings and bought pillows, two sets of sheets and pillows covers, towels, two woollen blankets, two plates, two cups, two spoons, knives, forks and wooden spoons, plus three pots and a frying pan. We had our new home all ready to go, fully equipped.

I felt I was out-of-this-world lucky to have new things and my own home finally! Anyway, it worked very well. Frank took the train to Cheltenham for work. Soon I found the Queen Victoria Market for shopping. Fridays and Saturdays, I would walk from Nicholson Street to the Victoria Market and buy fruit, veggies, whatever we needed. I worked out what to cook for the week. I bought live chickens because I could get a chicken for sixpence. I bought two for a shilling, I could get the things like liver and heart and the cheaper cuts of meat. It was great on Friday afternoon or Saturday lunchtime, around closing time, when they sold things off cheaply. My housekeeping was 'Two Pound and Ten Shillings' for a week and we still could save and have good healthy fresh food.

After a reasonably short term, I found a job not very far from the flat, in a little factory. They were making electric drills and I was given the job to clean them up and polish them ready for packing. I was earning at the time I think 6 pounds, which we saved.

Our entertainment day was usually Sunday, because Frank worked on a Saturday and I usually did the shopping. Sundays we would pack our bags up, walk across to Brunswick, from Nicholson Street, to Sydney Road and visit Panni and Bill. Together we might go to the park and sit and talk. By July, their son Bill jnr. (his name is Tibor/Tibi for short) was born. In the first few weeks, I splurged on a cheap sewing machine. I think the couple downstairs helped me buy it, so I could remodel my clothes. I also bought material from the market, so I made a skirt and blouse and so forth. I became Godmother to Tibi (Bill Jnr), and made a baby pillow (called a poja in Hungary), which is a long pillow with a cover. The top for the head is usually round with frills or lace, and then the sides just have the material to tie-up, which makes it look like it has wings. The pillow can be folded back with the wings and a couple of ribbons tied, so the baby can be carried quite securely, even in one hand, without being worried that the baby's neck is unsupported. You could carry the baby and a shopping bag: and the baby is nice and cosy.

I believe even today in Hungary, it's still used, because it's a very practical little pillow and so I made one. In Hungary, we used feathers for the pillow but because I couldn't get any feathers in Melbourne, I just used rolls and rolls of cotton wool to make the pillow. I made a couple of covers for Tibi when he was born. I also made him some little shirts, tops and little jumpsuits. It kept me busy and I saved a lot of money. I made some clothes, adjusted clothes for Panni as well, and some other friends too. The old gentleman downstairs was I believe a tailor by trade, but he wouldn't admit to it (he said he was an officer). He showed me a lot of sewing tricks and helped me to do some of the sewing. We were actually very happy living that way. After work we just sat around reading, studying, trying to learn English on our own, because there wasn't any school so, we just learned on the fly. Learned the words from the dictionary and read the papers to try to learn the language and find out what's going on. This was the happiest times and memories of my marriage.

One special and funny memory is that on one of the trips between Nicholson Street and Brunswick, on one nice hot day, in summer (Saturday afternoon) to visit Panni and Bill (now living in Albion Street) Frank said, "What about we have a glass of beer?"

And I thought well, "I could have a small glass of beer. Why not?"

So, the corner of Sydney Road and Albion Street is the Albion Hotel and we just marched into the bar and Frank ordered two glasses of beer and the next thing I know, the bartender jumped the bar, grabbed me by the hand and virtually walked me out of the hotel, my feet barely touching the ground. He virtually carried me outside and dumped me on the front of the door and said, "No women!"

Frank got so worried he just left the beer. We went on to Panni's and when we got there, we told them the story about me being bodily taken out of the hotel. They were rolling with laughter and said, "Don't you know that women are not allowed to go into the bar? You can only go into the ladies' lounge which is in the back."

How ridiculous that women were not allowed into the pub! So, that was a lesson! Anyway, we never visited a pub after that, because I wasn't going to be sitting in the ladies lounge on my own.

The Morrisons were very useful because they helped us understand the local 'rules'. They'd been in Australia since 1948, so they knew how everyone behaved. We could talk to them because they were Hungarians. She tried to explain to us that we definitely had to get private health insurance because in Australia the hospitals were not free and if you needed medical attention of any sort you had to have health insurance. So, we signed up for health insurance, which was a very hard thing to decide, because I think we had to pay a pound a week. That was quite expensive at that time too. That was sometime in late 1957.

Then I found out that I was pregnant. We tried to keep it quiet as much as we could for a long time, because it was a surprise to us as well. You didn't talk about it, because if they found out at work you would lose your job. I was quite worried because we didn't have an awful lot of money saved by then. I was just worried about how we would manage with having a baby and what kind of a job would I get. I went to visit an old Hungarian Jewish doctor, to make sure that I was really pregnant.

The birth control pills my cousin Jancso (he was already working as a trainee doctor) had given me back in Hungary as a wedding present had run out and I didn't know where to get any and wouldn't know who to ask or how to buy any.

So, I went to visit this Hungarian doctor in St Kilda, mostly to get some birth control pills, which at that time, wasn't legal in Melbourne, so he couldn't give me any anyway.

He said, "You are nearly three months pregnant," after the examination and I thought, "Oh dear. So, what happens now?"

By the time I was about four months along, I was not very well. I started to swell up and had problems of tiredness and dizziness. I had to tell the doctor of my heart history

He said, "Your heart is not strong enough, you won't be able to carry that baby. Even if you manage to carry to full term that's fine, but, I can't guarantee that there will be a healthy baby or that you will survive. So, why don't you have an abortion?"

I said, "No. No way, I won't have an abortion!" This was my first baby, and I believed at the time that if you aborted the first pregnancy you coulnd't get pregnant again. I did want some children eventually, just not right now. But I was pregnant, and I wanted that baby, despite what the doctor said.

By 5 and half months along, I was really showing and of course, at work they noticed it and I was given my marching orders. I couldn't be working because they thought lifting those six-kilo big electric drills from the ground, cleaning and putting it back down again would probably be too much. Besides, they didn't employ pregnant women. I was very unhappy because it meant that we couldn't save as much. And having the baby, how would we cope? My doctor had passed on by this point as he was quite old, and I didn't have a new doctor. The lady who lived downstairs worked in the hospital as a cleaner, so she took me to the Royal Women's Hospital, to register for hospital treatment. I went regularly to the check-ups, and she sometimes came with me to try and translate, as my English was still non-existent.

The doctors were getting very unhappy, because I was putting on so much weight. By 6- 7 months I was absolutely huge. I was so huge that I was too ashamed to walk out on the street. My feet were like tree trunks and my shoes didn't fit. I had to buy some men's slippers, because my feet were so swollen. I was putting on weight and putting on weight, but I didn't eat. I ate as much as I could but I got sick a lot of times, so nothing was working. When I went for my check-up, which was after seven and a half months, the doctor was really angry with me. He screamed and yelled. He said, "If you don't lose weight I am going to keep you in the hospital and starve you, because you're too fat!"

I kept telling him - through my friend the translator - that I didn't eat.

He said, "I know, all you bloody wogs, you say you don't eat but you're just shoving pasta and sausages in."

Anyway, he said I had to come back in two and a half weeks and I had to lose between eight and ten pounds by then! If I didn't lose the weight he'd admit me to hospital on a starvation diet. But I was hardly eating anyway! I was always thirsty and I knew I was retaining water because when I touched my legs with my fingers, the skin puckered in and didn't jump back - the hole stayed there for quite a while. I knew I was full with fluid. Anyway, as it happens my next checkup was the day after the Queen's birthday long weekend.

The people from the bigger flat upstairs had moved out a couple of months earlier and the landlord asked if we wanted it. He'd only charge four pounds and we'd have two bedrooms the kitchen and bathroom all upstairs. The front room was huge! A really large room furnished with a double bed and built-in robe, cupboards. It had three big windows to the street. It was a lovely room with decorated ceilings and it had red lino on the floor, which I kept polished beautifully. On that weekend I decided to do spring cleaning in June. I washed the windows, made-up fresh beds and tidied everything and polished the floor. By that time my stomach was so large that I couldn't bend, so I was on my bum slitting around the floor to polish it. I weighed 100 kilos. I was huge, absolutely huge. In the last couple of months, I would only go out in the street at night, because I was too ashamed to walk around in public. I was absolutely like an elephant.

So, I'm spring-cleaning and on the Monday night about 2 o'clock I had to go to the loo but I couldn't make it! My water broke and my beautifully freshly cleaned floor was all wet! At three in morning, I was down on my bum again, cleaning up the floor, and then the contractions started. It was getting fairly close. I had prepared the baby clothes, I had the bag packed, and everything was ready, except I didn't have a dressing gown. I had planned to buy a dressing gown the following week on sale.

Frank said, "Let's go to the hospital."

I said, "No I can't go to the hospital I need a dressing gown."

So, by 9 o'clock when the shops opened, he was at Coles and bought me a dressing gown. By the time he came back, the contraction was fairly close together and I wasn't feeling good.

He offered to carry me down the stairs. I asked him if he wanted to throw me, as I was too heavy and the stairs were so narrow, so I virtually bumped down the stairs on my bum because I couldn't really walk. I had to stop on the stairs for a contraction, and then bump a few more steps, and then Frank helped me into the taxi.

At the hospital, they put me on a trolley and the doctor, who was supposed to see me for the reduction diet, took one look at me and said, "My God there are twins!"

I knew it, all along! I knew I was having twins, and for the last few months I'd been telling them that, but nobody had believed me. I'd heard two heartbeats and they'd tell me it was an echo of a heartbeat, that I was only carrying one. I'd told them, "Well the baby must have half a dozen legs and arms because I get kicked from all ends of my stomach. It's up, down, everywhere!"

"No, no it's one very big baby. You will be in trouble because the baby is huge and we don't know how it will be born."

By the time I was on that trolley in the hospital, my stomach was like a tent. The middle of my stomach was standing up and one baby's head was on the right side of my tummy and another head on the left side under the ribs, sticking out.

The next thing I remember is a couple of injections and that was that for maybe five days. I was kept under sedation. Every now and then, I'd sort of come half conscious and I find myself strapped to the bed. Under the bed was a bucket and water was dripping into the bucket. They were draining the fluid from me!

After five days, when I finally became conscious, the doctor told me that I was very lucky, because I had two beautiful big girls and they're healthy and I'm still alive and all is well.

I didn't believe them, because I hadn't seen my babies. They helped me into a wheelchair and rolled me up to the nursery window, but I wasn't allowed to go in. The staff pulled up two baby carts to the window for me to look at.

"On the left, that's not mine, she's sick she's going to die." I was quite hysterical actually and obviously I wasn't really with it. The doctor went into the nursery, checked the name and it was true, it wasn't my baby. They brought the second baby along and I settled down.

"Okay, that's mine," I said, "But you said they were big girls. To me they're like little bunnies. They're tiny."

He said, "What do you want? They're nearly 6 pounds each. These are huge babies! If it was just one baby, you wouldn't have been able to have it. This is a fantastic result." And so forth.

I stayed for two weeks in the hospital, until I was allowed to get up and go home. I did not have any milk but the little I had, I had to pump. Five days after the birth I was put on the scales, I was 45 kilos (a change from a 100). All that weight was fluid from the babies!

I was allowed home after ten days and had to pump every 3 hours, trying to feed the babies. Well, I possibly had two cups for the whole day, which was virtually nothing of course, but thankfully the girls were on formula. I didn't have enough in one-day pumping that would feed one of them, (let alone both) for even one feed. So, the milk I produced was given to Pearly one day, and then given to Georgie the next day. For 7 weeks, I walked to the Women's hospital every single day to be with my babies. I learned to put the nappies on the Australian way, and bathe them and so forth. I was allowed into the nursery. They had to be in there until they were over 6 pounds. Georgie struggled to put on weight. She was always a couple of ounces behind Pearly. Pearly had reached the 6 pounds and Georgie was still about 2 or 3 ounces below.

They said, "Maybe you could take home one?" I

said, "No, no I take them home together, I won't take them one at a time."

Then I found out that the births had to be registered straight away. Frank registered them, because I was under sedation, as Ilona for Pearly and Rozalia for Georgie! The two grandmother's names. I was furious! There's no way they should be called their grandmother's names! I was called after my mother that was bad enough. I wanted them to have a second name, a proper twin name, which is seven letters and the middle of the name is different, an N in one and an R in the other, which is Gyöngyi and Györgyi

By the time I got home, I found out the other major things that had happened; my beloved husband, after the girls were born, got totally drunk, went over to Panni and Bill's and with everyone we knew present, cried his heart out!

"What am I going to do with two girls? I wanted a boy. And instead I get two girls! It's not enough that it's a girl but there are two of them."

I was devastated by his behaviour. He began drinking more and more. Then 3 weeks after I got home from the hospital, he decided that a small growth on his left wrist warranted an operation.

He was in a private hospital for three days. A part of it was paid by the health insurance, but it still cost quite a bit. My hospital bill had to be paid, because I didn't realize that I was already two months pregnant when we took out the health insurance. This meant we had to pay for the girls' stay and my stay in hospital as well.

It ate up most of our savings. On top of that, he went out and bought a new twin pram without asking me. Well, it was very nice but still, it was too expensive for our finances. And by the time the girls came out of hospital, we were at loggerheads.

Finally the girls could come home. I went to collect them, armed with their own clothes that I made and the two 'Poja' (the Hungarian baby pillows). The nurses made a big thing about the poja, saying, "You can't use these, what are you thinking of?"

But I insisted and showed them how they worked. Poja allowed me to carry both babies at the same time. While this was going on, my doctor arrived and he was enchanted with the idea. As soon as I got them ready, he picked up the two girls and of he wanted to show everyone in the hospital how pretty and practical the poja is. I had to wait over an hour before we could leave to go home.

On a happier note, a carpenter friend had made a double cot for the girls by the time I bought them home from hospital. A normal size cot would have been too small and 2 separate cots just didn't seem right. I wanted a special one, that way they were together all the time. The first week home was a nightmare. They got used to being fed immediately whilst in the hospital. So, it was changing nappies, getting bottles ready, settling one, then other one started. I was worn out and my decision was made - they had to learn a routine of feeding and sleeping.

I warned the neighbours that we would have a few rough nights and asked for their indulgence. So, the first feed was 6 am, then cleaned up and left for 4 hours. They complained of course and cried until 10 pm, when the last feed finished. Then I closed the door of the second room and tried to sleep. That was of course not possible as they cried and cried and cried. One by one, or in tandem. Then at 6am I was there with the bottles and mercifully they were quiet. This happened for two nights, but on the third night they had a bit of cry, then as I didn't move, they became quiet. They tried again a couple of hours later, until the morning. By the fourth night, they slept till 6am and the bottles were there promptly. After that, we never had any further trouble. They slept through the night, unless they had some tummy upset or other complaint.

When they were home, about ten to twelve days, I noticed that they were playing with each other's hands very happily. Later I would lay them head to toe, so they discovered not just their own feet, but the other one's as well. So, they played happily with each other for hours. They would not sleep if the other one were not in the room. Bath times were a bit of a noisy affair, as they did not like it when one had to wait for their turn for the bath. This was also the case when one had to wait for her bottle. But generally we managed quite well. I found that I had less of a problem than Panni, whose second baby Susy was born in September of the same year and young Bill was fourteen months old by then. We kept comparing notes, neither of our lives was a bed of roses. She had problems with Bill's drinking and the bad influence by his uncle and I had problems with Frank.

He was spending money like it's nobody's business and I was worried sick about how we were going to manage. I wasn't able to start working with the girls being so young and paying for child minding was not possible. What could we do?

By early October, Frank came home one Friday after work and said, "We're moving tomorrow."

I said, "What do you mean?"

He'd rented a house in Ormond, (without saying a word to me of his intentions or discussing anything with me). It was closer to his work, and he said we could get someone to share the house with us, so we could manage. Virtually in 48 hours, he packed us up and we moved. He got some friends to take our stuff.

It was a nice old three-bedroom house, but we didn't have any furniture and only the basic household stuff. Frank bought some furniture from friends and had a carpenter friend make us a wardrobe. He went around and bought second-hand furniture like a dining table and chairs, couch and a television (that was 'most important') and all on a system called hire purchase, spending every penny we had. From then on, we virtually lived pay cheque to pay cheque. It was unbelievably difficult. I couldn't do anything. I just had to follow on because I didn't work. I didn't have any money, I didn't know anybody, so I didn't have that much of a chance to make big waves. We had the two babies and I had to think of how we were going to manage, which was devastating. Really devastating for quite a while.

First shared house
Northcote

Independent first flat
Nicholson St

First time at the beach

With Panni & baby Bill
(just find out I'm expecting)

First Christmas with the Gang

Burke St. Father Christmas corner

7

I must talk about that time from settling into Nicholson Street (that little flat) and our independence before the children were born. That was just over a year. It was a difficult but also a quite exciting life, because we were all trying to establish ourselves. We were working hard and we were saving hard. The four or five couples we knew, from the various refugee camps, were all living like this. We kept in contact because of the times we'd shared together. We visited one another on the weekends, in our free time, as that was our entertainment. We did not know very much about anything but we also tried to get to know the town. We were constantly looking around and learning about Melbourne, Panni and Bill had their baby, Tibi who was born on 10th July in 1957. Shortly afterwards, they moved into a little flat, at the back of a shop. They rented the back of the shop to be independent, which was great for them in many ways, but also quite challenging.

With the new baby, they couldn't so easily move around, but we didn't have any responsibilities just yet, so we'd go with other couples and meet at their houses or find a place at the beach for the day, to see what the beach looked like and what people did there. We had little parties, which were quite pleasant. I become Tibi's godmother, as I said I made the 'Poja' for him which is a long pillow that wraps up the baby keeps it warm. It was July, so it was cold and it was very useful for Panni to have that special little wrap. Also, it was the Hungarian way of carrying a baby in a long pillow that was folded to support the head and then tied with ribbons. It looked really cute we had a lovely Christening for him in the Hungarian church and Panni was really happy.

Things were looking up, we had some fun but it was really a very cheap way of living. We were all very enthusiastic, very young and hopeful. Unfortunately, Panni's husband Bill got into the habit of drinking with his uncle. At this stage, Frank didn't drink. He told me that his father was a drunk so he didn't want any alcohol. He was very sober. We enjoyed ourselves together and we spent quite a lot of time with one another. It was one of the happiest times of my life and we really lived a loving, peaceful life

And then I found out I was pregnant. I was a little bit taken aback but I didn't tell anyone. We just kept it to ourselves. Frank was really happy about it, but by February, I was showing quite a bit. Also, Panni was devastated because she found that she was pregnant again and their baby was only seven or eight months old. It wasn't a very good thing for her. She'd just started work and then had to give it away. Bill was a really hard worker. He worked at the railways by the day, and at night time he cleaned the Royal exhibition buildings, so he was really doing the very best thing for his family. Things were looking up for them, so it was a devastation for them to think how they were going to cope having two children so quickly, one after another.

I told Panni that I was expecting too, so we were comparing notes. She was telling me all the things I should expect, how it went and what I needed to look for. So, the first part of 1958 was still in the 'happy go lucky' atmosphere. Of course that all went up in smoke, because by the time my babies were born, Frank was disappointed and devastated about having two daughters. Our relationship started to deteriorate, I found it hard to forget his behaviour after the birth. He just went on a rampage of spending and there was not much I could do about it. He even bought a car, on credit of course.

8

We'd moved to Ormond, to an old three-bedroom house. It had five fireplaces, so the heating wasn't very comfortable, and we used a kerosene heater as well. The bathroom had a wood-fired hot water heater and the laundry had an old copper, but no washing machine. Frank, as I said, had all the furniture on hire purchase, and we only had one income and had to pay the rent and the instalments on the hire-purchase. A week or so after we moved in, I got a kidney infection, which I'd had previously, (it had happened before, while I was pregnant.) Now it was back, and I was really in a lot of pain. I couldn't do a lot of things, and I was looking after the babies, changing them and bathing them and I couldn't stand up because of the infection and constant backache.

On all fours, I went in to the garage to get wood for the fire. A lovely old gentleman called in to say he wanted to welcome us to the neighbourhood. They lived two doors up from us in number 7 and we were in 11. He saw me on all fours packing the basket with wood and he asked what was the matter. I tried to explain that I had pains and I coulnd't stand up. I was taking painkillers for my back, but I couldn't take it all the time because they were upsetting my stomach.

Anyway, he helped me to take the wood in and lit the fire in there, in the dining room where the children were, and then he said farewell. An hour or so later, he came back with a big pot of vegetable soup, which was absolutely wonderful! That's how I got to know my neighbours, Alex and Lillian. They were in their sixties and they had their granddaughter living with them. We became quite friendly with them and I was very, very grateful for their help. Lillian started to teach me English.

Within about three weeks of living in the house, Frank found a young Hungarian couple with a baby of their own, (who was almost the same age as our daughters) who needed somewhere to live. As the husband was working nearby, they decided to share the house with us.

They had the bedroom at the back, we had the front bedroom and we shared the lounge and the dining room. The arrangement was that they would go to work and I would look after the three babies and maintain the housework. I washed and cooked and cleaned after everybody, four adults and three babies. I did the washing in the copper, by hand. At that time, there were only material nappies.

It was working out for us, because they were

paying half of the rent, plus they were paying for the baby-sitting of course. We shared the food bill but I can't even remember if they paid anything for my cooking and cleaning and so forth. Anyway, that was working out, but unfortunately the lady decided that if I was looking after their baby (their baby slept with them in their bedroom) and she cried at night, I was the one who had to get up and resettle her. All because her mother was 'working' and needed her sleep. I of course, didn't go out to work, I was home just looking after three babies and kept house for 4-5 adults, I was just a housewife!

So it was 24-hour servitude again for strangers! It worked reasonably well for a while, but then I decided I had enough and I rather take on a job at night. This meant Frank could look after the children and the other couple would do part of the housework and look after the children at night. So, the arrangement was that Frank went to work at 7 am and got back home at 4 pm. I took the 4:30pm train into the city, as I was offered a job working in a coffee shop, cooking and serving, for a Hungarian Jewish couple who owned the coffee shop. I was there until 11-11.30 pm at night, then had to take the 11:50pm last train back to Ormond.

The café was situated next door to the Lido Theatre, which had a lot of very good plays on, and at ten pm when the play finished, the coffee shop would usually be full. I had to cook some meals and I served coffees. A lot of the time I was on my own there, as the owners left me to do whatever needed doing. I'd also close the shop. They lived upstairs. It was a reasonably good job, it worked out really well and the pay was much better, as I got some tips as well.

One night I came home a bit earlier, because there wasn't much happening. It was the middle of the week and we closed up, as there weren't any customers. I came home on an earlier train, thinking how lucky I am to get home about 10.30 pm, instead of 1 o'clock in the morning. Low and behold, I opened the bedroom door and there in our bed was my husband and the woman who was sharing the house with us. Her husband was working nights as well, so the two of them were making good use of their evenings.

As it turned out, this had been going on for quite some time. I must say I wasn't very surprised about it, but of course I was terribly upset, as it's not the nicest thing to discover.

I said, "Well, that's it! You just have to leave because I can't live this way, it's not going to work."

I told her husband the next day, that they have to find another place to live, but I didn't say why. I gave him the excuse that as I was earning money and Frank was as well, we'd be better on our own. In two weeks, they moved out.

In the beginning, when they'd joined us, there were other Hungarian couples living nearby. One Saturday evening, we decided to go somewhere and have some fun. One of our neighbours looked after our three babies and we drove to Dandenong, in Frank's car. Back then, Dandenong was "in the country" and therefore didn't have six o'clock closing.

We arrived at the pub in Dandenong and had some fish and chips. The others started drinking. I've never been a drinker myself, so I was sober, but the two men and the girl were absolutely "legless" drunk and we had to get home. The hotel closed at 9:00pm, we had to get back to Ormond, but the men and the woman were too drunk to drive.

They decided I had to drive. Well, I can laugh at the memory now, but back then all I knew about driving is from watching Frank drive. I had gone with him for a couple of his driving lessons, so I only knew the brakes and the clutch and basics. The poor car suffered badly with my changing of gears. It was a 'Ford Saphire', a nice old, second-hand car, very solid, but on that drive home that night, I would have to pull off the road, every ten minutes, so that somebody could be sick.

It was a nightmare to get home, and disappointing that it had been the one and only time I went out to 'enjoy myself' with company.

So, once that couple left, it was Frank and I and the girls. Frank was supposed to look after the children while I was working. When he came home from work, I had everything ready so he only had to feed them, change them and put them to bed.

I was chatting with Lillian one day who said she was worried about the children, were they sick? She'd heard them crying a lot at night. That worried me. And then one night, just as I was coming home, I could see all the way down our street (Ormond Rd is a short street, off North Road), I saw a car pull into our drive. When I got home, I went to the garage. The car was hot, so I hadn't been seeing things. Frank was in bed pretend-snoring. I could smell the liquor on his breath. I don't know where he had been, but he'd had quite a bit to drink. When I told him that I knew that he been out, he got quite aggro.

Apparently what he'd been doing was putting the children to bed after I'd gone to work, then he would go out and return just before I got home. He'd been leaving the children on their own, for up to five hours at a time.

It couldn't go on. I had to resign from my job, because although it was a very well-paid job and I got quite a bit extra from tips, I just couldn't do it, because it was not possible to leave the children on their own. I was too worried and I couldn't depend on Frank.

By that time, he had left the factory and was working with a plumber. He couldn't work as a plumber on his own because he needed to pass a test to get his license, but he worked with the plumber, digging trenches and doing heavy work.

Then somebody recommended that I do some sewing at home which was great. A Hungarian Jewish Man was making electric blankets: I didn't know that kind of thing existed - it was really a new invention! Anyway, what I had to do, was to thread the wire into these blankets - he had the ribbing sewn by somebody else - connect the end to a plug and sew the joiner to the corner, so it could be fixed into place, and never move or shift. I was paid a fixed amount per blanket, which I could do at home. Luckily, he gave me a blanket as a template, which someone else had sewn, but the sewing was uneven and he couldn't sell it. So, he gave it to me, which was brilliant! I could have a warm bed to sleep in because the house was generally quite cool. I could only heat up the dining room with the big fireplace, and the kitchen was warm from the cooking. The bedroom was seldom heated, just a little heat from the kerosene heater to take the chill off for the children at night, so they didn't get too cold.

That reminds me of another incident with the girls: when I put them down for their afternoon nap, they liked to sleep in the play-pen. This was a corner, about 2.50m by 1.30m, bordered with a cot rail, sheet and blankets and at one end, and it had a cot mattress. They could play with their toys, until they fell asleep. One afternoon I thought they were sleeping too long, so I looked into the room and could not see the girls in the play-pen. I panicked a bit, rushed in and there are the darlings, in the wardrobe, which had sliding doors. They'd unpacked the bottom three shelves and were playing hidey. They did that a few times before I realised how they got out of the playpen. They had stacked the teddies on the mattress, which made it high enough to get over the top of the rail and had some good fun, rearranging the room.

Another time I remember well was when we had to go to the health centre nurse for their check up. I had knitted a winter outfit for them both, in lovely pink wool: pants, jumper, hat and gloves, got them all dressed and ready and then I needed to go to the toilet. So I left them sitting in their little chairs - two minutes I was away, but - when I got back to the dining room, (where I didn't have time to clean the fireplace from the night before), the two of them were sitting in the fireplace and painting each other with ash, head to toe. We had to have a wash and a change of clothes so, we were a bit late getting to the appointment.

When they were about sixteen months old, they could run like the wind; we were in the front yard, when I needed to go inside for a few minutes, leaving them near the porch. Next thing I knew, they were over the fence (80cm high, made of metal mesh) and running in opposite directions. I just stood and screamed 'Someone please catch that child!' Luckily, Rosalie got one and I managed the other. I had to have eyes in the back of my head.

Another couple that we knew were looking to share a house. They had a baby as well, so, they moved in to share the house with us. This time, we didn't share the housework as such or cooking or anything else, they did it for themselves. The husband had a younger brother who was living with them, so he moved into the third bedroom, which was actually more or less a closed-up sunroom. He paid full board for me to look after him, to do his cooking and washing. Then, that other lady went to work for a while as well, so I looked after her child too, did the housework, same scenario as before.

So, I was cooking for five adults and three children and washing and cleaning and so forth. Then the friend of the young man decided he needed a room, so he moved in to share with the younger brother.

Now, there were two men in the spare room, which meant six adults in the house. That also meant that we had help with the rent and I was earning a bit extra from the cooking, cleaning, child minding plus my sewing.

The new boy decided that he needed a fresh shirt every single day and it was part of the full board as far as he was concerned. I couldn't wash and iron that many shirts, on top of all the other washing I had to do, plus everything else. I told him, "Your board includes two washed shirts a week – one work shirt and one best shirt, but no more."

After that, he suddenly didn't need to change his shirt every day. But he, like every one else, thought he'd found a silly one in me, one who just did everything!

I did my sewing work at night, regardless of the housework for everyone else. Then the lady had a problem with her child and had to take time off work. She lost her job, so she was at home as well. By this time, Frank was drinking an awful lot, and often came home drunk, after going out with his work mates. One evening, he came home about, 11 pm. I was in the dining room doing the sewing, and the two young men were sitting and talking as they had just got back. Frank drunkenly crashed into the house and started yelling and fighting with the young men, accusing me of having an affair with them!

Somehow he thought I had an awful lot of time and energy left over, after keeping house with six adults and three children and doing the sewing on top of it. Obviously, I must have had so much time that I could afford to keep a boyfriend as well!

Home from hospital 7 weeks
(in Mum made "POJA")

3 month old getting to know the garden

Unhappy day in the park 6 month

In our 'Cherry' jump-suits

In the front garden from where we escaped 18 month

He made such a fuss, screaming and yelling, that the husband of the couple living with us ran off and called the police. The police came and took Frank away because he was totally drunk and out of his mind. So he spent a night in jail.

There were obviously lots of arguments and carrying on, it wasn't a very peaceful time. In the meantime, Lillian the next door neighbour and Alex had been absolutely wonderful. They helped me with official papers and Lillian was teaching me English. She gave me Georgette Heyer books to read. They are regency romances and very easy to read and beautifully written. I'd read them when I had a little extra time, just before sleep, reading with the dictionary in my other hand.

So that was my learning curve around English, there was no government support, there were no schools that we could go to, to learn English, there was nothing. We didn't get anything from the government. Not a penny of support, no child maintenance, nothing. It was do it yourself, not like today.

By that time, life was very difficult, Frank collected all the payment from the boarders and only gave me a small amount for housekeeping. He would do some shopping from the list I gave him, but small items and daily stuff I had to get. Sometimes I would buy things for the children and put food on credit from the corner Milkbar, so when he went for his cigarettes, he had to pay the whole bill, as the money he gave me wasn't enough. I would get two oranges or two bananas for the children, but if he found it, he would eat it, and I didn't have fruit for the children.

It got to the point, where I was getting quite worried and managed to talk Frank into going to see a doctor. He'd been very erratic. So, we drove to see this doctor, a Hungarian G.P. His father was a doctor too. The young one spoke Hungarian reasonably well so we could understand each other. I stayed in the car with the children and Frank went in. He was supposed to get help with depression.

After a while the doctor came out to the car and said to me, "We need to get Frank assessed properly, because he's emotionally unstable. There is something wrong."

I said, "If you get him to agree and organize it, I'm quite happy to support it in anyway I can, because he needs to sort something out, we can't live this way."

He went back inside, and next thing Frank came out and got into the car, didn't say anything, just looked like thunder and drove us back home.

As soon as we got inside, I put the children to bed for their afternoon nap. Then Frank started screaming and yelling, "You're conspiring with the doctor to put me into a mental hospital! He told me I have to go into a mental hospital and you conspired, I've seen it, you're trying to get me locked up!"

I said, "If you want to go and have a test, I will be happy to support you, you should do it, but it's your life, it's up to you."

Anyway, I went out to rinse out a few of the children nappies and the next thing I knew he called me to, "Come in here, come in, come in here," so I went into the bedroom and he stood over the cot with the big kitchen knife in his hand, and he said, "Pack your bag, we're going or I'll kill the kids. You are coming with me out of here; I am not having you put me into a mental hospital and having all your boyfriends here. We're going away. Pack your bag."

I said, "That is stupid we can't do that. We got this house, you've got a job."

"Don't worry about it, pack your bag."

I said, "I can't pack the children's stuff, it's still wet."

"Doesn't matter," he said. "Just pack it."

I really had no choice; he was standing over the children while they slept, with the knife in his hand. So I packed two bags, got some of the children's stuff, some food for them, just the basic things, then I got the kids dressed and got in the car. He drove to his work place, collected his wages and gave notice.

As it happened, it was payday, so he got his pay and told them to send the rest of his pay to a friend's place in Sydney. Then we started driving and I said, "Where are we going?"

He said, "Never you mind. We're going to start a new life."

After about six hours driving, I managed to get him to stop and have a bit of rest. But after that it was fourteen more hours of driving by the time we got to Sydney. He drove us to his friend's place (the friend from his school days, who's brother left Hungary with us) in Parramatta and asked him if we could stay for few days.

Well, this friend of his wasn't such a close friend. We hadn't seen him for a long time, we didn't correspond and previously we'd only stayed with them for a day. We drove up with the children to visit them, so they could catch up. This time he said we could stay a few days until we found somewhere to live. They had two children, he and his Australian wife. She wasn't very happy about Hungarians in the house and wasn't very keen on Hungarians anyway, as she didn't understand our language, plus our English was limited.

They had a little room that was virtually a single room, or rather a built-in veranda, which had a single bed, with a wardrobe in it. They put in an old cot, that had been used by their children. Now this was in May or early June Sydney, and the single cot was useless for the two girls to sleep in. We had a single bed, so I could not get them to sleep with us.

I didn't want to ask the woman to provide meals for us, so I had to ask her to allow me to prepare something for the children, so we were eating cold cuts and bread and cheese.

In two or three days Frank got some work with a development company, to dig trenches and what have you. So, we were staying there, in a very uncomfortable situation and in a very unsatisfactory arrangement. Frank didn't want to look for a place for us, as he said it's better to stay with others, as they will keep an eye on me.

While we were there, the routine was that if I went into their bathroom to have a shower, he would come into the bathroom with me, take every piece of my clothing and touch it right through to see if I had any love letters or correspondence from someone! He did the same to my pyjamas too, before he gave it to me to put on, to make sure there was nothing in it, that I didn't hide anything.

He even went to the extreme of wanting to come into the dunny (outside toilet) with me, which I absolutely refused. He stood outside while I was on the toilet and went in before and after. He was looking for a paper tucked away, a love letter or whatever; I don't know what he expected. I was just about at the end of my tether, his jealous rantings were very hard to take. After the fourth day at work, he cut his foot through the boot with a pick, I don't know how he did it, but he had to have some small stiches in it and wasn't able to work for a week. So we were there for three weeks in that condition and then he went back to work. In the meantime, the children started to have colds and were generally unwell, because we didn't have enough proper clothing, with us. The room was absolutely freezing, the days were hot, but the nights were freezing.

I had to take them to the doctor, who said they could get pneumonia. Well, by that time I was absolutely frantic and sent off an express letter to the couple that still lived in the house. I had said to her, "Please look after the house I have to go with him, I don't know what is happening, I will let you know." When we left. Anyway, I sent off an express letter to say we are here and the children are sick and I just have to get home. I don't know what we are going to do, please sell anything that you can lay your hands on. If you can lend me some money, I will definitely pay you back as soon as I get back. Can you send me an airplane ticket for me and the two girls, to come back to Ormond, care of the Post Office!

I went up every day to the post office, and one day, (it was now the fifth week, and the children were still unwell) the letter arrived, with the airplane ticket in it. That was ten in the morning. I could get a flight at three that afternoon, so I dashed back to the house and told Frank's friend that I was taking the children and whatever I can manage, and we're going back to Melbourne.

I said to him, "I am very thankful that you've put up with us I'm really sorry that we abused your hospitality this way, that wasn't my doing or wish, but I can't stay any longer. If you have any decency, you won't tell Frank about what time we left, when he gets home. He won't be back until four or four-thirty. That way he won't come to the airport and cause problems."

He said, "I understand what you are doing, I give you my word I won't say anything. Then he gave me 20 pounds as well to help. With the 20 pounds I got a taxi to the airport, we got on the plane and flew back to Melbourne. I had another taxi to bring us back to the house. The girl had sold some carpets and tables and chairs and what have you, but I didn't really worry, they were all on hire purchase anyway, I had the money I owed them for the airfares, plus I could return the twenty pounds to the Sydney friend.

I had to get a job, and luckily only a few days later, I managed to find work. I had maybe about forty pounds in the bank. I would need money for the rent and the car payments - even though Frank had the car - and hire purchase payments and so forth. I took any jobs for a few weeks to earn some money. I got a job very close to home, on North Road. It was a knitting factory and I got a job overclocking the edges of the knitted garments, as they came off the machine.

So I had the absolute minimum wage and I didn't know how I was going to manage. But the couple in the house had taken a bigger part of the rent to help out, so they were very good to me and agreed to look after the children and help in any way they could. My wages I think at that time were about twelve pounds. I needed to pay four pounds for rent and would have had to pay at least three or four pounds for the lady to look after the two children a week, and then we needed to eat as well, so that wasn't going to work. Somehow, I managed this sort of hand-to-mouth existence for a couple of months.

Frank didn't turn up or contact me for six weeks, which I was very thankful for, because I needed some time to get my nerves settled. I thought this was my new life now, I had to try to work something out. I was scared of what he may do again. I did not want any more trouble. I slept with a gun under the bed, expecting something bad to happen. I grabbed that gun from the back shed. No idea where it came from, it wasn't even loaded. So the gun was there and I promised myself, I wouldn't let him into the house.

Then six weeks later he turned up and he wanted us to get back together. I didn't want to be living this kind of life and could not get together with him again. I put up with an awful lot but when the cup is full, it is finished forever for me.

I only spoke to him from the veranda. He stood in

the front yard and said he couldn't have come sooner because he was so upset, He'd had a picture of the children in front of him and he'd had a car accident because he was crying so hard, and he hadn't been sleeping.

I found out later that wasn't what had happened. He'd been drunk and had an accident just before reaching Canberra and the car was a near write-off. It needed repairs, so he stayed in Canberra and got a job there, so he could repair the car and come back to Melbourne.

I said, "No way. You get a job, pay the children's maintenance, and if you don't do it I'm taking you to court, because I need to have help and you need to take some responsibility. I am working but I can't pay for everything!"

What did he do? He went to speak to the Hungarian catholic priest, Father "Varga". He was the biggest scoundrel you could ever have known, but I think I leave it for now for that will be an upsetting episode, so I'll come back to it later.

9

He wouldn't give me any support with the children, so I was called to the Hungarian church to Father "Varga" for reconciliation. I told him that reconciliation was absolutely impossible. I was still afraid for the children and for myself because Frank was not in his right mind. He threatened us with a knife and threatened the children with a knife. I couldn't trust him anymore around the house. He was irresponsible. He had drunk away all our savings. I just could not do it any longer. I'd had my fill.

Father Varga suggested, as I could not finance everything, he would arrange for a foster home for the children. I definitely didn't want to send them to the foster home, but he said it would only be for a few months. "Two or three months, until you sort things out. Maybe you can make up by then."

Frank promised to pay the people who were fostering the children the weekly allowance, but refused to give me any.

After father got our hair cut

All I had to do was provide them with sufficient clothing and so forth, to send them to the foster home for a couple of months. We would move forward from this arrangement.

I'd come back from Sydney in about mid August that year, 1960, so this was about October.

Well, they got me to sign the agreement. It was in English. I couldn't read it. I didn't have it long enough to study it. I didn't get a copy of it. I didn't quite understand what the legal terms meant in the papers anyway. The priest told me that the agreement was that Frank pays for fostering for a few months, no more than a maximum of six months.

So I signed it, because I had no other way to maintain us. I received the list of what the children needed; three sets of pyjamas, half a dozen tops, shirts, pants, a dozen underpants each. Twelve pairs of socks each, three pairs of shoes. (It was quite a list for 6 months!) I worked like crazy trying to sew all the clothes so I didn't have to buy them all. I had a big grey suitcase full of clothes for the children. I took them to church, then Frank and the Father were going to take them to the foster home in Werribee, to a lady I don't even remember. I think she was called Miss Grey. I was told I had visiting rights to the children. It was heart breaking to let them go, but I had absolutely no choice.

So the children went off that week. I had the job already at the knitting factory. I still had the sewing job, of the electric blankets. I had taken a night-time job as well, waitressing in a coffee shop in St Kilda, which was quite a problem to travel between St Kilda and Ormond in the evenings, however I worked it out. I can't remember now how I did it, but obviously, I did. I made arrangements with the couple that was living with us at the time. They took over the lease on the house and I rented a bungalow in Caulfield, sort of halfway between St Kilda and Ormond, where I had a little bedroom, kitchen and little lounge area, it was small and cheap so I could save some money.

While we were living in Ormond, the children became very friendly with Lillian's granddaughter, Rosalie. She was a few years older. I think four/five years older than my two, so they were quite devastated (and so was I) when I had to leave, but I kept in touch with Alex and Lillian because they were like a surrogate family for me. They were absolutely wonderful in every way to the children and me.

3rd Birthday with Rosalie

Anyway I started working my three jobs. I had Saturday off as the factory wasn't open and the restaurant was Jewish, so they observed the Sabbath. I packed a big basket full of food and gifts and whatever I could get and got a train to Werribee, which left at eight o'clock in the morning. There was one train in the morning and one train at four in the afternoon back to the city. So, I went out to Werribee to visit the children, taking the basket and we'd go to Werribee Park if it was a nice day.

I made us a picnic and got them dressed in clean clothes. I always took some fresh clean clothes with me and took the dirty ones back to wash. Sometimes I washed them at the tap in the park because they were not clean. This woman, a spinster, had six to eight children to foster, that was her livelihood. She had a teenage girl that she'd fostered and then this girl had stayed on, as she had no home and nowhere to go, so she stayed to help look after the other children. There were four or five of them in a room. Two to a cot, very unpleasant circumstances, they didn't get properly cared for, that's for sure. The clothes that I sent with them were worn by everyone else and they were dressed in all sorts of odd things.

They were always hungry when I got there. About three weeks later, I arrived to spend the day with the girls but when I got there, the children had gone out already.

Frank had arrived in the car half an hour earlier and taken them for the day. He had them the whole day and I didn't get to see them, before I had to take the train back to the city. That happened quite a few times. I'd arrive to see them, only to find Frank had taken them.

When Christmas came the woman closed the foster home for the holiday weeks, so I would have the children to look after for three weeks. I arranged with Panni, who, at the time was taking in borders, that she would look after the children for three weeks and Frank would pay her the money for the children's keep, and of course I was helping as much as I could. So on Christmas Eve, the arrangement was that Frank was to pick the children up from Werribee, he was to have them until three or four in the afternoon, then bring them to Panni's so we could all have Christmas Eve together, with both families.

Lilian our beloved 'Nina' with Rosalie

At Panni's place, we cooked, we prepared and we made the Christmas tree. I was filled with hope that we'd have a wonderful Christmas together. Panni and Bill had had their second baby born in September 1958, so we hoped the children would all play together.

Five o'clock comes, then six, and no children. By eight, Panni had to put her children to bed. I was running around like a fly, trying to figure out what happened. I called everybody we knew who might know where they were. By 9 pm I ran to the police station in Russell Street and reported my children missing. They laughed at me, they said they were with their father, they're a few hours late, what did it matter. They told me to come back in ten days if they hadn't turned up. The police could not care one bit, even when I told them about Frank previous behaviour.

I tried, everything under the sun, I couldn't find them anywhere.

Three weeks later, one of the boys that used to board with Panni, turned up and brought back the children. Frank was nowhere to be seen.

This boy told us that Frank had picked them up at Werribee and taken them to Mildura. Apparently, he'd decided to do some fruit picking with this mate, and for those three weeks, the children lived in the car with him. They didn't have a change of clothes, he bought a couple of bits and pieces, but he kept the children in the car for three weeks in Mildura, without proper food and care.

After three weeks, with Frank, who be drinking so much, Frank's mate said, "This is just not right, you can't look after these children, they're in miserable circumstances." So the mate packed up and brought my girls back to Panni's after three weeks.

By that time, I had discovered what was really in the agreement that Father Varga got me to sign. It wasn't an agreement for a short stay at foster care; they tricked me into signing over the full custody of the children to the Catholic Church!

I was devastated, I just didn't know what to do, where to go, how to manage to get them back. So I had virtually no choice but to leave my children at the foster home and visit them every week if I could, as many times as I could.

I worked in the restaurant at night-time, six nights a week until eleven at night. I'd go home, sew the electric blankets, then grab a little sleep and be in the factory the next day from eight until three. Every spare minute was spent sewing and I was saving as much as I could. I hardly spent anything on food, as I got some leftovers from the restaurant, I only paid out for rent and transport.

In the restaurant, I met the man who was to be my second husband. He was also named Frank. He was separated from his wife. He rented a bungalow at the back of the restaurant. He ate there every night. He had two sisters in Melbourne. They had families and a couple of times he gave me a lift when he was going to Oakleigh, to one of his sisters. He would drop me off, so we become friends. Then a couple of times he offered to drive me out on the weekend to Werribee to visit the children. He said he had nothing to do and it was good to get out of the bungalow. That way I could get there in time to pick them up, before Frank got there.

Frank would only turn up to take out the children if he knew I was coming on the train. This was done out of his typical spitefulness, which was always how he operated. Once he found out I had transport and could get a lift – and be there earlier – he stopped. He stopped visiting the children altogether.

One time, when he visited our daughters, he took them for a haircut. They had beautiful long hair before, but he had their hair chopped off. He must have been told it was too hard to look after. He bought them hideous clothes from Coles, just to say that he bought some new clothes for them. All the beautiful things I made for them and supplied for them, everybody else wore. It took an awful lot of energy, time and money that I didn't have, to make them and the result was devastating.

After about a year and a half of this lifestyle, I collapsed and was taken to hospital with exhaustion and a nervous breakdown. That meant I lost the job at the factory. I couldn't do the sewing, so I was in a pretty bad way.

My mind is buzzing around too quickly with all these memories.

In that time, I didn't have any social life. I kept in touch with Panni of course, but could not burden her with my stuff as she had a hard time of it as well. I had visited Lillian, Alex and Rosalie in Ormond and they treated me like family.

One day, I was visiting them on Mother's Day, as I was invited for lunch. After lunch, we were sitting in the dining room, talking about various things. Alex went to the kitchen to make a cup of tea, the next thing we heard was a big thump, I dashed out to the kitchen and Alex was lying on the floor, he had fallen over and was dead. He'd had a heart attack and he died instantly.

I was there until we organized an undertaker, got the daughters to come along and looked after them. I spent some time with Lillian; it was heart breaking, because Alex was a wonderful man. He had a heart problem, I was very sorry for Lillian, as he was her life.

Lillian and Alex lived a modest, genteel life, in the same house that they built when they got married. They were now retired. Their story was an interesting one; Alex came from a well-to-do, old English business family who didn't liked his marriage to Lillian. Lillian's father was an immigrant, an uneducated rower. He'd met Lillian's mother, who was a well-educated daughter of a prominent family - at the building of the first Uniting Church on the corner of Collins and Russell Streets, both being volunteers there. They fell in love and against family opposition got married. She then taught her husband to read and write and he became a well-respected, well-read manager of a large business. They lived a genteel, loving, family life and made sure their children were educated and knew the fine and honest way to live. I always thought this story was a wonderful romantic one, I felt privileged to have been told it and to know two such wonderful loving people.

That must have been about six/seven months before my breakdown. I just collapsed one day at work. I was two weeks in hospital under the doctor's care: they were not going to let me out, as I had no-one to look after me. I didn't need looking after any more, but they wanted someone to say they would be with me in case I had another relapse. I rang Lillian and asked her if she would mind if I gave her name?

She said, "I didn't know you were in hospital and I'm very upset that nobody let me know." She offered me a home right away and said I must stay with her, at least until I could make another arrangement.

She set me up in the back room of her house - a sunroom that was built in and was used by Alex before - and I stayed there. I was terribly grateful, that I had somewhere to go and reassess. I had been working three jobs, and I not only had to maintain myself but I had to save money, see the children as much as I could and pay back some of the hire purchase that was sold. Frank had earlier signed up for hire purchase on the furniture when he moved us to Ormond and of course, he didn't pay it, so I'd had to pay for eight months, which was stuff we'd mostly sold for our airfares back from Sydney. I sold off a lot of the other items as well, because I didn't need them. But I still had to pay for the hire purchase because Frank couldn't be found.

When I left hospital and stayed with Lillian, at least by this time I was debt free, which was a relief. I couldn't go back to working three jobs; it was physically impossible to do and to have some kind of future for the children I needed to do something different. I wanted them to be back home with me. With Lillian's help, I had a public solicitor look into it, he told me I'd have to go to court and ask for the custody to be given back to me again, and in order to get the children back, I'd have to prove that I had good living conditions and could provide for them.

Lillian suggested that I learn machine bookkeeping. She offered to pay for my six-week tuition. She wouldn't charge me or let me pay anything for my board for that six weeks. She said, "Office work is not so hard and in the office, bookkeepers earn good money, and machine bookkeepers get well paid also." She said I would meet a better class of people. This would give me a good future, so I could live better and have less stressful work. Physically it wouldn't be so hard, and I could then eventually get myself organized better and perhaps even work myself up to better position! So that's what I did and in the meantime, Lillian helped me to learn to speak English better, she tutored me while I lived close by and every time I saw her, she always gently corrected my pronunciation.

Machine Bookkeeping wasn't a hard job for me; I picked it up quickly because it was mechanical stuff, using figures and numbers. With Lillian coaching me in English, for many years afterwards, people used to ask what part of England I'd come from. Lillian had spoken the 'Queen's English' and made sure that my pronunciations were the best. You could say I had a very 'plummy English accent'. Unfortunately, I've lost that 'plum' by now, from the time I lived in Europe. By the time I came back to Australia, it had gone. But anyway, I thank Lillian with all my heart, because without her, I don't know how I would've survived.

On top of all that, when Frank and I split up, I didn't write to my mother about the unpleasant things at all. Just the usual things about the new world we found ourselves in. There wasn't any use telling her about the hard things. Soon after arriving in Australia, we did try to get a visa for my mother and brother, under family reunification. They were guaranteed to immigrate to Australia. My mother would be able to obtain an exit visa, but my brother couldn't get one. He was eighteen years old, and had to go into the army for three years. Until he finished his army service, he would not be able to get an exit visa. My mother wasn't prepared to leave Hungary without him so we couldn't do much about that.

I didn't realise Frank wrote to my mother a few months after we split up. He'd told her a pack of lies, of course. He said we'd split because I had a boyfriend and I didn't look after the children and I was living a horrible life. He claimed I didn't care about anybody, I neglected my children and home, I'd spent a lot of money, all I did was party and just left everything to him and he couldn't take it any longer. What a story!

I think this helped to bring on my breakdown as I dwelt on it a lot. I received a letter from my mother, in which she called me all sorts of names. She didn't ask for my side of the story, didn't ask what had really happened. Just berated me on how disgusted she was with me, that I wouldn't look after my children and I didn't deserve to have two beautiful children etc.

For a long time, I didn't correspond with my mother or brother. I did correspond with my cousin Jancso however, and eventually he talked to my mother to help her see what had really happened. Mum wrote again to say that she was sorry to hear that Frank and I weren't together, but divorce wasn't something that should happen in our family. I was the usual 'what would everyone say?' sort of thing. So now she knew what had really happened, but she didn't think I should be divorced? Well, I was getting a divorce, that's all there was to it.

Once I finished the machine bookkeeping course, the course leader organized a job for me in a company called EIL Services, which was part of the Astor group. Astor was at that time making refrigerators and washing machines, and then televisions: we were the service arm of Astor. We had service men doing maintenance work on the machines the factory produced. I was in the bookkeeping department. There were six of us in the machine bookkeeping section. It was a lot of work, but very good work. The office was in Sturt Street, South Melbourne which was a really good place for me as I could get the train in from Ormond to Flinders Street and then get a tram to South Melbourne or sometimes I'd just walk down Sturt Street to get to work. That was a really good job; I got paid three times as much as I got paid in the factory so that was good. I had managed to start to save more money, I still did a bit of sewing, but I couldn't do very much because I didn't want to disrupt Lillian in her house. I would have needed a lot of space to have the materials and the parts, I didn't want to do that to Lillian's house and to inconvenience her in any way.

I could do a few hours waitressing on the weekends, so that helped to earn some extra money.

I lived with Lillian for about eighteen months. In that time I had found a group that had solicitors doing 'pro bono' work, so I got a solicitor to put in an application for the custody of the children. It was Christmas, 1963 and of course the foster home would close for Christmas.

Back with Mum for Christmas Holdiays

I was getting them for the holiday period. I was advised by the solicitor to move away with the children during that time. He put in the request to the courts to get a hearing. I rented half a house in Balaclava, two rooms with a lean-to kitchen. We shared the bathroom with the landlady, and she had her daughter living in the house. I was advised to move to a place that Frank didn't know, so I virtually kidnapped my children, while I took them on holiday.

In the first week of January, as soon as court opened, I had a hearing. I had all the documentation of how they been taken into fostering, I had guarantees and character references, everything I needed to prove that I could provide and look after my children. I was given full custody of my children once again,

I was recommended another Hungarian lady who also had a young daughter, who would look after the girls while I worked. They lived nearby, it was a good arrangement. Until the following year, when they would start school.

Then, when school started at the following year, (darling Lillian came to the rescue once again offering to look after them) the children could attend preps at Ormond State School, where their friend Rosalie was in fourth grade.

So the arrangement was that Frank Nemeth (who was living in a boarding house in Caulfield, not too far from where I had the half house in Balaclava) was to pick up the children every morning as he was working in Huntingdale and it was on his way, take them to Lillian's in Ormond and from there they would walk to school with Rosalie. After school, they walked back with Rosalie to Lillian's who looked after them until five. Then Frank would pick them up and bring them home to Balaclava. In reality, darling Lillian has taken on the after school care for me.

I would be back home from my office job by this time, and I would cook dinner for all of us. Frank contributed to the food bill, but I did all the cooking so he wouldn't have to worry about his meals. I'd also make his lunch every morning, when he picked the children up.

We were good friends, he was alone and seemed to like the children very much, and the children quite liked him. Also, during this early time their father didn't have access to them for about six months.

Picnic in Ferntreegully – we are home for good!

The girls were very happy little children, back with me, in regular loving care, and I was certainly very happy to have us together again. That was the state of things for about two years until 1965. I didn't want to burden Lillian any longer and I didn't want make her life difficult. She had given me so much support and I'd depended on her so much for her love. Also, Rosalie was now in high school and Lillian's daughter (Rosalie's mother) had moved back in with her, so I didn't want to make her life any harder. She had given me virtually a life, a family and my children back and without her I would never have been able to manage our life.

Eventually Frank my ex-husband found us. Because the court has ordered him to pay maintenance for the children, he had to have access. And I was quite happy for him to have access: he was their father, so every second Saturday he could take the children away from 1 to 4pm and spend the afternoon with them.

However this arrangement was precarious, as a couple of times it worked out ok, but at other times, he simply did not show up. The children would be disappointed and upset. It was hard to keep their spirits up on those days. So I would dress them in pretty dresses, Frank arrived and he took them around to all the Hungarian people we knew and showed them off. What pretty girls he had – he also told everyone he'd paid for everything which was totally untrue.

I made most of my clothes and the girls', until they were 16. I could buy materials very cheaply, especially offcuts, that way the girls always had very nice and unique clothes. Especially while I lived with Lillian, as she was a very precise and a great sewer. She also made all her granddaughters' clothes by hand, in spite of having very severe osteoarthritis. I did most of the sewing with my trusty cheap sewing machine while I was there.

When Frank (their father) did have the girls, he'd

often arrive already drunk. Some times he'd take the children to a couple of places, showed them off (especially when they looked cute in new dresses), then plonked them in the pub while he drank all afternoon, with his mates.

So that wasn't a very good arrangement but I didn't want to rock the boat too much. I tried to do as much as I could to keep a good relationship going, between the girls and their father, but it was not an easy thing to do.

I had never said anything against their father while they were growing up. They can't help what he is, and it would upset them, so there was no point. I always thought the children would see his true colours, sooner or later and that would be a disappointment for them anyway.

However, every time he took them away, they would come back with stories about how "daddy said 'mummy is bad' and 'what a cunt mummy is' or 'what a whore mummy is". One day they came back and after dinner, Georgie sat on the toilet, in the outside loo and she just kept repeating loudly, "Mummy is a whore, mummy is a whore, she is very bad and 'Feri bacsi' (that translate as Uncle Frank) is a bastard, he is very bad, a bastard."

That was meant for Frank N. my friend of course, because he was a part of their lives by now, he was coming every day, driving them to school, here for his meals and so forth, and I thought. "What am I to say to her?" I just got her and I said, "Darling these are not nice words, and little girls don't say, things like that."

"But daddy said you are a whore."

"Well, you don't know what that word means, it's very naughty and please don't say it again, that's not nice. Nice little girls don't say that. These words are not nice and Daddy was very naughty to teach you these words."

Naturally I had to have a few words with they father about it and that didn't go too well.

One time their father turned up with horrid pink dresses from Coles, the worst that I had seen and some plastic sandals. When the girls came home, he'd changed them into these awful clothes.

They were saying, "Daddy bought it! Daddy bought it!"

So, on the next visit, I dressed them so he could show them off in the clothes he'd bought them. Apparently, they didn't go anywhere interesting on that day, and they were home very early, because the "Daddy's clothes" didn't look as good as the clothes I sent them in normally.

The child maintenance payments were very irregular after the first couple of months, then the visits started to get less and less. I would not get the children specially dressed unless their father was at the door, as they became so upset when he didn't arrive. About six/seven months on, the visits stopped altogether, so did any payments. Then I heard that he'd left Melbourne and was living in Canberra. That made our lives more peaceful. The children quickly forgot to ask about him and I never really counted on Frank's payments.

I worked at E I L, at the bookkeeping office, I always tried to keep ahead of the new technology. My bosses and colleagues appreciated and respected my work ethic. I was sent once to Sydney to teach people how to use the new machines. I spent three or four days in Sydney and the children stayed at Lillian's.

I received a job offer with Olivetti Machines to travel all over Australia, teaching people how to use the latest bookkeeping-machines. It would have doubled my wages, but I had to let it go - with two children at home that was not possible, but it was good to know that I could do that job if I wanted to or if I had the choice, but my choice was the family and the children.

Alas, the girls contracted measles. I had to stay home to look after one, and then when she was better, the other came down with measles! I was home for six weeks. The boss was unhappy and said if I couldn't come to work, he'd have to let me go. By that time, I was running the bookkeeping department as second in command, doing most of the important jobs, and I knew that he couldn't really get rid of me that easily, because it would be difficult to find someone to replace me. So I just said to him, "Look if you give me the increase which I asked for, and if I had the same wages as you have, which means that you can afford to keep your wife at home to look after your children, then with the same wages I could afford someone to look after my children too at home and I can be here twenty-four seven, if that is what you want."

Of course that didn't go down very well, and by that time, there were stories of decimal currency coming in, which as far as I was concerned, was a good idea, because that would not cause me any difficulty. I had no difficulty with pounds, shilling and pence calculations either, I can calculate very quickly in my head all the currencies but of course decimal currency was so much easier.

During this time, Frank N. and I decided to get a house together. Instead of renting two places, we could put our resources together and make housing repayments. We might as well do it, he'd been very helpful, he'd been behaving nicely, he wasn't drinking (that I could notice) he cared for the children, he's always very nice with them, he helped with everything. I was living in Balaclava with the children and he was in a boarding-house near by. When I cooked a meal he would wash up, clean the children shoes while I bathed them and put them to bed, and helped with everything around the house. We were getting on really well and so I thought it wouldn't be a bad idea if he wanted to live with us. That would be a better solution; maybe there is more of a family look about things?

So we were looking for houses and we found a house off Huntingdale Road, where a new housing estate was being built. His sister lived in Oakleigh and their families got together quite often. They had three children, the other sister had two, and we would go on picnics together in the holidays, or visit them on the weekend, so all the children got on well. We put a deposit on this land and house package. The total cost was three hundred pounds, which was a lot of money for a house at that time.

Then I read in the paper that the builders went bankrupt!

We were going to lose our deposit of one hundred pounds, so I got into action and rang everybody, went and banged on the builder's door and harassed the company for aid, because we just made our deposit on the Saturday and the following day the announcement came out about the "bankruptcy".

I said they couldn't bank our cheque, they wouldn't have been paid, and they needed to pay it back. Long story short I carried on and I got my boss to ring them and threaten them with everything under the sun.

Finally I got the deposit back. Then I decided that no, we shouldn't buy a house. It would cost too much, I would have to get the children in day-care, which would cost extra money. I was also worried about my job as it would be much harder to get to the city. The solution came to me that we could buy a business, we should get a milk bar. That way I'd be home all day, we'd live behind the shop, I could look after the children, I'd be there with them all day, earn the money, hopefully a little bit better than if I was working and Frank N. could carry on with his job. So we went looking for a milk bar. I resigned, and in the mean time I got a temp-job, through an agency, helping people prepare to switch over to decimal currency that was starting on February 1966.

I was paid twice as much as I normally earned and some of the weeks I only had to work two/three days, so it was a really good job. I could have worked 24/7. In the meantime, we found a milk bar that was suitable and we could afford it.

It was in Elsternwick and the house could be divided into two flats, so we thought we could rent out half of the house and make money out of that as well. This would then go towards the rent, while I worked in the milk bar.

Frank N. was working as a welder in Huntingdale, he'd been there eight years so was well established. The milk bar was very run down. It was owned by an English couple that had six children - teenagers to babies. The wife who ran it was worn out, near to collapse. Everything was filthy dirty, the business was not profitable, and the house was a mess! The price reflected the condition, which was why we could afford it. We did everything we could to clean it all up and get it going again.

10

We lived in Grosvenor Street, Balaclava about three years. The first real Christmas we had once the children came home, we made a big Christmas tree. I wanted to make it a special Christmas, I didn't want them to miss out like when their father pinched them. So we had a big Christmas tree, and they wished for Teddy bears. They were just five years old, and being twins, they were so particular about having their own things. Everything, as far as they were concerned, had to have their own specialty. This is mine, this is yours, that sort of thing. So Frank N. and I decided to go to Myers and shop for teddy bears. We made sure that the teddy bears had to be exactly the same. Every stitch we checked, we selected colours and sizes. We went through about 50 teddy bears before we picked the two that we thought were exactly the same and special. Under the tree were the teddy bears, toys and clothes. Anyway, we came to Christmas Eve, and had the Christmas tree ready. So, when the door opened, my two darlings, dashed to the Christmas tree to look at the toys, and picked up a teddy bear. This was what they most wanted, their own teddy bear. They picked it up, turned it around, up and down, looked at every corner, and then swapped, turned them around again, then switched back, and said, "This is mine, this is yours."

I was absolutely gob smacked! I asked, "Please tell me? What is the difference? They are the same. I'm sure Father Christmas made sure it is the same."

"No, it's not: this is mine."

I said, "How do you know it is yours?"

"Well, it is mine because it's a little bit crooked."

That must have been 3mm out of whack, the stitching wasn't quite in the middle, and they picked it up. So I tell you, everything they had when it was new, got the same treatment. "This is yours, this is mine." And they were happy with the teddy bears. Forever!

My twins, they look alike, 9 people out of 10 couldn't tell them apart. From very early on they had separate sleeper earrings. Pearly had yellow gold, Georgie had white gold. It was so their father could tell them apart, because he never could.

I had no trouble from day one, knowing who was who. I always knew, maybe it was a mother's thing. But most of the people wouldn't know them, even in pictures they're so much alike. But by nature, they are totally different. You wouldn't really believe that twins could be so different. They have so much similarity in many things. They would come from two different directions, arrive in the same colour dress and clothes, their hair done similarly. They just looked alike. There would be an argument: "Why did you buy this? I wanted it before you." They didn't even know that the other one had bought it, yet they would buy exactly the same thing! It was amazing while they were growing up, the similarity between them, but also the differences.

Well, while we were living in Balaclava, we spent quite a lot of time, visiting friends and Frank N's sisters and their families. We would sometimes spend a weekend there with them. And all the children had great fun. We organized a picnic, because Frank N had a VW bus/van that he'd bought in Sydney, for deliveries, (before he'd split-up with his wife). He was planning to use it for a job here too eventually, so it wasn't worthwhile selling. In the back of the van, we would pack in the kids. Sometimes, there would be seven kids and even some of the adults. Frank's two sisters would sit up in front with him while he drove. We used to put in the camping chairs for the adults to sit on and a baby mattress on the top of the motor for the kids. We'd drive from Oakleigh to Deer Park, to visit the other sister, or pick up the Deer Park ones and bring them over to Oakleigh.

These times were quite pleasant. We enjoyed doing things together and it seemed to be working quite well. So that was the motivation for me to agree to move in together with Frank N. We were talking about buying a house together, but I changed my mind and said no, I wouldn't be putting money into a house. That's dead money. But investing in a milk bar was a chance to save for our future.

We found this old milk bar and signed up to move into it in Elsternwick. I think it was just in the New Year, 1966. Just before the decimal currency came in. So I was doing temp work when we bought the milk bar's 'good will' and all the stock in it. We had just enough money left to buy two beds for the children and another two beds for us. But we only had the mattresses. We didn't have the bed bases.

I scrubbed the living room floor in the middle, so there was enough of a clean surface to put the mattresses on. The children stayed with Frank's sisters in Oakleigh for a couple of days while we cleaned.

One of Frank N's friends, Matthew, was a painter by trade. He came over and we closed the shop for 24 hours and solidly cleaned and painted. The shelves, the fridges, the windows and we threw out a lot of stuff that was out of date or damaged.

Many friends and Frank N's family members helped us clean and get everything sorted. We had the shop open the next day, and in between customers, we cleaned the living room which was right behind the shop. We washed everything down in between serving and organising. And the next thing was the kitchen, bathroom and then the children's room. Everything really needed scrubbing, washing and disinfecting!

In that first week in the milk bar, we only had enough money to last us for food for that week, until Frank N brought his wages home and on Thursday, we had to buy stock. From then on, each week we bought the things we needed, second hand bedroom furniture, second hand lounge furniture etc. A couple of weeks later, the children had second hand bed bases, (but new mattresses) and a couple of second hand wardrobes. We bought a table for the kitchen, and a few chairs. So gradually, within about six weeks, we furnished the house. It was now a clean place but it needed a lot of repairs. It was hard work as the place was awfully dirty and very neglected. The bathroom was in the middle, with two doors and on the other side were two big rooms and a kitchen. The shop was originally a large family home. So they had two rooms and a kitchen on the other side. The bathroom could be reached from both sides of the flat, and there was a big backyard there. The laundry was underneath the back veranda, nothing was closed off.

This was our livelihood from now on. Every week when Frank brought his pay home, we would buy a small piece of furniture or some stock, as well as various other things we needed. All the takings went right back for stock. It was very interesting, because I never ever had been into the milk bar, other than to buy milk and bread. And I didn't know ninety per cent of the stuff that was on the shelves. Some of the things I had never seen before, never used them. I didn't know what Spam was, for example.

At that stage, we had many salespeople bringing their deliveries to our shop. At 6:30am, the milk van would drop off the crates of milk, which needed to be put straight into the fridge, and then along came another with cream and cheese. Then there was a different deliveryman who would come with stuff like cigarettes from different cigarette companies. They just sent a driver that week on a truck and you ordered what you needed and put it on the shelf.

So I said to every salesman that came into the shop. "I'm new to this business, we've just taken it over, I have no idea how much I need, what sells, what doesn't, at the moment. I don't even know what the stocks are. I'm in your hands. If you help me to order the right things, and I can sell it, I will make sure that you get all my business in the future. But if you try to cheat me and you give me bad stock, one bad thing that doesn't sell, and you know it doesn't sell, or things that are of no use in this business, I won't deal with you ever again. You will lose my business, which I know will grow!"

I said that to every salesman: to the cigarettes, the ones that brought cream, the cheese, (we had in the fridge, packets of ham, cheese, cream), the baker, the same thing. The baker brought in different kind of breads and rolls and I said I didn't know how much I'd need, so he'd take back the bread that didn't sell. There were so many deliveries, such as ice creams, soft drinks, lollies, chocolates, various people and trucks.

I had a very cordial and friendly working relationship with all the salesmen and no one ever tried to put things over me. Most things were delivered, except for groceries like flour, sugar, and stuff like that, which, I had to go and buy at the wholesalers. That was a bit of inconvenience because somebody had to stay in the shop while I went to the wholesaler. But the wholesalers were open late at nights and I could go after Frank N. came home from work. He looked after the shop for an hour or so, but generally, he was pretty useless in the shop.

Anyway, the first months we were getting on all right. It was still school holidays and the girls were home. So, we were managing quite well. But obviously, I was on call 24/7. And then somehow, (I don't really know how it came about), but Frank N. and Matthew and his partner were talking and they said to Frank, "Why don't we share the shop?"

Matthew and his partner could move into the flat. Matthew was already helping with the painting after work and on weekends. His partner could take over the shop at school pick up times, allow me to get stock, or whatever was needed. So we could share the shop. She takes half a day, I take half a day, then another few hours or whatever. We would share the profits and expenses!

They were not going to put money into the purchase of the business at that time, as they didn't have any. I said to Frank N. "I don't want any partners in the business. I mean, it's bad enough, the two of us are partnering on just a verbal agreement. But, I don't want a different partner in the business, because, that never really works out!"

I wasn't sure about Matthew's partner. I had met her a couple of times, but she was in her late fifties by then, closer to sixty I suppose. At that stage in 1966, I was 26 years old. Frank N. was 18 years older, so he was, 44. So I said I didn't want to do it. Frank said we must do it because it would help me and I could spend more time with the children. He argued it would be best for all of us, as she was a 'business woman' - she had run boarding houses for many years. I didn't know (I had to find out later) that she was renting large houses and subletting rooms that was her 'business', and the lease had run out on the house they were in, so they needed to move somewhere.

I was overruled as usual (it was getting to be the pattern of my life.) My nature is to do anything to keep the peace, whatever it may cost, in the strong hope that our life could be secure, so I submitted. And Matthew and his partner Babs moved into the flat and she became a partner in the shop. No contract, no agreement, only verbal promises.

I wasn't confortable with the arrangement. I quickly found out that she didn't know how to work the till, and she didn't understand the prices. I had everything marked, but she couldn't see it, as she didn't want to wear her glasses. She had trouble, didn't know what was what, she had no idea how a shop worked. She would be non-functional until about lunchtime, and then would spend 3-4 hours in the shop. Then she had to lie down, so there was no time for me to really do any of my own work. Once she went inside, she had a couple of beers, so when she came back into the shop I couldn't let her stay, because she was reeking of beer and was slightly under the influence and was more confused by the shop then ever.

So I battled on about 4-5 weeks, but it was getting worse and worse. She was less and less useful in the shop or with anything else at all. She could not calculate the prices, she wouldn't pack stock, she wouldn't do any heavy work. She didn't come out when it was time to get the children. I was doing all the work once again.

Luckily, opposite the shop lived a lovely family, the

McKenzies, a young couple with three children, two boys and the middle one was a girl, Jenny: she was the same age as my daughters. They went to the same school, Ripponlea Primary. Mr. McKenzie drove the children to school every morning. In the afternoons, the children used to come over and play with the girls. When Mrs. McKenzie got herself a job, we arranged that Mr. Mc. would take the children to school every morning. Then they would walk home from school in the afternoon, as the boys were old enough, so they could all come home together. When she was working in the school holidays, the children would be in my place; in the back of the shop, playing with the girls. Also, when they went out on the weekend to the beach, they would take the girls. Or they would take them to the football in the wintertime. It worked out beautifully.

I was really struggling with having Babs in the shop. I found sometimes after balancing the till, at closing time, it was less than it should have been. I started to count the till before I left the shop for my break and in the evening. It was less after she was on duty for a couple of hours. About five weeks after Matthew and his partner moved in, I caught her taking money out of the till red handed!

She could not understand that whatever was in the till wasn't all ours. She thought that whatever money was in the till was all profit, and that she could take half the money because the shop was half hers. Well, it took some time to explain that it didn't work that way! I explained the stock had to be paid for, the electricity had to be paid for, blah blah blah. Only then could it be divided up and this too was subject to how many hours had been worked in the shop. I worked it out later on, I was working for something like one or two Pounds an hour. When I was in the office I was getting 15 Pounds an hour and now I was working 14 - 18 hours a day in the shop. But anyway, long story short. I said to Frank N, this has to end!

He asked me where they would go; because they'd have to find a house. I said I didn't care; this arrangement was not what I wanted.

So, I sat them all down, and laid down the law: "I'm sorry, the partnership is not working."

They couldn't come into the shop anymore. They didn't put any money in it, so there's nothing to share. Babs was taking money that wasn't hers to take. So, I said no, it doesn't work that way and I won't do it. I put the suggestion that they could buy the shop, as I'd be happy to move out. If I gave them the shop, they of course would have to pay us out for what we put into it. And they could have the shop. "No-no," they said, they certainly could not work it etc. (I knew of course, they couldn't do it.) So they had to move out. I had a long talk with Matthew and he understood the situation and didn't hold it against me.

They lived on in the flat for another 4 weeks, before they found somewhere to go. She was supposed to be a businesswoman. But she ran a boarding house. Running a boarding house was not exactly a proper business. But she was convinced that she was a good businesswoman. Unfortunately, she liked the bottle far too much and spending time in the pub with the boys. And would you believe it, Frank N. started drinking more and more. So, it wasn't a very good time.

Once they moved out, Matthew would still come every weekend and sometimes during the week, when he didn't have any important big jobs on. He worked for himself as a painter, so if he didn't get a job, he would work at our place for 3-4 days, only for a thank-you and a good meal. Frank N, when he came home from the factory, would do a couple of hours work on the house. They painted the whole house, top to bottom. Everything was freshly painted and we got some carpets down and bought some other second hand furniture. So, we had a reasonably nice home. The living room was used mostly for business. When I brought the groceries in, I would price them at night-time in there.

For a long time, the flat stayed empty. I didn't want to rent it, it would be too difficult to have strangers living there, with all the stock spread out even to the front yard.

It took the first year to finish refurbishing the whole of the house. On the Christmas holidays, (between Christmas and New Year,) we unpacked everything from the shop, and painted the whole shop out one night, with Matthew's help. By the New Year, it was all finished. We painted the front as well. We had it cleaned before, but then when it was painted it looked much nicer. We had rearranged the stock a little bit and rearranged the counter. Frank's brother-in-law, (yet another Frank!) who was a carpenter, made some shelves and a proper counter for the front. This meant nobody could just walk through to the private area. It was nicely done and I was happy about it.

We were doing reasonably well. The business had increased tremendously in the first year, as I kept improving it, getting new stock with more variety. I had good customers. They realized I kept good quality stuff and the prices were reasonable. We didn't inflate the prices, I made everything as near to cost price as possible with just a little bit of profit. We were able to save quite a lot, because I didn't need new clothes. All I had was 3-4 uniforms a year. Three good pairs of shoes, that I could walk in all day. I was in my uniform virtually 24/7. And I didn't need anything new. I made the children's clothes (in my spare time of course.) Frank's other brother-in-law, Steven, was a tailor. He was working on contract for Myers, making lots of dresses and coat supplying other shops as well. He gave a lot of his cut-offs to me, so I could make the children quite pretty things, very cheaply. All I needed was maybe to buy the buttons sometime and not even that, because he would have some buttons and bits and pieces of whatever was left from the tailor shop.

So, the children were very nicely dressed. And they always had good Italian shoes because their feet were very narrow. The normal children's shoes in Australia were far too wide for their feet, they would be wobbling in them! As soon as they started walking, I had to get them good Italian shoes. Growing up, as the daughter of a shoemaker, I knew the value of good shoes! Italian shoes were the only ones that fitted them properly. I learned from my darling father, the only thing you should look after (and not scrimp on) was shoes. They carried you all your life. And if you don't have good shoes, your feet will suffer and then you suffer as well.

But I didn't need extra clothes or shoes, and working in the milk bar, I didn't need any transport. Our only private expense was Frank N's car.

After the first year, once we'd finished painting the house and shop, Frank quit his job as a welder. He decided that he would take on a delivery job, so he could help more in the shop and use the car for the reason it was bought for. That was the idea.

However, as that second-year journeyed on, things became more difficult. He found being in the shop uncomfortable. He had difficulty understanding some of the customers. He read a lot, especially the papers, and he understood English, but had a problem speaking it. Because his pronunciations were not always perfect, he'd developed a complex about it.

He also started saying: "This is not a good thing, I don't like to be called Mr Kontos", (because I was Mrs. Kontos). The girls had their father's surname of Kontos as well. In the shop, everybody called him "Mr. Kontos", so he was very upset about that. Then he said, "This doesn't look good." He also said it wasn't so great for the children or for good family life, just living together, so why didn't we get married?

Well, I didn't want to get married. I was quite happy just living together. I somehow felt that by living together I'm not committed so much. If things didn't work out, I could take my share and move and have my own life. But he seemed to love the children and looked after them and behaved well. He helped and worked hard with the painting and at the hard jobs. So, I eventually allowed myself to be talked into it, "for the children's sake." Definitely for the children's sake! That was his mantra for getting married. As my divorce became final, the pressure mounted with Frank N to make our arrangement legal!

So, one nice day, his niece Anne, who worked in the milk bar part-time, after school, came and stayed for a few days. We got married in the registry office, with his two brothers-in-law as witnesses. I became Mrs Nemeth and we arranged with the solicitor that the children's surname be changed by deed poll. Their father would not agree and sign the adoption papers, and anyway, I didn't really want to involve him at all.

By this point, Frank K had been missing for quite some time, and we didn't hear from him. Of course, we didn't get any money either. I think the whole time, after the children came home, I don't think he paid me child maintenance more than 6 times in 3 years. So, it wasn't anything that I relied on. Anyway, he found out 'through the grape-vine' that we got the milk bar. One nice day he turned up to visit the children, with out any warning, just turned up, with two great big dolls.

So, once again he started coming around and taking the children out on a couple of Saturdays. I wasn't happy with it, because he was unreliable. He just started off again arranging when he would come to pick up the children. Then he started to miss the arrangement and the girls were again disappointed. By the time he brought them back home, he was drunk (most of the time). A couple of times I refused to let them go, because he was too drunk to drive.

One day, after I got married, he came to pick up the children. Frank N invited him into the kitchen. Not through the shop; but through the back door, and offered him a drink. And, while I was back and forth from the shop and the children were playing, the two men were having a good old "chin wag". And there they sat, drinking beer and all of a sudden as I was coming in from the shop, I hear my ex is telling my new husband how untrustworthy I am! "You have to watch out, because she likes the young boys," and so forth. I was so flabbergasted. I just said to them, "Excuse me, what's going on here? You can't listen to this kind of rubbish! How dare you? First of all, how dare you talk like that about me in my own home? You don't know what I like, you've never bothered to find out. And secondly, you my 'darling new husband' what kind of a man are you? Where is your decency in listening to someone rubbishing your wife? And you, out you go and don't ever think that you can step into this house again!"

I picked up a bottle of beer, threw it out the backyard, pointed at Frank K and just said, "Out you go!" So my ex left

Frank number 2 got very upset; which I didn't take very well. So we had a ding-dong of an argument. I said, "From now on; I forbid you to invite him into my house. I always handed over the children at the door, and picked up the children from the door. He's not coming into my house. And he's certainly not going to rubbish me in my own place, to my husband! What kind of life is that?" Anyway, I was very upset about it, I can tell you. So, that was that.

After that, there were even fewer visits from ex-Frank. Then he disappeared again. We hadn't seen him for about 18 months beforehand. Then for about 3 months he came and took the children out a few times, and after that, he disappeared! Then I heard that he had moved to Canberra; which was fine by me; because that meant that at least I was spared that kind of annoyance and the girls didn't get upset so often.

However, the year after we got married, things didn't work as well. The milk bar was doing well; I had good relations with the salespeople. We were able to save quite nicely. But as Frank stopped working as a welder, he took on a job delivering bread from a Hungarian bakery. The Hungarian baker was in Glenhuntly and he was delivering bread to milk bars and supermarkets in the area. Anyway, he was working on a commission for how many he sold (that wasn't very profitable). He also got some extra bread from the bakery, continental bread which we sold in the shop. That was part of his wages. He was supposed to be finished about lunchtime, by the latest. But he didn't arrive home until about 1 o'clock or after. So he got up at 6am and started work at 6:30. I got up at 5:30 every morning anyway, to get the milk and the shop ready to open at 6.30am. So I didn't think his getting up at 6 o"clock was such a hardship. So, he started at 6:30 and usually finished by 10-11am. But, instead of coming home, he would get himself a coffee and a paper and park the car somewhere, on the beach or wherever, and read the paper until 1 o'clock.

He said it was because he couldn't get peace and quiet at home to read the paper, and he had to read every paper every day, English, Australian, Hungarian, whatever he could lay his hands on, (he was a good reader.) Okay, he was an 'educated man', he had his matriculation. He worked as an auditor in the Hungarian National Bank. His family spoilt him rotten, because he was the handsome, young, smart one of a family of six, who managed to get an education and work himself up from porter to auditor in the bank. And that's probably why his first marriage didn't work. Because, he was just too smart for his own good.

As it turned out, he was smart enough to work out what would suit him best and how to get it and I was the meal ticket he was looking for.

Until the marriage certificate was signed, he was caring, helpful and generally a nice guy. But as our marriage was now official and I "couldn't kick him out" then it became another story. From then on, he became less and less helpful. He would not help with any housework, any of it. He came home as I said about 1 o'clock from 'work', then he went to bed to sleep, after his lunch, because he had to get up "so early". So by 2 o'clock, he was in bed until about 4 - 4:30pm. Even though the afternoons usually weren't too busy, I still had to do the laundry, which was down the end of the corridor at the back of the house. Obviously if the bell rang from the shop, I would rush back from the laundry to serve customers. Then as soon as the door closed behind them, I rushed down to the laundry to hang out the washing or do whatever needed to be done. This created sulking and arguments, because I was so inconsiderate as he couldn't have his well-earned rest, he would sulk. I often had to leave everything whilst I was preparing dinner and rush to the shop. Sometimes, I had to get the pot off the stove five times before I got to the point that it was ready to simmer. So, I tried to put my bits and pieces together and do as much as possible in the lounge room because whenever the bell rang, I jumped and served.

Frank was supposed to be serving in the shop, especially after school times, because we'd get a lot of school children buying lollies and drinks and so forth, as Caulfield Grammar School was at the end of our street. It was good business in one way, but the school children were very difficult to control sometimes. They were noisy, rude and tried to steal. So it wasn't a pleasant time to be in the shop alone. Frank couldn't manage them, and I was worried he'd hit them, so I had to be in the shop with him. When he was on his own and a couple of people came in, he would push the bell for me, because he couldn't manage: it was too much and he got so flustered.

After he'd get up from his sleep, he'd sit in the lunchroom reading the paper as I was trying to cook. If the article was interesting, he wouldn't get up. So I had to run in to serve in the shop. I did all the housework, looked after the children, as well as buying for the shop and stocking the shelves. I didn't really mind, most of the time. I enjoyed the shop. I thought it was good for us. We did well. And I had a good relationship with the customers, with the clients, with the salespeople. I didn't have any problem with anybody.

There were a couple of people who didn't like Frank serving them. His English wasn't bad; he had the usual Hungarian accent. However, he had this idea in his head that he wouldn't speak unless he could pronounce it 100% correctly. So it was quite difficult to get him to talk. He understood everything and he knew the words. So it looked as though he wasn't friendly in the shop, which wasn't that good for business. But, we (or I) were doing the best we could and earning a living.

It meant working 16-hour days: the shop opened at 6:30am and closed at 9:30pm. 363 days, of the year, Good Friday and Christmas Day we closed at 12 o'clock. So the afternoon was free. That was it for holiday time.

My other time off was when I'd leave the milk bar to do the shopping, to go to the warehouse for whatever I needed to have for stock. That would take a couple of hours a week, and about every fortnight, I would take off to go to Lillian's for an hour and take her some groceries, to make her life easier. Which gave me 2 hours out of the shop. Half an hour there, half an hour back, an hour there for visit. I would do some shopping for her, or just spend a bit of time with her. As far as I was concerned she was my Mother. More of a Mother than anybody else in my lifetime, and I just needed to be with her, to refresh my soul.

As the year rolled on Frank became more and more lazy and self-centred. He wasn't kind to anyone, anymore. All his good qualities that were so relevant beforehand, seemed to have disappeared. He was drinking more and more as well. Which certainly didn't help me at all. I didn't like the idea of it at all, never did. So there weren't too many happy days anymore.

The third year that we were in the shop, we had enough money for a deposit for a house. I decided that we needed to buy a house and start paying it off. The money we saved was just sitting in the bank and not producing enough security. Everything else came out of the shop and was paid for. Virtually all our food was bought wholesale, and some of it even written off as tax deductions.

I found a small house, not very far from the shop, in Elsternwick. It was part of a block of six: 2 bedroom, detached houses. We put a deposit on it. In truth, I bought it. I had a look at it worked out that it was a good buy. I gave the okay for Frank to go ahead and have a look too. Then I signed the contract.

I had a very good relationship with the bank manager, from the very beginning. Because he realized that we had potential for further business for his bank. I told him that it was difficult for me to go to the bank with the takings, (couldn't leave the shop and it didn't fit in with Frank's hours) plus, I didn't like carrying cash around anyway. He suggested that he'd come to the shop every week, on his way to work and take the money into the bank for me. We had joint accounts everywhere in the business, but I don't think Frank had signed more than 2 cheques in the whole 5 years that we were in the shop. One of them was actually the deposit for the first house. He signed a cheque for the deposit because I said to him 'go and see it, ask these questions from the agent and if the answers are what we want, give him the cheque for the deposit'. An hour later I got a call from the bank manager, (who was checking in with me,) 'You know that Frank signed a check for 'X' hundred dollars?'

I can't remember how much it was, but it was a big amount. I said, 'That's right, it's the deposit for the house that we talked about." And, so we bought this house and started paying it off.

The following year; we bought another weatherboard house in Oakleigh, opposite his sister's place. So we had one house paid off in 18 months, the other in about 12 months. We were coming up to five years in the milkbar, about the end of 1970, and I said, 'I can't do it anymore. It's wearing me out.'

Our best friend 'Pajty'

When we'd been in the milk bar for about three years, I had a run of tonsillitis, one after another, for about 12 months. I had to have them out. Otherwise, it threatened to infect my heart as well. So, I had to go to hospital. Anne, Frank's niece came to stay with us, to look after the shop and the children for the 4 or 5 days I was in the hospital. Prior to that, I usually dashed to the doctor to get penicillin injections to hold me over until the next time and then went back to work in the shop, regardless.

But that year was so bad. I think it was 1969 that I

had to have my tonsils out. I was out of action for about a week with it. Anne stayed at our place, in the girls' room, then stayed on, as she didn't want to live at home.

Ballet recital

She was helping out in the shop for her board and was meant to go to school. But, she didn't go to school and wasn't very much help in the shop either, we lost a lot of stock due to thefts. She was also teaching things to my daughters that were not appropriate. So she lasted six weeks. Then I said, "Sorry, you'd better go home to your mother. Because I can't deal with this." I wasn't the favourite with her mother either; because the mother was not happy that she'd left home. She was needed at home. I did not need the hassle either; I had enough on my plate dealing with her uncle.

A few months later I had a real surprise waiting for me. One nice sunny afternoon a taxi pulled up outside the shop and a young man with a suitcase walked in.

I said, "Can I help you?"

He started swearing at me in Hungarian and said, "Is that a nice way to greet your relation?"

I certainly did not recognise my brother Jo. The last time I'd seen him was as a 15 year old and 13 years on, it made quite a difference in his appearance. So, he arrived without one word, or a note or any kind of information to expect him: the usual treatment that I'd always received from my family.

He told us that after finishing his army service, he signed up in the army-reserve, and at 28 years old, he could get a tourist permit to visit Austria with a bus tour. It becomes the expected thing that quite a few of them "lost" their way and did not return with the tour. Instead he sought asylum at the Australian Embassy.

As he had relatives here, he received preferential treatment and after a few months, was transported to Melbourne and took a taxi straight to me.

I was happy to see him of course, but slightly apprehensive as well, as to how it would work out. As the flat was empty, we put him in there and that was supposed to give him his independence. We came across an advertisement by 'Siemens' (the German electrical company) looking for electricians, a couple of weeks later. As Jo is qualified, I rang up for an appointment: he went and was accepted, because he spoke German, (very little English) but all of the equipment and instructions were in German, so he got the job.

That helped sort his life out, as he had a well-paid job, free independent accommodation, instant friends, (as we introduced him to all of ours) and the family around him. That only left me, with now another person to look after! We agreed that he should help with the heavy things, like sorting soft drink delivery and filling the fridge with drinks and thinks like that while he lived with us. But he soon saw that Frank didn't do a lot around the place and was waited on 'hand & foot', so he adopted the same attitude.

The girls enjoyed having an uncle around: he bought a TV shortly after arriving, and put it in the flat. I didn't allow TV in the house because that would really mean an end to any help I may get or any schoolwork that had to be done. On the weekends, I would catch the girls at 6am, sitting in front of the TV, in Jo's lounge, with the sound turned really low.

I was getting very tired, the work load was

wearing me down, so I was thinking that there must be some change due in my life.

Anyway, as the 5th year finished, I said, "I can't do this any longer. We have to sell the shop."

Frank wanted to do another year. But I'd really had enough. I just couldn't cope with it any longer. The girls had started high school. And I said, we should sell the shop and go for a 3 months holiday in Europe, visit the family, show the girls where we came from and then come back and start another business.

What I wanted to do was to get a sandwich bar in one of the high-rise office buildings, or a canteen, that would be open from 8 am – 3 pm and only on business days (Monday to Friday) so that I could be free on public holidays and enjoy other holidays etc. That would have been an ideal business to run and was reasonably easy to buy. We had the 2 houses paid out. We had enough savings to pay for the trip. And we had some investments; we invested money with the solicitors in property trusts. So we decided, or rather I made the decision to sell the shop. Whatever we got for it, we would use it for the trip. By March 1971, we sold the shop, we didn't get a very good price for it. But I wasn't really worried about getting too much for it. I was more concerned about having the stock paid for. There weren't many people who wanted that kind of business any more, as the competition from supermarkets was getting stronger.

We booked to go on a ship, because Frank refused

to fly. I don't know why, he didn't want to fly to Europe. He said he wanted to go on a ship, have a real rest (in his case, I don't really know from what). At that time, there were problems in the Middle East and the Suez Canal was closed. So, we had to go the long route, from East to West; through New Zealand to South America, Panama Canal, to South Hampton England and then from there to Rotterdam.

This sounded very idyllic, 36 days on a ship, but it wasn't like that for me. We had to get passports, so I needed my ex-husband Frank K's, signature, for the girls to be put on my passport. Legally he had access to them though he hadn't used it for the last 3-3 1/2 years. But we needed to have it by law so we wrote to him, sent him the forms and asked him to sign. It didn't come back. We wrote again but he ignored all our letters. So, we packed up the car and drove off to Canberra to get him to sign the papers. We managed to meet up and that day the girls spent the last afternoon with him. He signed the papers on top of the car. He took the girls for an outing for a couple of hours and came back to the camping place where we were staying, for the night. We stayed in the caravan, on bunk beds, and in the middle of the night, Pearly screamed and jumped out of bed and started to run away (she was still dreaming and sleepwalking.) When I managed to get hold of her, she started to sob and say, "I don't want to go with daddy I don't want to go with daddy."

Apparently, while they'd been with their father that afternoon, he'd told them that after they got back from their holiday, they had to go and live with him. And that obviously had her terrified! It took quite a time to settle her down, Georgie didn't say anything but she was very subdued as well. So, it took me a long time and a lot of explanation, to reassure them that this was not the case.

When we got back, we found out that Georgie's birth certificate was incorrect. (The original birth certificates where taken by the church when they were in foster care, so I didn't have a copy). Instead of Georgina, (the Hungarian spelling was G-y-o-r-g-y-i) they wrote in Erica. We had to prove that she was never called Erica, had never been Erica, blah blah blah. That of course, took days and we could not finalise the booking until all the passports were at hand.

So by that time, the ship was booked out. We could only get a very low deck cabin, which wasn't a very good position. I was seasick a lot of time, which was awful.

We left Melbourne on the 29th of May 1971. We left on a Greek ship that was carrying 2,000 passengers and 1,600 staff. The official route was from Sydney. It only stopped in Melbourne as the end of the round Australia trip, and then proceeded to Sydney for a 3-day stay, to take on the majority of passengers.

The last 4-5 weeks after we had sold the shop were pretty hectic. We had 4 weeks to pack up, sell our things, mostly furniture and whatever we could. A couple of pieces we kept and Panni kindly said she'd look after and store some items for us.

Everybody always said to me, "Why don't you make Frank do more? Why do you always do everything for him and everybody else?"

My explanation was always the same, "It is easier for me to get on with it and do it, rather than keep reminding him and argue about it, just to get it done." And the other thing was, whenever help was needed in the shop or in the house the girls had to help too. (I needed to teach them some responsibility). But there was always the fact that Frank wouldn't help and the girls would say: "Well, Papa (they called Frank Papa, which means Daddy in Hungarian) doesn't help! Why doesn't he help? Why do we have to help?"

Then he would turn around, and say, "Why don't you get the girls to help? Why ask me? Why always ask me" Why don't you get the girls to do it?"

So, with him, I didn't want to argue about it all the time and would do anything for peace. And with the girls, I mostly let it go, because if he didn't do it, I couldn't ask the girls to do it. It wasn't fair, they were children. So, everybody got the easy way out of life, and I was left "holding the baby" at all times.

The three weeks or so when we had no home, before we left on the ship, Panni and Bill offered for us to stay with them at their house in Brunswick.

So, while we staying at Panni's, she said, "Frank can talk you around to do anything and you do it for peace sake", "And secondly, you find it easier to do it, than to put up with the remarks and argument, just because he can twist everything around."

I said to her "I'm sick and tired of arguing. It's

easier most of the time not to argue. If you knew it was black and he said white, you'd just eventually agree, as he could turn it around and you'd say, yeah, yeah OK, it's white." Then when you go away thinking, "why the bloody hell did I say it's white, when it wasn't?"

Anyway, one morning Panni came into the room (Frank was still in bed,) and brought him coffee Frank just laughed at her. He said, "You see, even you bring me my coffee.'

I thought Panni was going to pour the coffee over his head. She got so mad. She didn't realize that he had manipulated her into doing something that she didn't really want to do. And that summed up Frank very well - he could manipulate you into doing things and you didn't realize it, until you'd done it. And then it was too late.

Anyway, long story short, we finally got on the ship, got to Sydney, and had a sightseeing tour. We looked around Sydney for a couple of days and then we were on our way to Europe.

11

To go back a step or two, during our time in the milk bar, Frank sister's kids often spent time with us. They were a big boisterous group of five children and it seemed that everyone was getting on reasonably well. I did realize though, that as the children were growing up, Frank's sisters (especially the older one) were trying to muddy the waters every now and again, between us.

The relationship was cordial but I didn't really get close to either one of them. I didn't particularly want to be a drinking buddy. They both drank excessively, especially the younger one. I never liked drinkers and I did have bad experiences with the first Frank, so I wasn't very keen on the idea of drinking and going to drunken parties. But life rolled along in that respect with his family, and I always made sure that the children were remembered on birthdays and Christmas and had decent gifts from us, even if Frank couldn't care less.

The milk bar was always a very attractive proposition to all the children. Mind you, I was very strict about them touching any of the stock without asking. They weren't allowed to go into the shop and just help themselves.

Anyway when we left for Europe, the friendship between Panni's two children and mine was more sincere, more of a real family situation likes cousins. We were very close and as we stayed with them for the weeks before we left for Europe, the kids definitely became closer.

Thirty-six days on the ship wasn't a pleasant journey for me as I was seasick most of the time. I don't like travelling on boats. I don't like to be closed in by water. I can't swim, so it was a very insecure feeling for me. The girls took to ship life like ducks to water. Being twins and being very pretty, they quickly became the darlings of the whole staff. All the waiters and stewards were going out of their way to make them feel comfortable and they had a great time. They really enjoyed it; they were in everything and everywhere. They couldn't get off the ship, so they couldn't get into a great deal of trouble and I was happy they enjoyed it so much.

They had their thirteenth birthday on the ship after we passed Ecuador. The staff made an awfully big fuss at the dinner that night. They got special cakes with candles and the steward had made a special dinner for us, so they were the stars of the ship on that day: they were absolute little princesses as far as they were concerned. They had always been very pretty. They were good, well-behaved girls always, so we didn't have any worries in that respect. They were spoiled by all the staff, from the captain to the last cook. They had free reign to run around the ship: they could virtually do anything they wanted, which was a good thing, because I wasn't terribly lively with all the seasickness, so I was thankful that they had such a good time.

Wherever the ship stopped, we would go out sightseeing with the tours. We stopped in New Zealand, Tahiti, Panama and possibly a few more places that I can't recall anymore.

We arrived in England, at Southampton, for only a stop, because we were going on to Rotterdam. I received a letter from my dear friends Stephen and Annus, whom I'd spent so much time with as a teenager. They left Hungary at the time I did, in 1956, but instead of going overseas, they settled down in Sweden with their daughter. We had been corresponding over the years. I was very sorry that we didn't catch up in the refugee camps. I didn't know they'd left Hungary too and where they were, I only found out about a couple of years later that they were in Sweden. So we'd been corresponding all the time and I was always hoping that they'd come to Australia to visit us. But anyway, in that letter, we got a message to say that Stephen had an industrial accident some time back and was not expected to live very long. The letter was forwarded to the ship, (as it first went to Melbourne) so I didn't know if he was still with us.

He was an electrician. He had worked on the high

voltage power lines. Somebody had switched on the voltage and he got electrocuted and had suffered greatly. In that letter, Annus was saying that they only gave him a couple of months to live. And if we wanted to see him we better go to Sweden because he may not live long enough. So I said, "Well that's it, we're going to Sweden first." It wasn't the exact plan, but that's what we decided to do when we arrived in Rotterdam.

We had made some friends on the ship with some Dutch people, so they helped us to buy a car, we got a Renault. The Renault is a French car, it was second hand but it was in really good condition. It was a very, very comfortable car for the four of us and all our luggage. The large trunks we sent on to Vienna to be stored. We decided to drive to Stockholm from Rotterdam. We stayed in a youth hostel and spent about five days there, until we got our luggage sorted and got the car. It was quite an experience, being an old couple with teenage children in a youth hostel, but it was great fun as well, especially for the girls.

The girls made friends with everybody. Georgie definitely picked up an American accent: she is very good at accents, Pearlie is not bad either, but Georgie can talk to a person for a couple of hours and she's got the accent down pat. We drove through Denmark and stayed one night in another youth hostel and then we virtually drove eighteen hours solid to Stockholm, in one incredibly long drive.

We didn't realize that we went through the longest bridge, that connects Denmark and Sweden over the ocean, because it was night-time and the fog was so thick we could only see the rail of the bridge as we drove.

It was strange driving on the right side of the road, after all that time driving on the left in Australia. Somehow, I was navigating. I had all the maps on my lap. Anyway, for some reason or other, we got off the main highway, because we were going to find a guesthouse, or some kind of accommodation, to stay for the night. Frank had been driving for fourteen - fifteen hours, he was getting really tired. I did have a driver's licence but I refused to drive with Frank, because he was a terrible 'backseat driver' and could not navigate.

We got off the main road, finished up in somewhere in a field and he somehow drove into a ditch, while trying to turn. I jumped out with all the maps on my lap. He gave me his watch beforehand to wind up, because he had the old fashion one. In all the fuss, we lost the watch. It was very late in the evening and pitch black, but we simply couldn't find it. We did find it on the way back. We were lucky there was a farmer who was driving past, with a sort of industrial vehicle. I flagged him down and asked him for help (luckily he spoke a bit of English), so he could help. He understood, saw what had happened where we were in the ditch, so they tied the rope around the car and pulled us out of the ditch and pointed us to the right direction. We never managed to get to a hotel, just kept driving.

They said just follow us, we're going to the main

highway and that will get you there, but the nearest hotel is probably two hundred kilometres away.

We were just on the outskirts of Stockholm by then, so we drove all the way and got in very early in the morning, around 4-5 am.

It was a very happy reunion with Stephen, who by then had recovered enough to be home, but in a wheelchair. Their daughter, Edith, was on summer holidays, so we didn't manage to see her. As it turned out, by the time we got there, he was over the worst and was back at home.

He had lost one of his legs, (it had to be amputated), because it wasn't getting the proper circulation, but he was his happy self again. So we spent about a week together, having a wonderful time in Stockholm with them. Through a lucky bit of organising, we managed to stay in the flat next door, so we were virtually independent from them because I didn't want to be an extra burden on Annus.

It was quite an experience for everybody: we had dinner about seven o'clock and would sit around with a glass of wine and talk about everything. We had beautiful sunshine the whole time, so we just kept talking and talking.

Of course, we didn't realize that July in Sweden (summer) is a long day with a very short night-time. I was getting awfully tired one night and I said, "Jesus it's still beautiful sunshine but I am so tired. I should be going to bed." I looked at the clock and it was two o'clock in the morning but the sun was still shining.

So anyway, we went to bed and about 2.30 am or so when the sun dips, and at 5 am the sun is out again, so it was a couple of very short nights we had in Sweden.

While we were in Stockholm we bought some camping gear. We bought a tent, some air mattresses and for cooking, a little stove with a pot, plus bits and pieces we needed like blankets. So we fitted ourselves out with the minimum of camping gear, because we thought on the way down to Hungary, we could go into camping places, because a hotel for four would be quite expensive.

We could have afforded the luxury, but we were conscious about spending too much money, the old saving and frugal living was always with us. So I think we only stayed in motels about twice in that four weeks, going from Rotterdam to Stockholm and eventually to Vienna. We stayed in various camping places along the way from Denmark, Holland and then through Germany, and Austria and when we got to Vienna we stayed in a camping place a bit out of town. There we met an old couple, who were in their late sixties holidaying. They lived in Vienna, Frank spoke quite good German, because he studied it in school when he was doing his matriculation, so he could communicate with them.

He'd been born close to the Hungarian - Austrian border, in the village of Farad, so lots of people spoke German there. His grandmother was Austrian and she apparently hardly spoke Hungarian but mostly German, so he had a reasonable German and the old gentleman spoke a little bit of English. So, we made ourselves understood and became quite good friends. The girls loved the old couple, as they also had a little dog that was quite a hit. We told them, well when we come back from Hungary, we want to stay in Vienna for a little while and they said, "Oh just get in touch with us when you come back and we will help you find somewhere to live."

So that settled the matter and we were on our way to Hungary. It was quite a shock to arrive at the Hungarian border in 1971. There was supposed to be a relaxation of the communist rule, and of course we had to have visas to visit Hungary, with our Australian passports. Also, about a year or so earlier a general 'Amnesty' was issued for all people who had left after the revolution. It would have been prison for us if we had returned to Hungary before then.

Our car was packed full with camping gear, gifts and what have you and as we drove up to the Hungarian border from the Austrian side, there were boom gates that were as thick as a big tree trunk that blocked off the road, they were huge! On either side of the gate was a tower, where soldiers were standing with machine guns. On the other side of the boom gate were more machine guns: and a big building full of soldiers - not police - just soldiers in uniforms, most of them with guns on their hips and machine guns in their arms.

It was terrifying!

The girls were frightened, we had to quiet them down and we said, "Just don't talk, don't talk, definitely don't talk and try not to talk in English," as their Hungarian was quite limited.

We went through the border check, and a passport

check, as they looked at our car. I was very, very thankful that they didn't ask us to unpack it because, while we were waiting in line with our car, they stopped other cars and virtually stripped them of everything, and unpacked it all onto the tarmac.

Anyway, we got through the border reasonably well after driving through 'no man's land' for about five or six kilometres. We certainly let out a great big sigh of relief. Then we drove the next sixty or so kilometres to the village of Frank's birthplace, Farad where his brother and his family lived in the old family home.

By the time we got back in 1971, unfortunately Frank's mother had passed on some years before hand, so we were visiting his brother and their four children. They were lovely and loving and caring, they had virtually nothing, and they lived very, very modestly. The old house had two rooms and a kitchen in the middle and no running water. It was pretty primitive and they lived like many small country families. My sister-in-law worked in a metal factory, which ran two shifts, till midnight and that was very heavy work. Standing eight hours by a big machine, lifting heavy things, by an open door, winter or summer also looking after a family of four children.

Frank's brother was unfortunately the same as Frank, (if not worse). He used up most of his wages for drinking and they had problems all the time. He was a very difficult man in many ways. We stayed with them for a few days and the children had a wonderful time, they become experts in Hungarian in no time. Their 'cousins', two boys and two girls, just took to them like old loved family. The girls went with them everywhere, got introduced to every one, as they went shopping. Everybody knew the Nemeth twins had arrived and the little village made a great big fuss of them, so that was extremely pleasant. My sister-in-law Rozsi (she had an even worse time in her marriage than I did) and the children, truly become our family, and even now I miss them the most.

We had a lovely time and I really, really loved my sister-in-law and we're still the best of friends. I just wish I could do more for them, because she's a woman with a golden heart and the hardest working woman I've ever known. We were all sorry to go, but my mother was waiting for us, as well as the rest of Frank's family in Budapest.

After that, we arrived in Budapest, at my mother's place, where we settled in for a little while. What I've left out of the story so far is my brother's part in it.

I will regress and go back a couple of years. About two years after Frank K. and I split up, I had received a letter from my lovely brother. I never had very much correspondence from him and my mother was a bad correspondent too, (so am I actually,) but I tried to keep up the correspondence with my mother when we were on good terms.

Anyway, my brother sent me a letter and he wanted me to send him a Harley-Davidson motorbike, with leather jacket, helmet etc!

At that stage I was working three jobs, trying to provide a home for the girls and save money. I ignored the letter and didn't bother answering. Some months later, I got a very nasty letter from him saying that I was too lazy to help him. He said, 'Money grows on trees in Australia; you're too lazy to pick it. Everybody would be rich by now, so you must be very lazy or too selfish to share.' That was my brother's expression. I did not hear from him for some years, until he just showed up at the door of my milk bar. And from then on I had two children and two adults to look after!

He then lived with us about eighteen months after he'd arrived. When I told him, "You better get out on your own and find your own feet. I'm not here at your beck and call and we are going to sell the shop." That didn't go down very well! Eventually I had to find him a little bungalow flat, furnished in the next street.

I said, "You're welcome to come around every now and again for a meal, but I won't be cooking for you every day and I won't be washing your clothes and so forth and so on, so get yourself organized and make yourself a life." He was very nasty about it. After we sold the shop, we had a couple of small parties with our friends and Panni and Bill. At these parties Joe got drunk very quickly, he was obnoxious, he insulted some of my friends and I had quite a problem with his behaviour. He always threw in my face: "You don't care about your family. You don't have a family, you're just too selfish to look after anybody."

(I just wondered what it was that I was doing all this time??)

So, we didn't really part with a very good relationship at the time and, as it turned out, we never really managed a proper one.

In his childhood, while we were living with Mum

on our own, he tried to play the big man of the house. He was quite a worry but Mum always thought that the sun shone out of his backside. He was the star in her eyes until she died, it didn't matter what he did, he was always 'my darling son'.

So, by the time we got to Hungary, he'd written to Mum to say we didn't get along very well and I hadn't really welcomed him or helped him. Mum, of course, questioned me, asking why I wasn't a better friend with my brother? But she would not listen to anything against him because in her eyes, he was perfect.

That meant our arrival at my mother's house in Hungary wasn't as happy and welcoming as I'd hoped. She was very happy about the girls, but she wasn't quite happy with me. Anyway, we stayed with my mother for a few weeks, and then went down to the town of Kiskunfélegyháza to visit other relations there. By this time of course, my mother and my aunty had become bosom buddies again, and so we had to go and visit my aunty. When we arrived, there was the usual big story and big fuss about everything and everybody.

We were meant to stay for two days and arrived the late afternoon. So the next day the girls, Frank and I went to look around town to show them the old familiar places I remembered as a child. We naturally went to visit my cousin Jancso and his wife, because we were the closest my whole life. I loved him very much, because he looked after me when I was a kid. He'd always been very good to me. He, being the doctor in the family, was a big feather in my auntie's cap, as she treats it as her own achievement.

We spent a couple of hours with them and had a good chat and enjoyed ourselves. It was great to see them, everything was lovely. When we got back to my auntie's house, we found Mother in hysterics in one bed and my aunty crying in another.

"What's the matter?"

My mother said: "How dare you go and visit and talk to Jancso, you must know we are not talking!"

"So? What's that got to do with me? I've come from the other end of the world after so many years. And you expect me to help you argue and help you to keep score with other people? Besides, I have nothing against him, that's your problem, you sort it out."

But my mother said, "How can you do that to your aunty, after all that she's done for you?"

"We'd better not talk about what she's done for me. Because if I list what she's done, it won't be very nice, so I don't want to talk about it." I said: "OK we are leaving now". I wasn't staying to listen to hysterical theatre. My uncle (he was very upset) asked us to stay longer, he said he'd talk to them and sort it out. Because I loved and respected my uncle, we stayed another day, which wasn't very pleasant or good for my peace of mind. But, I went to see Jancso once more regardless, our trip back to Budapest was in a sombre mood.

Before we left, my aunty pulled me aside and told me that my cousin, her son (the one I changed and looked after as a baby) was getting engaged. They wanted a gold engagement ring, with two diamonds and a sapphire, plus a wedding ring in eighteen carat gold. Would I buy it for them in Vienna?

"First of all, have you got the money for it?"

She said, "You can give it to them as a wedding present."

I said, "No, I worked for the money I have and I'm not going to spend it on his wedding. If he wants to get married, he'd better save enough money to buy the rings and if he hasn't got it, he hasn't got it. Secondly, I would not do it, because that would be smuggling. I could get caught at the border, put into jail or my passport taken away. I am not going to risk that for anybody and especially not for a spoiled brat."

And that was the way we left them, it wasn't a very happy re-union I suppose.

We visited Frank's three sisters and families in Budapest and his other brother in another small town, to get to know every one. I caught up with a friend from the old days. I didn't have many before I left, just a couple of girls from my school days. Frank, on the other hand, had many, as he'd worked and played sport for many years before he left. Some of them became good friends to me too, for many years. Unfortunately, most of them have now passed on, as they were all much older then I was. Only one girl, a daughter-in-law who is younger then me, is left and we are still very close friends.

So, after about six weeks in Hungary, we then decided to go for a couple of camping trips around the countryside, including the Balaton (the largest lake).

Then it was time to head back to Austria. We went back into the camping place in Vienna and then caught up with the old couple, Mr & Mrs Sceener, who invited us for coffee. They lived in the second district and they said, "We're going to help you find a flat within a couple of days."

He worked as a porter in one of the ministries, a government department, so he was a 'very important man' in his own eyes, but a very friendly and helpful person as well.

Because Austrians care a lot for appearances, they were very happy to say that he was a government employee. He worked in the government ministry, so he was somebody really, really good. And they had a little dog and the girls loved the little dog, so we had coffee with them a couple of times. Anyway, he came one day and said there was a flat not very far from where they lived, in the second district, which is very close to the city, with good transport and so forth. It was a downstairs flat in a four-story house; one and a half rooms and a kitchen. Not very comfortable, but better then a tent, and we thought we could settle down for a little while until we worked out what to do, because in my mind, we were going to stay for six months in Europe and then come back to Australia.

So we stayed six months in Europe we thought renting this flat would be cheaper than living in hotels plus living in camping places is not a good idea long-term. So we rented this downstairs flat, which was originally a 'Porter's Residence' (they didn't have porters anymore.) We had this very narrow kitchen, with a narrow room opening from the kitchen onto another big room, which was the main room. You had to go through the kitchen into the so-called 'half' room.

We made up the main room as a bed sitting room we got some bed bunks and a couple of second hand chairs and tables. We bought two couches for the girls to sleep in. The kitchen had a little gas stove that didn't work (I used our camping stove for a while) and the toilet and water tap was outside in the passage, just opposite our kitchen door.

I wasn't terribly impressed with the situation because to have a bath I needed to heat water on a little stove, then I had to get a big plastic basin to wash in, then carry the water out to the toilet.

Everybody had to carry out the water, and to do any washing! I mean we didn't have first class luxury in Australia in the shop, but we did have a proper bathroom and automatic hot water and we did have a proper toilet and our own rooms!

September came and Frank said the children had to go to school, so we enrolled them in a school, (which was in the next street) and we tried to find work. He wanted to go to the Australian Consulate to ask for recommendations for jobs, which of course they couldn't give us. But they did help us get visas and work-permits to stay and work in Austria, which was very handy, so we got that organized.

At the consulate, Frank asked if they had any jobs for us? The answer was of course, "Sorry there is no opening," then my darling husband turned around and says to the secretary we were talking to, "We didn't think about working in the consulate as such but maybe cleaning or something like that?"

I felt as small as a dust mite, I felt so embarrassed, so terribly embarrassed, when I told them that we came from Australia. We have money behind us. We've run a business, they knew what a milk bar was, it wasn't a big business, but even so it was such a stupid, stupid thing to say. Australians are not fussy about what you do, if you are a cleaner or a company director, you still say 'Hi Joe' and 'Hi Mac'. Still you need to keep some kind of base line, re how far you're prepared to go. You have to have some self respect and not behave like a beggar.

Anyway, one way or another I think Frank got in touch with the Hungarian club. They had their meeting place in the Hungarian House, not very far from where we lived. It belonged to the Hungarian government and the consulate managed it, mainly for social functions. Somebody there recommended him to work in this plumbing business in the warehouse. So, he got a job in a warehouse as a storeman, the children were in school and for me I needed a job too. One where I would be there for the girls when they came home from school, because they finished school at one o'clock, (there's no afternoon school or no late school in Europe.)

So Mr Scheener, who was our Austrian friend, got me a job working with the cleaning company that worked for the ministry. Well that was OK, I started at five o'clock in the morning and finished about eleven and I was home by twelve. This company was doing major clean-ups in the schools and government offices, like spring-cleaning times. After about two months living in Vienna, I decided that I had to learn German, as the girls would finish out the school year. I was also learning beside the children, as they learned the language. It was difficult for the girls to get used to the school, as it is so different from Australia. Not just the language they had to learn, but also a lot of the subjects were totally new to them. We spent every afternoon doing homework and trying to catch up on the new subjects. Most of the children and the teachers spoke English as a second language, but they did not make life easier for the girls, they were not a friendly lot. One girl called Ilse, was friendly to them, as she was also new to that school: previously she'd lived in the country with her Grandmother. She had an unhappy time in the city, with her mother, so she spent a lot of time at our place. The three girls become very close.

Everything was going OK at work, but one day about three months down the track, we had to clean a sports hall. There had been a fire and some rubber mats had burnt. The ceiling to the floor was covered in thick black soot. It was a really high ceiling, and because I was the youngest there, they sent me up on the ladder to wash down the walls and the ceiling. About three and a half meters or four-meter-high ladder, up and down, it was absolutely filthy work. I was so black and dirty I looked like a chimney sweep when I finished work. And I couldn't get on a tram because I was so dirty, so I had to walk home. This was quite a distance away and when I got home I had to get quite a few buckets of water to wash myself down and then get my clothes clean. I said to myself, "This is it, I will not do this job ever again."

That didn't go down very well with Frank because he said I couldn't simply give up. I spoke to the manager and he said he'd organize that my jobs from now on would be cleaning offices.

This is my story, of the happiness of our Vienna holiday.

12

The reason I wrote this memoir? One morning I woke up, early as usual, and just lay there thinking about my life. Not just the daily happenings, but also my life overall. There are a lot of underlying things that have happened in my life, which created the life that I eventually led.

To begin with, after my father's death, I felt very, very lost. I knew instinctively that my mother favoured my brother in everything, and I had an awfully big need to be loved and cared for. So for that reason, I tried always to please everyone and in every situation, to make it easy for everybody around me. 'Don't make waves, don't do anything, and don't ask for anything'. I realized that very early on, when living with my aunty, my willingness created a situation where I became virtually an unpaid servant for the whole family, and I would do anything to just get some quiet and be left alone.

But it didn't quite work that way, it didn't change

the situation. Eventually we went back to live with my mother, where I was the housekeeper, maintaining our life, virtually cooking, cleaning, washing, doing everything that needed to be done around the house as much as my twelve-year-old abilities allowed.

I kept thinking of why my first husband Frank K. decided to marry me. He was nine years older, so he was twenty-five I was just over sixteen and, what was the motivation that he wanted to marry me? I never really worked it out, it may have been the possibility that our life looked like a more affluent one, or if not affluent, a more structured family life. His family life was quite a mixed bag, not knowing his father, looked after by a drunken grandfather, a very nervous insecure mother, so maybe that was it. Or just wanting to be independent, and someone to look after him.

We were both a bit insecure and just looking out for one another. Has that got anything to do with it? I don't know. For me I certainly wasn't the big love of his life. My motivation was a hundred percent selfish though. I liked him quite well, he was quite good looking, good company, good fun for dancing, he had a good job, so I did like him but I wasn't in love with him, madly in love with him, in the sense that I would call true romantic love.

My motivation was more that he had the ability to provide a home he was supposed to receive a flat through his work, I would be independent from my mother and I could live my own life. My mother had not given up totally on the idea of marrying me off to some old Englishman, (or anybody from a western country,) so that I could then provide my mother and brother with more comfort and financial security.

My dream was always to have a happy home: where everybody loved one another, cared for each other and have children I could love and care for and then I would have a happy life. But the flat fell through, the Revolution happened and terrifying times unfolded.

My mother started working on Frank, to talk him into getting out of the country. My thoughts were, we might as well go this way I was at least going with someone I knew into the unknown. Well, I knew him, but I didn't realise how very little I *really* knew about him. I left my country with misgivings but still with hope for something better, and went into the unknown. God only knew what would happen to anybody back then: all was uncertain, all was in chaos.

When you're young and hopeful you seem to be able to do anything. Then of course, in the refugee camp, life went on. In my own way I tried to help everybody the best I could, I tried to help with the children, helped other people if I could, that's how we became good friends with Panni and Bill. I was trying to manage with what we had or what's been given to us. I had a little bit of an idea how to sew, so all the Red Cross clothes we got I could adjust so they'd fit better and look nicer. It kept me occupied, because if I wasn't doing anything I couldn't have managed the long months of camp life. The best thing for me is reading, but in a refugee camp there were very few books, so we could try to study, but it wasn't very much you could do in there.

Then arriving in Australia, falling into the situation by sharing a house with a family and two children, trying to keeping the peace and have good relationships, I would do all sorts of things that normally wouldn't be accepted by anybody else, but I thought for peace and quiet I'd do it.

The first year and a half when we were married and starting off life in Australia was lovely, we never argued, always talked to one another nicely, and we just had a really happy, peaceful loving life, because there was no reason to argue about anything. I'm not a person that puts her wishes ahead of others. Unfortunately, I am very biddable and for the sake of peace I would do anything. My worries started of course, after having the children, which created more responsibility. That's when Frank K. went off to the rails, devastated by having daughters instead of a son (that I can't forgive him). His reaction was to start drinking, spending money and making all the decisions without me, (his version of a 'real husband,' in his mind). He changed completely, nearly overnight, and that was a real shock for me.

After we separated, I had to get myself together and try to build a life for my daughters and myself. Then the second Frank came into my life, offering a friendship. He was apparently nice and a little lonely, and he loved the children. As it turned out (20 years later,) I found out it was quite a calculated decision on his part. His brother-in-law, (his younger sister's husband) told me after we split, that when he announced to his sisters that we going to be married, they both were very much against it, especially the older one Terry. 'No, no, what are you thinking marrying her, she's got two kids, what are you doing taking on somebody else's children?" And his reply was, "Look, she is eighteen years younger, she will look after me, she's biddable, she's a hard worker and through the children, I can always control her."

So, okay, my reason for marrying him was simply being worn down by his persistent arguments for it. "It will be better for the children and would look better in the shop etc." Just living together wasn't really that *'au fait'* with everybody else at the time either, in the late 60s, early 70s.

As it turned out, marrying Frank the second was the worst thing I could have done, for the children. There have been lots of things that I've done "for the children's sake" which turned out badly. You live with regret: "Why did you do it, why did you put up with it for so long?"

I regretted it as soon as we married. Frank's caring and helpfulness around the house, and with the children ceased virtually overnight. As soon as we were married that was it! From then on, he was the king of the castle and he would only help if he absolutely had to. I would do ninety per cent of the work around the shop and one hundred per cent around the house.

I still made the children's clothes until we left for Europe. I made sure that they were always nicely dressed and had good things, even if it meant I had to sew all night. I made sure that we all looked decent and I tried to make up for the time that they didn't spend with me, by having things that other children had. Except, I could not erase the memory of that time.

The girls had to go to school in Vienna, it was the law. I had always intended to come back to Australia. I didn't want to live in Europe and at one stage, Frank was working very hard to convince me that the children needed to learn to speak German and a bit more Hungarian, as it would be good for their future.

He wanted to go back to Hungary to live at one stage. He said we had enough money to live comfortably in Hungary, we could even have a business, plus the children would have family in Hungary. I flatly refused (one of the few times when I stood my ground) to even contemplate it, as moving back to Hungary was never what I wanted. That would mean that he and I would have to give up our Australian passports, but the children wouldn't have to. That meant that the children could leave Hungary any time and I would be stuck there, I would never ever get an exit visa again.

I enjoyed the visits and looking at places in Hungary that I hadn't seen before, but that was all. It definitely wasn't right for me to live in Hungary again. I am an Australian (true blue) The politics of the time still presented a very restricted situation: there were still lots of things you couldn't do, couldn't say, couldn't buy, still lots of shortages of a lot of things. It just wasn't the life that I wanted to have and definitely didn't want my children to be subjected to.

So we stayed in Vienna. Well, six months is nothing I thought, so we stayed until the children finished their year of school, which became another six months. It went on for four years in this horrible little flat. Frank kept promising, "Just stay six months more, then we go etc."

Eventually I got to breaking point once again. I had to carry every drop of water into the tiny kitchen, heat it on the little gas stove, carry the water out and so forth. The girls were growing up and needed more privacy and we needed more comfort.

We had visitors from Australia and Hungary all in that poky place.

That's when I said, "We either get a decent flat and settle down in Vienna, or we go back to Australia."

Frank opted to find a decent flat by that time the children were apprentices, having just finished school. It was Frank's idea to get them the apprenticeships, as they didn't really want to stay in school, plus a trade learned in Europe was always much appreciated in Australia.

By habit, I always glossed over the unpleasant things, the hard things in life so, I never told the children anything bad about their father, I left it unsaid. Yes, they knew about their father, and that we didn't get along and that was the reason we lived apart. They knew their father loved them and that was the main thing. They didn't have a lot of very pleasant memories. They never really talked about it and that was a subject we just let go. However, their father used every opportunity to try to get them to hate their mother, or at least disrespect their mother, with whatever reason he could come up with. And that seems to have stayed with them!

I suppose their father's stories about me, have in some way become deeply embedded in their heads. Possibly that is the reason why the close relationship I hoped for and craved with my children never eventuated. A happy close family never really happened. Whatever the reason, it's most probably my fault of course, because I created the lives for them. I may have been unable to provide the kind of foundation they needed, to have this close relationship with their mother. I don't know, but it never worked out and that is a deep regret for me. The reason for my life and most of the things I did or put up with, was only for one reason: to make my girls' lives happy and better than mine had ever been. I seem to have failed on all accounts!

I did not have a good relationship with my mother, as much as I would have liked to. She always thought of me I suppose, as a child she didn't want, right up to the end of her life. She believed that it was my responsibility to look after her and provide for her, if need be.

The loving mother-daughter close relationship just didn't exist for me, not with my mother and unfortunately not with my daughters. So it's not very easy, to look back and say. "If I'd done it differently, would it have made a difference? What could I have dome that would have made it better or different?"

I don't know, I just don't know.

The relationship with my brother, of course, is a totally different kettle of fish, because he always felt entitled to whatever he wanted and my mother had always made sure that he had everything he wanted. All his life, as far as I can remember, while we were growing up, he got into trouble for lots of things, but at the end of it, he always got what he wanted.

With my brother living with my mother for many years on their own, their relationship deepened. When he arrived in Australia, he felt entitled and believed that I should provide and look after him. When I told him that he had to leave that flat in the shop, (because we were selling the shop,) he was very, very upset. He accused me of packing up and leaving him without any support. What a joke, a grown man that needed support.

Well, by that time (1971) he was thirty years old. Why would I stop my life for his pleasure to provide a home for him, when I had my own family, and I had my own life to live? That didn't go down very well, because I insisted it was up to him to build his own life. I did my own building, doing the best I could without any support; he had to do it for himself now. That just about finished up anything that we might have had as a brother-sister relationship because with that, I obviously sinned against him in such a way, that it was unforgivable. Later on, this played out in a pretty nasty way, more for my mother than anything else.

Well, I suppose this is enough of my bleeding heart. I don't feel comfortable about getting these feelings out. But it needs to be said and I suppose by hiding, and pretending that it didn't happen and that everything was and is a bed of roses, does not cut it, as that is not exactly how my life played out. So I'm going to leave it here and go back to the day-to-day routine of where we left off.

13

We left off in Vienna with me refusing to work on the heavy cleaning, and instead I got the work in the Ministry of Interior, cleaning offices. This meant starting at 5 am and finishing at 12 noon, so I could be home for the children, same as before. The girls could get ready and go to school with Frank, when he went to work and I was there in the afternoon when they got home. That was an okay job, but absolutely boring. I had virtually finished before 9 am, because everybody started to come in at 8 am to work, so once the bathrooms and hallways were done, I still had usually about two hours or so where I had nothing to do. I just sat around in the lounge room, with the cleaning brooms: there was about a half a dozen of us. Everybody had a floor, (I think it was a six-storey building,) you were officially not allowed to read, or do anything else, but had to just sit there or work.

I very quickly managed to clean up the rooms allocated to me, as they were absolutely disgusting. They generally were only cleaned when you could see the table, as usually there were a lot of papers over the desks. Generally most people packed all the papers away. Anyway, within a very short time, I became a well-liked cleaning lady, as all the office workers were very thankful and kept telling me, "Now I can wear a white blouse because my desk is clean, so I don't have to get dirty."

That didn't make me very popular with my colleagues, but that didn't worry me. Their company was so damn boring, they didn't have anything to do but gossip and just say bad things about everybody. They just enjoyed having dramas. Vienna for me was not a happy place to work. It's wonderful for a holiday, everybody was very friendly, very nice and clean and so forth, but if you start working there, as a foreigner, they think you are below them in every way, not good enough for anyone, because you're just not Austrian. The Viennese people are quite big snobs; it feels as if they are only happy if somebody has some problems. It's not a very pleasant atmosphere between neighbours and work colleagues. There are of course exceptions to the rule, but that was my experience.

I worked about four or five months, until I decided that this wasn't for me, sitting around and doing nothing for hours, I felt my brain just freezing up. No mental stimulation, no intelligent conversation. I told Frank that I'm going to go to school to learn German properly, so I can go back to bookkeeping. He wasn't very happy about it, but I resigned from the job. I went and enrolled in the best language school in Vienna, (The Berlitz School of Languages) which taught five or six different languages. It was an intensive course for three months. I had to go four times a week, sometimes in the evening, as well for another three hours to have lessons and practice conversation in German. It worked pretty well for me, as I became more confident.

Frank would belittle my pronunciations, but other people understood me and I managed to make myself understood, so I become pretty proficient in German in spite of him. Frank had originally learned in school and he knew much more German than I did, to begin with, but when we had to do any official stuff, it was always me who had to do the talking because he wouldn't talk. He was not going to be laughed at, because his pronunciation and grammar weren't perfect, or at least that was his excuse.

I couldn't care less; I was just talking like I did in English. I talked and if they didn't understand, maybe they have to ask me again or I'd explain it in another way. I was not worried by what they thought as this method had stood me in good stead for a long time. When I finished the three-month Language Course, I got my diploma from them and a reasonably good mark.

I was quite happy with my achievement even if he wasn't, and started looking for a job as a bookkeeper. I came across an advertisement by total accident -

General Motors was creating a bigger sales office in Vienna, as they were getting more sales and therefore expanding the operation. They needed a bookkeeper that spoke English, because they had to report every three months to the head office in Detroit, USA. They needed somebody proficient in English. I applied for the job and I got it!

That was a normal office job as well as much better pay. Better than Frank would get in the warehouse or what I was getting as a cleaner, of course. Machine-Bookkeepers were always well paid at that time, and that was pre-computer times. GM still had the old Remington Bookkeeping machine, which I started on originally. I had no problem speaking German and English, all the documents were in English, so that was even better. Very little German was used so that was a blessing for me and the office was fifteen minutes from our flat, so I could walk there. I worked normal office hours and by that time, the girls were finishing their school year.

I was going to send them to Hungary for holidays, but we decided to send them into a camp in Austria so they could practice their German a bit. I thought, "They are now fifteen; they're grown up enough to look after themselves for a couple of hours in the afternoon."

While I was working as a cleaner and home in the afternoon, they had a couple of friends come over to our place, nice Austrian girls, and a boy they befriended, so they came over to study together. I felt they had good company and they were doing well.

Back tracking a little again, I don't seem to keep a chronological order in my story telling. Things pop into my head at any odd time – the girls went to ballet school in Melbourne when we had the milk bar, one of the best ballet schools in Melbourne, The Soymosy Ballet Academy. The owner was the principal dancer of the Budapest Opera Ballet Corps. He left Hungary and had come to Melbourne around the same time as we did, and started his own school. The girls were going there for three years, though by the time they turned thirteen they weren't as keen as they used to be. In Vienna they started to attend a ballet school, but they got sick of that quickly. Then they decided to go to judo, near the school, so they did judo classes after school. Anyway, the point is that I was working in an office, I was getting reasonably well paid and we were settled in, but I wasn't happy about it. I wanted to come back to Melbourne, but Frank said, "Wait and let the girls have another year in school, let them finish their schooling here and I will see after that how we go. You have a good job and we have joined the Hungarian club and we have a lot of friends."

We got to know quite a lot of people in the Hungarian Club in Vienna and Frank became one of the office bearers, so we were doing a lot of good work with them. It was a reasonably settled time. People started to come from Australia and Hungary to visit. It was a little bit difficult in that crummy small flat - the ones coming from Hungary (my mother and

Frank's eldest sister) came one year to visit for two weeks. That meant that the girls had to come in and sleep on their camping mattresses in our room, whilst mum and my sister-in-law slept in their room. It wasn't a very comfortable arrangement, but they wouldn't notice it anyway, they had a good time and we started having more and more visitors. Panni came with her children, then Bill, visiting his family. They all stopped at our palace for a couple of days.

Then a couple of Australian kids came along, plus a friend's daughter came to stay in Vienna to study. She rented in some boarding house or student accommodation with another student, Susanna Agardy. Her father and Frank worked together in the Hungarian National Bank and Mr Agardy, was also called Frank (goodness the Franks in my life, such a lot of them), he was our accountant in Australia, so we were good friends. His daughter came to Vienna to study German in her gap year and in the boarding house where she lived, she met up with a couple of American kids and an Australian. She used to come to our flat at the weekends for home-cooked meals and some family time, bringing her friends. Then our house become a sort of a student get together.

I was always very happy having Australians around; they made life so much more bearable and it was good for the girls to remember. I wouldn't have minded at all, except the accommodation wasn't ideal as I said: I didn't have running water in the kitchen and we only had limited room. We made the best of it. The years passed and I wanted to come home, come back to Australia that is, because as far as I was concerned, Australia was my home. Anyway Frank said, "Let the children learn some trade."

The girls didn't want to go to higher education, because they had a very hard time in school in Austria. The curriculum in Europe was very different from Australia. They had trouble picking up on Geography and History and the language was a problem, so they weren't very happy in school and they never were studious types. Which for me was a big disappointment, because I couldn't study when I so wanted to. I was happy to help and support my daughters in school, to go as far as they wanted to in higher education. But they said they were done with school.

They'd loved school as entertainment, but they didn't want to study anymore. I said they had to learn a trade. They chose hairdressing and beauty treatment. So both of them went and got an apprenticeship, which would be for three years. Frank said we had to stay until they finished. It wasn't what I wanted, but I thought it would be a good thing for the girls to have a proper trade as the Viennese trade schools are excellent and have a good reputation. I thought it would support them in their future.

In the meantime, three and a half years had passed and every six months we talked about going back, but it was always, "Another six months,"'and I was getting really impatient. I said the girls could finish their trade in Austria but we had to move to a decent flat to live in, I could not live in these conditions any longer. After four years of living in that terrible flat, I put my foot down and I said, "That's it. Either you find another flat, a decent flat for us, or we're going back to Australia."

Frank talked to friends at The Hungarian club and one of the couples there said there was a flat in an apartment house they lived in, closer to the city. We found out it was available and we could buy it. So we looked at it: it needed a lot of work of course, because some old couple had it and they hadn't updated it. We made arrangements with the house-owner to buy the flat. We had the money, so we just sent a telegram to Australia to transfer money from our savings, because we still had the two Melbourne houses and the income was coming in from that. So we didn't need the income from Australia, because we were earning money there and paying taxes. I paid the Health Insurance in Australia for three and a half years as well, to make sure that everything was running perfectly. We also paid taxes in Australia, the whole seventeen years we were away, because we had the investments and that was taxable income of course.

We decided that we were going to get this flat and I said okay, but we have to renovate it, to make it suitable for us. The apartment had a long and very big entrance hall, plus two big rooms, and a smaller one (they called it half room) as well as a kitchen. The house was 300 years old with three and a half meter ceilings. A lovely old house, well kept, but we had to bring the flat up to scratch. The landlady had the painter and decorator business that she operated in the ground floor. She had the flat on the fourth floor, for herself. The arrangement was that she would paint the flat for us in the price, but first we had to get some major works done. New electrical wiring needed to be done, because some of the wires were covered in paper for insulation! That was dangerous, so I wanted to make sure that everything was okay so we had new wiring put in. We had central heating put in, and an instant hot water service. I got an idea to make it the way I wanted it. There was a toilet in the flat itself, but no bathroom as such, and the landlady, she was very, very proud of the fact that she had a bath in her kitchen (bathrooms in Europe in old houses were not that common). The kitchen was a tiny galley kitchen, it was really very narrow and not very long, but she had a bath tab put in. On top of the bath was a board that she used for storing things, or to sit on when not in use.

With two teenage daughters, I really couldn't have a bath and kitchen together. What would happened if the girls wanted to have a bath and their father wanted a cup of tea or something like that? No, I wanted a proper bathroom, so I worked it out that if we took part of the entrance hall, (which had huge double doors and was nearly three meters wide), it was as wide as the first room. So we built a wall in the passage, extending the front of the toilet door (because that's where the toilet was), next to the entrance door. We'd enclose it up to the kitchen wall, so it would give us room for a shower, but the girls wanted a bath, so we put on what they called a three-quarter bath, which wasn't very long. Frank couldn't get right into the bath, because it was only one meter fifty. However, it meant that fifty centimetres of the bath had to go into the kitchen. So there was a little section cut off from the kitchen. We used besser blocks because they were lightweight. In old buildings you couldn't really put up a heavy brick wall, not on the third floor, above your neighbour. We had the wall built and took off the toilet door and put the door on the bathroom. Opposite the door was the basin and next to the basin the bath, (which took fifty centimetres off the kitchen), with the shower above.

We had an indoor bathroom with hot water, a proper shower and an indoor, closed toilet! (That was a really big deal for me; finally I could have proper comfort for my family, a civilised life again) even though it wasn't 'Australia'.

So life started to work a bit better. We managed to find second-hand furniture, which is not very easy in Austria, they are so conscious of appearances; they are such snobs, that 'no decent person' would want second-hand furniture. Anyway, Frank had a cousin whose daughter and son were living in Vienna. She got married to an Austrian some thirty-forty years before, so she was a much older lady, (it was a cousin to Frank, his father's sisters daughter or such). Her son was moving into a bigger flat and they had a wall unit they wanted to get rid of, so we bought it off them, along with their dining table and four chairs. The dining table and the four chairs I still have, but the wall units we got for the girls to have long gone. We got a couch bed, that could be pulled out and made into two single beds and a couple of armchairs to go with it, and that was the girl's room. Then we bought another wall unit and a couch with a sideboard from another acquaintance. It is a fine piece of furniture that is still downstairs in the house, as it is very well made; a beautiful mirror finished wall unit combination, of hanging space drawers and crystal cabinets. In Europe it's common to have living-sleeping arrangements in one room, as the flats are much smaller.

We had the lounge room fitted out and the girls' room fitted out. We used the girls' couches from the old place for our bedroom. I got a very small washing machine fitted just behind the section that came out from the bathroom and we got a new fridge and freezer. We had a proper sink put in and we even had room for a tiny table and chairs. All four of us could sit down to dinner in the kitchen; I then didn't have to bother getting up to serve dinner, because I could reach the stove and the sink from my chair. It was pretty tight fitting, but it was comfortable and clean and was what we needed.

By this time Frank had got himself a job in the office, with my help. It was in the plumbing business, (where he first started) sorting and filing. He was there all those years I was working with General Motors. The girls were doing their apprenticeships, so things seemed to settle down a bit. But I still wanted to come home to Melbourne. All these years in Vienna I was very, very home sick.

14

Just as one thing settles, something else comes up. We started to have problems with the rental of the house back in Australia. In the space of about ten months we had three lots of people renting the house, who walked away with the hot water service! I had to buy three new hot water services, and we always had repair bills. We were so far away, we relied on the agents, but it wasn't going well. At that stage, the interest rates in Australia were climbing very high. I had the idea we should sell the houses rather than deal with the headaches and worries of renting: invest the money, (as second mortgages), through our solicitors, like we had the rest of our savings.

We were settled into the new flat, the girls were growing up; they were at the end of their first year of trade school. I was still working at General Motors.

We didn't want to leave the house sales in the hands of agents, so it was decided that I would come back to Australia to sort everything out, because Frank would not have been able to do it.

I left the family behind in Vienna and arrived in Australia. It must have been February. It was still hot in Australia, which I enjoyed very much at that time, because I hated being in these European winters. I stayed with Panni in Brunswick in their house. Quickly I bought a cheap little car to get around, to see agents and visit the houses.

I organized a meeting with the solicitors, found agents and put the houses up for urgent sale. I managed to sell that little detached house in Elsternwick very quickly, for a reasonable price. I cannot remember now what it was, but it was profitable.

The second house was in Oakleigh and was opposite Frank's sister's house. They never so much as looked into it or let us know if there were any problems: such as the agent not doing the right thing or if the tenants were not being trustworthy. The Oakleigh house was more difficult to sell. Somehow there was not much of a market in Oakleigh at that time and being a weatherboard house, it needed some work done.

I would ring Vienna once or twice a week to tell Frank what was happening and what was going on. I needed some papers for him to sign, which he did, and he faxed them back to the solicitors, because everything was in our joint names. I had Power of Attorney but I wanted to do everything correctly.

When I told him I bought a car, he nearly hit the roof. "What an idiotic thing to do, what an expense!" I don't know how he thought I could get around Melbourne, making it cheaper with trams and taxis, as well as the time factor and the distances. He was always very careful with spending on anything or anybody, apart from himself. As it happened, the day before I left, I sold the car for the same price that I bought it for, so I did not lose anything.

As I was in Melbourne, Panni and I went to check out the house and meet with the agent to arrange the sale in Oakleigh. I told her we must say hello to my sister-in-law, as they lived opposite. Terry was at home obviously, because she never worked. The kids must have been in school and Steven of course at work. He had started off working for himself very early on, as a tailor, so he was always at work.

Anyway, this was about 2.30 in the afternoon. It looked like nobody was home. We knocked and waited, and waited, then knocked again. Terry put her head out the door, "Who is it?" she called.

I said, "It's me, we've been to the house and I thought we'd come over and say hello."

She reluctantly opened the door.

She'd just got out of bed; she was still in her dressing grown. The house was all dark: curtains and blinds were down. Anyway she let us into the living room, opened the blinds a little bit and let in a little bit of light. The place had rubbish everywhere: lolly papers, drink cans and stuff. On the coffee table was an ashtray that was over flowing. There were beer bottles and glasses … the house looked an absolute mess. She apologised by saying, "These kids, they never put anything away."

I asked for a glass of water and she said, "Don't you know anymore where it is?" (so she told me to help myself).

I went to the kitchen! The kitchen was full of unwashed dishes, pots, pans and leftovers everywhere. There was not a clean glass to be found so I decided not to have anything at all. She did not even offer to make us a cup of tea or coffee. Mind you, we would not have accepted because I was not sure she could rustle up a clean cup anyway.

We spent about ten, fifteen minutes there and it was time to go. It was about three o'clock, and the children would be home from school soon. It seems she stayed up half the night drinking, watching television and smoking. Then she'd spend most part of the day in bed and when Steven came home, she would ask him, "What did you bring home for dinner?" Or, "What are you cooking for dinner?"

I remembered an earlier time, before we used to go out together. We went to pick them up to go to a picnic at ten thirty or something. She was not dressed because she said, "This horrible man has not ironed my skirt." So we had to wait another half an hour before she could get herself ready, so that's the kind of sister-in-law I had. That was the one and only visit I made to her place, while I was here.

I had visited Steven at the factory, but I was not here for visiting, I was here to do a job, to get the houses sold. It was very iffy at one stage. We had an offer; I didn't think it was a reasonable price for Oakleigh. We haggled for quite a bit, and even though I did manage to increase the price I still thought it wasn't reasonable, so in the end I told the agent no.

They come back with another offer, closer to what I expected, and that gave us another five hundred dollars more. Long story short, the house was settled the day before I had to leave to go back to Vienna. So I only had enough time to sign the final papers and with that, I went back to our accountant. He was astounded, so was the solicitor, over how quickly I'd organised the sale and what good prices I'd achieved for both properties. I actually stayed only four weeks and in that time, I was able to complete it all and get a good price. I was quite happy with my achievements and got on the plane feeling good.

Well, I was not happy about going back to Vienna: I would have loved to have stayed here, but of course, I had to go back, I had my girls there. I knew there were problems, there had been friction between Frank and the girls for years. I knew there would be a struggle when I got back because of the phone calls. There were a couple of messages that warned me about what to expect.

When I got back to Vienna, I arrived to an absolute disaster scene with the family. At home in the house was world war three.

The girls did not talk to Frank and Frank was hysterical. "They did not do what I tell them!" The girls were telling me he did not do anything and expected them to do everything. This was the usual routine, no surprises, but he expected the girls to run around after him too. Of course they wouldn't! They were working and did not sign up to pamper him: they actually worked longer hours, as they also worked Saturday as well. He was at home and would not do anything.

It was not friction, more like a full-scale war! They were not talking to each other at all by the time I got back. So, that took quite some time to settle down and reorganise. I tried to explain that going back to Australia was something I really had to do, there was no one else who could have done it. I was sorry that I left them on their own, but I thought they would be able to manage. I could not do anything about Frank's behaviour, that was beyond my control.

As was obvious, I had done everything for Frank, our whole life together, like a mindless little woman should. But the girls would not have a bar of that, and rightly so. He had that ability to turn everything around, to convince you that you were wrong.

I realised, after a lot of soul-searching, the efforts and reason for me to keep up the appearance of a 'normal family' was, that I felt responsible for every one and I was too ashamed to admit that I had chosen another user and had another failed marriage. I needed us to look like a family to the outside world. I had created a rod for my own back and alienated my daughters.

I'd always done most of the things for the girls as well, because if I could not get Frank to do it, I could not expect the girls to do it. That was always his motto: "You do not get the girls to help you. You want me to do it, they should be helping you." Then, the girls would turn around claiming, "Papa never does anything, why should we have to do it?" So to get out of an argument, I would simply do what needed to be done, to keep the peace.

I had been so well indoctrinated with the fact that I just had to do what everybody around me wanted me to do. Even today, I will do things for strangers because they expect it or I think they expect it. They probably do not expect anything, but I think it's expected of me to do this or that, for whomever.

I am just a doormat by nature, that is what I am, and I admit it. I realize that now. It took me years and years to realize that the circumstances of my life have made me this way, but it's such a part of me, I just keep on doing it. It is not an easy thing to admit, and sometimes I want to rebel or mainly just rage at myself.

Anyway, I just did whatever needed to be done and in a couple of weeks, I got things back into some sort of even keel and the family functioned once again, in a fashion.

Then a fresh friction came up, around Pearly's boyfriend. Because our house was always open to the girls' friends, this meant their boyfriends came around as well. Pearly had this very serious boyfriend; I wasn't happy that it was so serious. I liked the boy, he was decent, kind and hardworking, but his family was questionable. His mother was spending a lot of time in the gest house (sort of a pub). She wasn't a very pleasant family connection. Anyway, you cannot argue about boyfriends with teenagers. The girls spent a lot of time entertaining their girlfriend Ilse at our place. Ilse did not get on with her mother (as previously mentioned), so she spent an awful lot of time at our place and was virtually part of the family. The three girls did a lot of things together, and then Harry came on the scene.

Then one night my darling daughter said to me that Harry had to leave home. The grandmother had died, leaving a flat nearby. Harry's mother had told him to move into the flat (he was training to be a motor mechanic) and she'd give him an allowance to supplement his pay as trainees earned a pittance.

My darling daughter hit on the idea that I should be the one to supply his meals every day and Harry should come and eat his meals with us. He could give me a little money and I'd do his cooking and washing and look after him. My daughters did pay a little board as a small token to contribute to meals (from their traineeship,) but it was only a token, so they'd learn what life is about.

I said defiantly 'No' to looking after Harry. I told her that if his mother doesn't feel it is her duty, why should I take on that responsibility? I may not have the energy to provide a full meal every day, we managed maybe on left overs between us. It was not likely that he could pay to cover the costs. We didn't need the extra money and I already had a full-time job.

I was working quite a lot of overtime, (as the company expanded) as well as cooking and cleaning. Looking after our family was more than enough. By this point, Frank was in the habit of criticising me more and more and nothing I cooked was good enough. He had to have soup every day, claiming that without soup there was no meal. He'd have a spoonful of it and then say, "This doesn't taste good." He would just pick at whatever I cooked, claiming he wasn't hungry. Then 10 minutes later he would go to the fridge and stuff himself with cold cuts, because that was his specialty, he loved the hams, sausages and cold cuts of all sorts, because he could drink with that. The heavier meals went better with drink.

So you can imagine I wasn't keen on adding another person to the table when all this was going on. I felt sorry for Harry, but he had to fend for himself. Pearly was naturally upset and became very difficult to manage. The next thing she came up with was: If I won't take on looking after Harry, then she will move in with Harry. They will manage for themselves in the flat. That sounded fine to her. Then she added that I needed to give her the same amount of money that Harry's mother gave him, so that they could buy all the things they needed. Of course I said, "No way! You're just 17, you are not going anywhere, you are still studying. I am willing to pay your way and keep you until you finish your studies. But you're staying home until you finish your apprenticeship and until you earn sufficient to maintain your life, that's all there is to it. And Harry is not coming here."

Then came a terrible day, which I am very, very sorry to remember, but I had reached the end of my tether.

I came home from working overtime, (as the end of the month was always busy) absolutely exhausted. When I got home I could not be bothered with cooking. There were some leftovers and I said everyone could eat whatever they liked, I couldn't cook tonight. The girls came home from work about the same time.

I think that must have been on a Friday as the shop closed late.

Pearly got in, opened the fridge and started screaming that there was nothing to eat in this house. "Why do I pay board when there is nothing decent to eat, no meal, not a proper provision for my needs, when I am tired coming home from work?"

Well I am afraid I lost it. I really, really lost it. As they were growing up, very seldom would I smack their bottoms. Anyway, on this day I lost control (all my frustration seemed to surface). I grabbed Pearly and shoved her into the corner and started to slap her. First she got two slaps across the face because I just let it fly. I shook and shook her and the thought come, "I am going to kill this girl in a minute, I just cannot take anymore." It was like it wasn't me: another person had taken over and was letting the rage explode. There must have been a lot of other reasons why I was so terribly at the end of my tether. Frank and Georgie pulled us apart and we went into separate rooms to settle down.

For quite a while there were very, very bad vibes and the relationship between the girls and myself was sorely tested.

I can't quite remember the exact time I got a letter from Panni, where she told me that the girl's father, Frank the first, had died (on my birthday). When I told them the sad news, it didn't seem to make a deep impression, they did not show a lot of emotion, they just accepted it. They very seldom mentioned their father after we left Melbourne.

Some time later, I received a large official letter from Australia; actually it was addressed to Pearly. It turned out that she had written to Australia asking about her father's estate. I think someone talked her into it, in case there was some money outstanding. Well, the 'whole estate' was in that envelope. A few pictures and some insignificant things. I was very upset that she had done this behind my back. I would of course have made all the effort to find out whatever she wanted to know about her father, there was no reason to be sneaky. Anyway, I did find out afterwards, that he had died penniless, leaving behind debts and that the Canberra Hungarian club paid for his funeral (which I would have done if I'd known about it.)

Shortly after, they got their apprenticeship papers and finished their training. As soon as they finished their training, Pearly moved in with Harry, a couple of streets away. I saw her on the street, she hardly acknowledged me. She came home once a week maybe. This was quite an unpleasant time. She was really very, very difficult to manage. Then a little bit later, Georgie decided to move out too. Officially it was said that she moved in with some friends and shared a flat with someone, but as it turned out, she moved in with an older man, a much older man. He was divorced or something, but anyway, he was much older and a similar sort as Frank, so I don't think she did a very good job with it, (unfortunately they did not learn from my mistakes) but by that time, both of them were madly in love. I knew the reason they left was the resentment towards Frank, but I did not know how to remedy that without leaving. I was trapped by my own mind. The girls didn't tell me that of course, as I wasn't their confidante.

I am sorry to say that this was a real heartbreak for me. I always dreamed of having a very close and happy family. Before my father died was the happiest time of my life, when we were all together. After my father died, life was not happy for me. I dreamt of having a lovely, loving family of my own that I could look after, but that did not quite work out. When I realized that, I just had to accept what is!

When I woke up in hospital and was told that I had two daughters, I thought how wonderful, we can do things together; we can be good friends, as well as mother and daughters. It won't be like what I had with my mother, we will be close and loving. I don't know, maybe it is my nature, but for some reason or other, my daughters and I have never managed it. Every so often, there is a little period of time where it looked like they were closer to me and we were having a nice, really nice relationship, but then it cools and then disappears. I don't know if anybody really has this ideal close, loving relationship with his or her daughters! Maybe that's just in books and in stories. But, when I see mothers and daughters in a loving, caring relationship, the lack of mine is much more pronounced. Unfortunately, I did not have that dream come true and I regret it very much, very much indeed.

With Panni we kept in touch by telephone or by letters: they visited about two or three times while we lived in Vienna. They always stayed in the 'Helen family hotel', where friends from all over the world would come and stay. Even while we were living in that horrible small flat, in very, very tight uncomfortable conditions. I had people visiting from Hungary, from Australia and as I said some students, at least for 18-months I had them for dinner 2-3 times a month. I used to cook big pots of soup and then at one stage I think I was cooking pancakes for hours on end. I think that was 85 or 90 pancakes that I baked at one meal, because the kids all liked it so much, so I kept on mixing more and more. Those were nice times and good times, and in company, Frank was always the perfect husband, the perfect host. However, with the visits from various people and relatives from Hungary, well sometimes it was pleasant, sometimes unpleasant. We were so involved with the Hungarian club, we were friends with many Hungarian couples. We had a busy social life, which was both good and sometimes difficult.

15

Frank was very much Hungarian-oriented and as the Hungarian club was nearby, he got more and more involved. That of course meant I got dragged into club activities and work as well. Which was OK, it provided a social life for us. After the girls moved out from home, more and more time was spent in the club and with various Hungarian people.

Then the news came that Panni's daughter was getting married and wanted the girls to be bridesmaids. By that time, they were both living independently and working full time. They wanted to go to the wedding in Australia. I was happy for them and tried to help out to make sure that they had a good time and enjoyed spending some time in Australia.

Georgie had teamed up with Ilse, and by this point, she too wanted to go to Australia, to see the country. So, we helped to organise Ilse's visa.

Because the girls were going to be bridesmaids, I made beautiful silk bridesmaid dresses for all three of them. Lovely materials, beautiful pale colours. I made sure that they were happy with them and so they set off to Australia, with Ilse in tow.

Pearlie didn't want to leave Harry. We tried to talk him into going as well, but he was just too much of a chicken and he wasn't really a guy that wanted to improve on his lot. He worked as an Auto Mechanic and was happy about that. He wasn't happy that Pearly wanted to go to Australia, and tried to talk her out of it. Luckily, he didn't succeed. He promised her that he would go after her later in the year. That, of course, never happened and it made Pearly very unhappy.

I secretly hoped that they would not come back to Vienna, which would give Frank and I a reason to move back to Australia as well. And so the girls left.

Unfortunately they only arrived about two days before the wedding, as they could not finish work earlier. On top of that, the airline lost their luggage, so they didn't have their bridesmaid's clothes to wear. They had to borrow clothes to go to the wedding

Panni generously offered for them to stay at her place, all three of them. She was working full time, she had her mother over from Hungary also, so she had her hands very full. I'm very, very grateful that she did give the girls a home for some weeks. I think they stayed with her for about five-six weeks.

Then they decided to get a flat to see if they could extend their stay a bit longer. Of course Frank's sisters kids were in Melbourne, so they virtually had their social life set up. As hairdressers, coming from

Vienna, getting a job was not a problem: they both got one in Melbourne and they got themselves a townhouse to rent. I did as much as possible from Vienna to try to help them and arrange things for them. So they stayed on, and I was quite happy about that. We kept in touch by phone calls and letters but mainly phone calls.

Back in Vienna, I started working on Frank, encouraging him to go back to Australia. But he was holding on, as it was only a year or two until retirement, when he could apply for a pension from Austria. He could also apply for a pension from Hungary, but that was too complex, even though he did pay into a big fat pension fund originally while working in Hungary, but that of course got confiscated by the Government. It was very minimal, so it was not worth bothering about.

So we stayed on in Austria. Then the opportunity came to get a garden, which in Vienna is on the outskirts of the city. It is government-owned land, which has been parcelled off, like community gardens. You could get a fair size block, you could have a little house put on it. Sort of a holiday house, that you could stay in there for a couple of days. Grow vegetables or flowers or whatever you wanted, but that meant that you could enjoy the weekends and holidays in the green of the garden, rather than in the concrete jungle in the city.

We had a very nice flat already, that's for sure; it was a beautiful flat, in a lovely old house. It was very well situated, very bright and sunny, which is not very usual in Vienna. But I did miss the greenery, so when this offer came up (from one of the Hungarian couple, who had a garden) we said yes.

They encouraged us to apply for the land and we secured a ninety-nine year lease on the garden, but it didn't have any house on it. Then I found an advertisement in the paper, for a wooden cottage for removal, from a similar garden setting, on the other side of the city. It was a log cabin type of thing, which they had to move from the block. So we organized to buy this little cabin, have it dismounted from its foundation and put on a truck.

As it happened a couple of days before the weekend that it had to be moved, the two boys, young Frank and Stephen (Frank's sister's boys from Australia) arrived in Vienna from London: they were on a European tour, spending three or four months travelling all over.

They arrived from England on the train, totally worn out. I picked them up from the station early in the morning they'd travelled overnight and apparently they had to stand most of the way, or just sat on their backpacks, because there wasn't any seating! I don't know how they did it! They were hungry and they didn't have any money left. So I got them home and made them bacon and eggs, which was a kilo of bacon and 24 eggs and a big loaf of bread. The two boys ate the lot and we had a lot of laughs about it afterwards. They offered to help (well I don't know, Frank got them to offer to help us) and so I was driving the truck, because I was the only one that had a licence and could legally drive. By that time we had to sell the Renault, because it was too old and needed too much work, so I bought a small Volkswagen beetle and got an Austrian driving licence.

We got the house loaded onto the truck and I drove it from one end of Vienna to the other. We hired someone to put the cottage together. It was a very cute little house, with one room, built in beds, a wardrobe and a kitchen. It was quite well fitted out with everything. We got a gas stove and a little fridge. The, block luckily had running water and electricity which was a big plus, so we had a lovely summerhouse and a big garden with some lovely big fruit trees.

This became our weekender and summer holiday place, which was all very nice and beautiful. I planted flowers and some veggies. It was really quite enjoyable, I was very happy about it. However, Frank spent most of the summer weekends and the wintertime as well, at the weekender. He would sleep there, even though it wasn't very warm in the cold weather. The heating wasn't particularly good and in the winter time, they turned off the electricity.

He decided to dig a big hole and make a wine cellar in the back of the garden. He dug out most, then hired help: they used concrete-blocks to stabilise it. Then he covered it back with soil on the top, which was supposed to keep the stored vegetables fresh. But it was mainly to keep his grog as he'd started to drink much more.

During the week while he worked, he didn't drink that much. Thank God, so he could get up and go to work, but from Friday onwards, (he usually finished early on Friday) until Sunday afternoon, he was totally washed out.

Anyway, it was his idea that now we had a garden he would invite people to the garden for the weekend. For about three years every summer, as soon as the weather broke, it was time to go to the garden. I would go out after I finish work, about three o'clock on Friday I would pack up two big baskets with food and fresh linen and whatever needed to be taken. Got on the tram and train and slogged it out to the garden. (We'd sold the Beetle by this point as it was costing too much to run, according to Frank.)

Frank, as per usual was quite sloshed by the time I got there. He'd taken nothing down with him as he went straight from work. Carrying everything was difficult, so he bought a bicycle for 'me' so I could go to the stores, (about 2km away) and bring back more beer, soft drinks and things that I could not carry from home. Then I would have to cook for four, six, eight, sometimes twelve people over the weekend. Lunches and dinners on Saturday and Sundays. On Sunday, in the afternoon, I'd clean everything up to go home so I could go to work on Monday. Of course I also managed to get in some gardening - that was the point of having the garden block - but by Monday morning, I was totally exhausted and glad to go back to work.

That went on for about three years until I got terribly fed up and said, "That's it".

Because he enjoyed company, in the wintertime, he would invite people to come for dinner, without asking me. Then on the day he'd get quite drunk, he would start to clean the house by moving furniture and getting out the vacuum: "Because the whole place is absolutely filthy and I can't stand it." He could not let people see the squalor we lived in. By that time he got the furniture moved around and the house totally disrupted, I was trying to cook a meal for 6-8 people. I had to dash around, try to tidy up the place and put the furniture back to get the house presentable, while he slept off some of the drink.

When we sat down to dinner, I would hear him apologising to everyone, "You have to excuse Helen because she doesn't really know how to cook, this might not be as good as you usually have and the place is a bit of a mess."

That was the whole story year in and year out. And about three years on I really, really was over it and said, "This is it. I am not going out to the garden anymore, if you want to entertain, you have to organize it yourself. You cook, you do whatever you want, if you invite people, I am not doing it. There's nobody invited, I'm not cooking all weekend and besides, it's costing me a fortune in drinks and food, mainly the drinks."

The two-three dozen beers and five, six litres of wine and what have you, went on every weekend. I was virtually working to pay for entertaining the neighbourhood and I was just totally fed up.

A few years after the girls come back to Australia I did manage to get Frank back to Australia for a holiday, because the girls had stayed on. We stayed with everybody in the family for a couple of nights each, just to see how everybody was going and enjoy a bit of Australia. My idea was that with his sisters' help, we'd try to get Frank to come back for good.

While we were here, I also needed to check out the mortgage funds, as they were not earning as much anymore and I was thinking we should get a flat or an apartment or house. The house would be more inconvenient, because renting a house would mean difficulties around the gardening and so forth.

So I was thinking about buying an apartment. First of all it would be a growing asset. It still would bring in income and wouldn't have the same maintenance costs as a house. We looked at a beautiful old flat in Glen Eira Road. It was absolutely gorgeous, an art-deco type. But it needed an awful lot of work and I no longer had the inclination to take on something like that, as it would be too difficult to organise if we were not here. We visited the old neighbourhood of Elsternwick and there were some flats being sold at auction. We were looking at places one Saturday with our accountant (Mr Agardy), Frank was nervous about bidding but I thought this was a good position and I had a price in my mind for it, so I got in there and bid. I won the bid so I bought one of the flats.

Frank was having kittens!

It was a security for when we came back, so we arranged all the paperwork and quickly signed what needed to be signed and arranged for the agents to manage the property for us. Mr Agardy was very complementary that I got the apartment for a good price, in a very good location and in a nice block. As usual everyone thought I did well, except Frank.

We headed back to Vienna because Frank was going to retire the following year or in the near future anyway, and he agreed to come back once he'd retired. So, things settle back into their routine in Vienna. The Hungarian club once again became the centre of his world. We had holidays when our annual leave came up.

One year we decided to go on our own to Germany, but as it happened, we got to the first stop in Bavaria to the hotel we'd booked for a night. Then Frank decided we should stay for a couple of days, so we extended it for three days. Then Frank wouldn't get out of bed, so we were in town and I walked around a little bit on my own. But he just wouldn't get out of bed during the day. In the evening we'd go down to the restaurant for a meal, where he get himself sloshed, then bought another bottle, and we went back to our room. He finished the wine and was then dead to the world for the following day. So after four days in Bavaria, we just packed up and went home.

After that experience we did some bus trips to Hungary with the Hungarian Club to various places, so that was good for weekends or three day trips to Hungary. Which is ok, because it only takes about four-five hours to the furthest point of Hungary, in a car or bus. We also got to see new places that I hadn't been before, plus we saw family.

While we lived in Vienna, we went to Hungary every few months to visit our families. The girls especially loved the visits to Farad, to my sister-in-law Rozsi's place. The house was quite primitive but the love and welcome we received from her and the children made up for everything.

We would also take our annual leave, usually twice, in two week lots, and see a lot of Europe. At these times, I would book a bus tour for ten days in the spring or autumn. The bus tours appealed to Frank's vanity, as he could show off how good he was to everyone else on the bus and at the club after, that he was taking me on a tour of so many lovely places Italy, France, Denmark and most of the European countries.

The good part about these bus trips was everything was organised for us, which was great, and as there were always other people around, Frank was too vain to misbehave. He wouldn't show his true nature until it was just the two of us. He would be the first at the bus in the mornings (no staying in bed) then he'd be the life of the party at dinner, even his drinking was moderate.

By the time he did retire and he didn't have to go to work each day, he was virtually drunk twenty four seven. He wouldn't do anything. He wouldn't go out, only to the garden some time. He wouldn't do anything around the house. He still expected everything to be done for him, so I virtually wiped his nose.

And because he had nothing to do all day, he was bored stiff and he used to sleep most of the day, then wanted to talk and be entertained at night, keeping me awake or waking me 4-5 times a night.

We were having arguments constantly; it was really a very, very nasty time between us by then. He was officially suffering from depression, and he got it into his head that he was very sick. He needed to have check-ups. As I mentioned before, his cousin was living in Vienna and her daughter and son-in-law lived close by. We got very friendly with them, Renate and Louis, were a very nice couple. Renate was very show-offish, like most Austrians, but Louis was an absolute angel. He was really such a good-hearted man, and would do anything for you, even without asking. By that time Frank cousin Tercsi has passed on. Louis worked as a Salesman for a medical company and so he knew all the doctors at the hospitals, all over the country. Louis promised to find someone to check Frank out; he knew an internist professor, who was Hungarian so Frank would understand him properly.

So, he arranged a check up for Frank at that major hospital, the best hospital in Vienna. He organised with this doctor that it will be paid for by the government's health insurance, so Frank got checked out, top to toe. He had X-rays and scans, everything under the sun. At, the final appointment with the professor. The doctor was very annoyed. He just growled at Frank and said he was the biggest hypochondriac and even though he was in his late sixties, he had the body of a thirty five year old. "Nothing under the sun is wrong with you. You are the biggest hypocrite show-off that I've seen and I don't want to see you, ever again I have sick people to worry about." He told Louis that he was most disappointed how such a healthy strong man could let himself go so badly, and he should go to a psychiatrist instead.

Of course that was out of the question because Frank said he wasn't mad, he didn't need a psychiatrist. This is Vienna, surely there were some other good doctors around and I should find someone else!

At this stage I was working full time and doing everything in the house. I was getting fed up, and we were arguing an awful lot. It was a terrible time. He started carrying on about how I had to look after him, because he was a sick old man. In company he was the life of the party. His famous argument was that I was the one who never could be happy, it was all my fault. Because nobody was good enough for me. He said, "You were never happy with your first husband, he was no good according to you. You have trouble with your Mother and brother, so nobody can please you."

Well after all, the true reason I stayed with him so long was because I felt responsible. I felt ashamed. I felt absolutely ashamed that my second marriage had gone on the rocks as well. It must have been my fault. It couldn't be anybody else's fault. It must have been my fault that things had gone that way. Something must be wrong with me and that made me responsible for him, because he couldn't manage on his own anyway. I took that on, as my responsibility, and I made that promise when I married him.

And for that reason and all the reasons he installed in my head, I couldn't possibly leave and get a divorce again: that would be unthinkable, so now I just couldn't leave. What would everyone think of me?

One day he got extremely drunk and very argumentative. He started carrying on and he screamed and yelled. I went to bed, but he woke me up again, in the middle of the night, carrying on. I was awfully concerned about what the neighbours might think about hearing us screaming, yelling and arguing ... then he dashed into the kitchen and picked up a big kitchen knife and I thought he was going to kill me: he was coming at me.

He was six foot, I was five foot nothing and he is a strong man when drunk. I tried to grab the knife out of his hand. I got myself cut and then managed to run into the kitchen and close the door. He slammed on the glass window of the kitchen door and smashed it.

I managed to grab the knife out of his hand, but by that time he managed to cut my wrist and I was bleeding very badly: it was near the main blood vessel. I wasn't sure if he managed to cut an artery. The next minute he just went and lay down on the bed and went fast asleep. I tied up my hand and got myself off to the emergency department and had it stitched and bandaged up. I had a couple of cuts on my hand and and also on my shoulder and I just said I'd slipped and cut myself with the knife, which of course they could see wasn't true, but they were not going to pressure me to go to the police about it.

The argument started off because he'd got it into his head that I was insisting he see a psychiatrist, which obviously meant I wanted to lock him up in a mental institution.

And here I am, not wanting to get the police involved because they would have locked him up.

Maybe if I had he would have sobered and been normal.

But he couldn't be normal, because his whole family were full-fledged alcoholics, every one of them. Sorry, the exception was his older sister Mici, she was the only hardworking decent woman in that whole family: she left home when very young and always helped the family. His eldest brother died as an alcoholic so had the other two. So the whole family were virtually all alcoholics.

So I could have got him locked up but I was too ashamed, I couldn't do it. So, I told the story in the hospital to get myself sorted out.

When he sobered up the following day (I think the following day was a Saturday or weekend) and I was at home, I sat him down while he was still sober, and I said if you ever do that again I will put you away. And I guarantee that if I put you away, you will never get out of an asylum. That frightened him a little bit and for a few months at least he was less argumentative and he drank a bit less.

The usual quantity of alcohol that he went through in our house, per week was six litres of wine and two-three bottles of brandy. If he consumed only two bottles of brandy, that was quite good, but sometimes he went through for or more so it so it was costing an awful lot of money. He also created a lot of very, very unpleasant situations.

If we had company, he was the life of the party, he was the most charming friendly and loving man; nobody would have believed me with regard to the way he'd behave or the way he treated me at home, when there was just the two of us. Honestly. I wouldn't have said anything to anybody, because I was far too ashamed to admit to what was really happening!

By 1987, Pearly called us and said she was getting married to an Australian boy. I arranged for my mother to come with us, mostly to be at her granddaughter's wedding, but also to see Australia and just because I thought this would be a nice gesture for Mum, who loved travelling and loved her granddaughters.

I booked all the tickets, but all of a sudden, Frank decided that he would not go to the wedding. He rang Pearly and told her that he was not going to give her away. That of course caused a very big upset for Pearly and for all of us. I tried to calm her, reassure her that everything would be all right. I cancelled his ticket. Then two days before departure, he decided that he would come after all.

I had it all planned, because Georgie was living in Perth at the time, so the plan was to visit her for a week, then fly together with Georgie to Melbourne for the wedding and stay for the remainder of the six weeks all together.

It was incredibly difficult, but I managed to get Frank a ticket. The only thing I could not get was a seat together from Singapore to Perth. He made a big fuss that he wouldn't sit separately. Luckily, the flight attendants found a way to get us all sitting together, so no problem.

Mum was funny on the plane at first, she was hanging onto the arm of the seat for dear life. By the time we were flying over Salzburg, I said to her, "It's OK, you can let go, we're in the air now." She thought we hadn't taken off yet and was waiting for some turbulence!

I didn't let Frank drink on the plane. One drink with a meal and that was all. I wasn't going to have him get drunk and create a scene. We got to Hamburg for our connecting flight to Perth, flying via Singapore. We had a long wait in Singapore. I asked Frank to stay with the luggage while I found the bathrooms for Mum, and when we came out, he'd left the luggage unattended and I couldn't find him. At the end, I needed to get the staff to help look for him. He'd just wandered off and got lost. (I started to wonder if he was getting Alzheimer's or alcoholic dementia). He said he had no memory of me asking him to stay with the luggage and he did hear me saying where we went, he was looking for us.

We arrived in Perth and we spent the week with Georgie, which was lovely. She showed us all around and we met some of her friends. We had a really good time and Mum enjoyed it. Frank had pulled himself together a little bit, so we did not have any dramas and then we all flew to Melbourne for the wedding. We stayed with Pearly, because by that time, she had bought a house in Richmond – I'd helped her with the deposit so she could buy it a couple of years before.

It was a two bedroom house, so we stayed in one room and I think Terry, her husband to be, slept in the kitchen-lounge area. Mum and Pearly slept in the other room. It was quite an old, little house, very much in need of repairs and renovation. Terry was driving taxis for work. He didn't really behave very well to Pearly. I wasn't very happy about it, but it was Pearly's choice.

Also, because Frank had been so difficult and said he wasn't coming, Pearly had asked someone else to give her away. Now Frank wanted to do that duty so they had to reorganise this and it was really very embarrassing. The wedding went very well, she looked lovely and everyone had a good time. I was very proud of her and both my daughters were lovely.

Mum enjoyed herself very much and she loved the attention. We travelled all over the place. I took her to the Victoria market: she nearly fainted from the quantity of meats at the butcher's and the hustle and bustle of the place. We visited everybody that we knew, so it was quite a lovely time we all spent together.

I had to go back to Vienna for work and I did say to my mother she could stay longer. Panni wanted to have her stay with her and the girls said., "Just stay grandma, that will be fine, we'll make sure you get back with someone we know." But no she wouldn't stay, she came back with us.

My mind was virtually made up that I wasn't going to stay in Vienna much longer.

16

As I mentioned we had done quite a few trips with the Hungarian Club. In 1979, I remember we had a trip to Szeged, where I met up with my cousin Jancso. We didn't visit my aunty after the last fiasco, but I definitely kept in touch with my cousin, whose marriage unfortunately had disintegrated.

His wife left him for someone else. He was devastated for a couple of years. Anyway, in '79 when I told him we would be in Szeged, he said I definitely have to come and talk to you. It is only about 50-60 km from his home. So, when we arrived, late in the afternoon, we had dinner and by the time we finished dinner, he was there. He said, "I have got someone here with me to introduce you to," and he introduced us to Marika a very, very shy, pretty young woman and really very young. He pulled me aside and he said, "Well what do you think? I want to marry her."

And I said, "What's stopping you?"

He said, "Oh, she's so very young."

Well, he was forty-seven and Mary was the same age as my daughters, which was twenty-one. So it was quite an age difference but as I said, "It's really up to your heart if you feel that you would be happy with her, and she suits you and of course if she agrees, then why not!"

She was a lovely looking girl and terribly, terribly shy: she was hardly able to get out a couple of words. When I asked her a question she stuttered with the answers: I didn't try to be too probing. He said, "Well I do want to marry her and she's pregnant." That of course sealed the deal.

I knew his heart's dearest wish was always to have children and his first wife refused to have any. He was pretty unhappy about that. So, when this happened I said, "Well, in that case, you'll have to marry her if she's pregnant, so there's no question about it". They did get married and in February 1980 their first little girl was born and she was absolutely lovely. My aunty (his mother) was living with them at the time, as she was pretty old and helpless by then. Marika looked after her and the baby. She was very hard-working and she still is. Anyway, they got married and ten months later the second little girl happened. And I said, "Well, how did that happen so quickly?" Obviously he wanted to have as many children, as quickly as possible. He'd told his wife that she couldn't fall pregnant while she was breastfeeding, which was very sneaky, as he knew as a doctor that was a myth.

Luckily everything went well, and two very healthy little girls were born and he was deliriously happy. My aunty passed on, before the second baby was born. They had a really happy life, until unfortunately in 2017 he had a stroke and within weeks, passed away at eighty four. Which was devastating for the whole family, me especially, as he was my only relation that I felt truly connected with. The girls are beautiful and we keep in touch, but unfortunately, I don't see them very much nowadays, we just talk on Skype at times.

Nora, the younger one, visited us, (twice now), first for a few days and then the last time just virtually for a day. She's an air hostess, so every now and again she gets a job to come to Australia, so then I can see her. My cousin Jancso always wanted to come to Australia, he would have loved it here, but unfortunately it never came to pass.

Where I left off …(before I regress on another tangent) it was Pearly's wedding that brought Frank and I to Australia, along with my mother.

She got on very well with my future son-in-law. She loved to cook and enjoyed the fact that you could get any ingredients you wanted: he was always ready for eating. Three weeks after the wedding our time was up, so we left to go back to Vienna, back to work, the usual story. My mother had the best time here in Australia.

It was April 1987 when Pearly got married. A few weeks later, after we'd got back to Vienna, I had an inflammation. My ovaries absolutely flared up and it was a question of not if, but when to have a hysterectomy and I was put into hospital.

The previous time I'd been in hospital, a few years earlier for a minor thing, Frank was having hysterics and driving everybody insane about what's going to happen to him if I passed away: what if I didn't survive the operation and blah, blah, blah. The hospital had to get some friends to come and take him home. It wasn't the point that I might pass away, it was all about what's going to happen to him!

This time, it was a more serious operation, a full hysterectomy. After two weeks in hospital, they were sending me for four weeks' stay in rehabilitation. I wasn't allowed to lift anything or do very much. I needed some rehab, as the doctors realized that I was not just physically exhausted, but mentally as well.

Frank was asking about what would happen to him while I was in hospital. I told him to go to Hungary and stay with his sisters. He did spend about six weeks in Hungary, and then rushed back as soon as I came home from rehab.

Two of his sisters were trying to talk Frank into staying in Hungary and to bring "his money" with him, (that was the main thing.) They were thinking that if Frank and I were able to have a flat in Australia and a flat in Vienna, we must be really rich, that was their idea. Everybody thought we were absolutely loaded and his two sisters had the idea of "how to fleece" us. Anyway there were secret phone calls followed when I wasn't there.

A big telephone bill came in, once I was home from Rehab and I said, "Well, what's going on?"

He went on to give me the explanation, which was: "Oh well, this is not going to work out; I want to go back to Hungary." (I did say that I want to be back in Australia but he didn't.) "It's not working out and I might be sick again and who will look after me? I need someone to look after me."

His biggest fear all his life was the idea of dying alone with strangers, not to have his family or his relations or someone who 'loved him' beside him. That terrified him.

By this time, after the operation, I was pretty low in my emotional state, with the constant arguments and drunkenness, plus waking me up all the time. He slept all day and didn't do anything around the house. I couldn't ask him even to get milk he carried on so much; he simply wasn't capable of anything. He'd totally lost it and the situation was very bad. I thought I just couldn't bear this anymore. There was no point in me staying in Vienna, I didn't like it and the girls were in Australia.

So I said to him one day, "I am going back to Australia. I am going to give my notice at work after Christmas because I can't do this. You make up your mind, you come with me or you do whatever you like with your life. We can split our money because everything was always in joint names, so it would not be complicated."

There were hysterics, jealous arguments, because in Frank's mind, I must have someone else and I wanted to get rid of him. So these kinds of stories went on all the time. He still wanted us to move to Budapest, to be near his sisters. If I wouldn't, then he told me I must also arrange a flat and get him settled in Hungary and organise someone to look after him!

I said if we are together I would look after him, if he came to Australia with me, but there was no way I was going to live in Hungary or run-around settling him in another place, once we are apart. If he wanted to go to Hungary, it was his business how he arranged it. I would not lift a finger.

I told his sisters that if they wanted him in Hungary they could look after him and do whatever needs to be done. I'm not taking any part of it. And I would thank them very much if they could take themselves out of my life. On one visit, when these discussions were going on, his sister sad to me "why do you want to go to Australia, you have everything here, what have you got there?" Well, I did lose my cool a bit and told her off properly, and said that I have my girls in Australia and they are my reason for life. That is my home, because where they are, is where I want and must be.

Just a side note; every time we went to Hungary and that was quite often, I always had some gifts for everyone. Things that weren't available there. Like toiletries, nice soaps, deodorant, raiser-blades etc, and of course chocolates for the kids. One year his sister Minka wrote a list of things in quantities (12 of deodorant 12 of other staff etc.) she wanted me to take. When we arrived with just the usual gifts, she got very agro and said, "I had all these things in order from my collegues and they already paid for it, what am I to tell them now?"

I said, "You just have to repay them, I'm not a supplier."

She was going to have a nice little business; by me paying for it and she collecting; not silly is it?

I handed in my resignation right after the Christmas holidays, Frank didn't believe me that I'd resigned, he just could not imagine it, that I would do what I said. (He still did not know me.)

So, I worked through my two-month's notice. In this time I trained someone to do my job. What had started as a little sales office, with sixteen or seventeen employees, had grown into a company of three thousand employees. It now had a big manufacturing section, where the motors and gearboxes were made. These were put into Holden cars, all over the world: mainly the small Astras and Berlinas and my job was to price the motors.

It was quite a complex job: every screw, every washer, everything had to be priced. When a new model came or was planned, I would get a description of what's going into the product: then I had to research the costs for the outside parts and all the materials that were needed, including the labour. Then I had to calculate the cost and the profits - it was a very interesting part of my job.

The bookkeeping department was by that time 35-40 people, so it was a big department. My section was the pricing, and it needed someone who could keep up, because they only had one other girl working with me in pricing. Anyway, I did get someone, one of the girls from the bookkeeping department that helped me out a few times: she wanted to do it, so she came in and I trained her.

After two months, I said to Frank 'I am not going back to work anymore, I am finished'.

I set about to sell the flat and sell the garden, to make money off everything that we possibly could to recoup the costs that we'd spent. We emptied out the things from the garden; fridge, extra lot of linen and cutlery, little tables and folding chairs and so forth to get rid of. A lot of it went to Hungary because one of the daughters, Marika, had just got a little flat, so we gave her a lot of furniture.

I organized a shipping container to pack everything in. Frank still hadn't decided if he'd come with me or not. One day he'd be coming, the next he would be staying and so on. He could see that nothing was going to deter me and I would not organise his separate life. So he made the decision that he couldn't manage on his own, so he would be coming with me.

Regardless, I just kept on with the packing. It was done and we were booked to come in April to come back to Australia. All our belongings, everything, including brooms and shovels, dusters etc were packed into a container and that left us with a couple of suitcases to fly home with. I think the last night someone lent us a mattress to sleep on, in the flat. I was able to sell the flat for a reasonably good price: the landlady wasn't happy that we were leaving, but she understood.

A young couple had bought the flat and wanted the fridge and washing machine, because no other models would fit the tiny spaces. They were happy to take it over partially furnished, and so we left Vienna.

We flew back to Melbourne. I had terrible trouble

with Frank on the flight back. He was hysterical, argumentative, he wanted drinks and I refused to let him drink. He already had memory problems and I did not want a scene on the plane. We had a stopover in Singapore, had to wait five hours: there were more hysterics. He didn't even want to let me go to the toilet; he wanted to come with me to the ladies toilet! He was more trouble than a two year old.

Anyway, we arrived back and stayed with Pearly in Richmond, I was pretty devastated that in over a year, nothing had happened in the house, no improvement at all. Her husband, hadn't even put in so much as a nail to make it more liveable, he was absolutely useless. They gave up their room for us, and went into the second bedroom, but the second bedroom was full of junk. I don't know how they manged there: it was not very confortable.

We started looking for somewhere to live, the flat was rented out on a long-term lease and anyway I did not want to live in a flat again, I wanted to have a house. And so we had about 7-8 weeks to find a house, because the shipping container was arriving in mid-June. Frank wanted to have a house near Oakleigh, near his sister, I refused, but there weren't any there anyway that I wanted. I was looking at Elsternwick and Ormond, the areas I knew well as I was quite at home there.

Unfortunately the prices were so high at the time, we couldn't possibly afford it. In 1988 in Ormond, the houses were already above what we could afford. Even Oakleigh was pricy. Panni wanted us to look for something around Brunswick: but even in Brunswick the houses were very expensive. Most of them were too big and I really didn't want to have a big house and I was most comfortable in this side of town. So, his other sister lived in Box Hill and urged us to look around here.

We needed to have a car to get around in Melbourne. My only regret is that I had bought a Holden Astra in Vienna about a year before Pearly's wedding. I got it at wholesale price, because I worked there, so it was a very good buy. It was one of the latest models and it was a beautiful little red car. I let myself be talked out of bringing it to Australia with the argument that it would cost more to transport it and change over from right hand drive to the left hand drive, we could get one here for the same price and would be costing more than it's worth, so I sold it in Vienna.

So we had to buy another car. Of course the cars were much dearer in Australia than what I paid for my little car. Through a friend of a friend, I bought a little Toyota Corolla, that was a few years old, but in good condition. Well, it wasn't a cheap car, compared to what I paid in Austria for mine, but at least we were able to get around.

By that time, Frank definitely didn't drive: he still had his Australian licence, (he had never been able to get an Austrian one) but he was far too demented and just about always drunk. I also still had my Australian as well as an Austrian driver's licence.

I have to tell you a bit about my brother. (I regress again as memories pop in to my head.) We left him here in Melbourne when we went to Europe, in a good job and a comfortable flat. But shortly after he went to work in the northern territory, in the mines, as an electrician. He made good money and saved a fair bit. Mum wanted to marry him off, so she went with this girl (the niece of Annus and Pista) on a holiday to Stockholm, and arranged for my brother to visit too. He wasn't that young anymore, he was over thirty and she was getting on in years and not married either. Anyway, he traveld to Sweden on a holiday and they did get married there. He came back to Australia and she followed six months later: they settled in Sydney for a while. They bought a house, but she wasn't happy, moved to Melbourne then they finished up going back to Europe.

He made a nuisance of himself with my friends here in Australia: with Panni and with some other friends, so it was a bit of an embarrassment, but what could I do? I knew he was always selfish and self-absorbed, so I didn't expect anything else. They eventually settled in Germany and had two children very quickly, one after the other, two boys. He became what we call in Hungary a total "slipper husband," which means that he did everything his wife wanted: she could use him like a slipper.

She couldn't manage the baby, so he had to go home during lunchtime to feed and clean, and change the baby: he was doing everything around the house. One time they visited us when we were in Vienna. I was working full time, when they stopped over with us. She just sat in the kitchen and expected to be looked after. The baby would not stop crying. Well excuse me, it was her baby but she expected me to pacify it. Anyway, I wasn't terribly happy about it and didn't run around after them that much. They were most upset and told my mother that I am really not caring enough to welcome the family.

I earned his scorn because I wasn't staying home to look after them when they visited. I couldn't, because that was the end of the month and I had to do the reports it was the most important part of my job. I couldn't possibly take days off, at the end of the month. Besides, I wasn't informed until the last minute of their visit, until they where on the way.

But that was typical of my brother, only turning up when he wanted something. As I wasn't able to provide anything or give them anything by that time, I was written off.

In Hungary, my mother some years before, had moved into a little half-house, just around the corner from where we used to live. It was more confortable; it was a room and a kitchen, with an indoor toilet, but no bathroom. When we got back to Europe I tried to help Mum as much as I could and to make her life easier. I organized for her to have a shower put into the back of the kitchen and put in a hot water system. I bought linoleum from Vienna and put it down in the kitchen so she wouldn't have to walk on the stone floor. I organized blinds, curtains and carpets, whatever she needed in the house: I did a lot of renovations. When we went there visiting, I would do things or organize for things to be done for her, to make life a bit easier. She was still working, (which she enjoyed) as a tea lady, in an office, not very far from home. Oh, they loved her in the office and she loved going and that was keeping her occupied and happy to be with people. She worked for 2-3 hours per day: she loved it and she wouldn't have stopped.

I tried to make her life as comfortable as possible. The only thing I couldn't arrange was a telephone for her, because in Hungary, home telephones were as rare as "hens teeth" they didn't have enough lines to go around. It would have been helpful to have had contact. Next door had a telephone and they would have being willing to share a line with her, but there was some arrangement already made by the telephone company about a shared line. It didn't matter what kind of money, goods or bribes I tried to provide, there was nothing available. We could not get her a telephone.

But she was comfortable and had a very lovely little garden. She was quite happy actually in her little house and had wonderful neighbours: she got on very well with them all and everybody loved her.

She was always very very popular with the people she worked with, as well as her neighbours, which was a great thing.

So now I can follow on about my story of returning to Australia, to try to find a house. Time was running out and I was quite concerned that we wouldn't be able to find anywhere. I did not want to rent something, as then you would have to have a contract. You can't rent for just a couple of weeks and even so, getting a container full of furniture couldn't just be put into a rented property.

I was getting quite stressed about how we could settle down. I didn't want to spend more than what we got for the flat, the garden and my car in Austria. I did not want to touch the savings we had.

Anyway, as it happened, one day we were visiting Frank's younger sister here in Box Hill. Talking about the challenges of looking for houses and so forth and the other Frank, (his brother-in-law) said, "Just around the corner, there is a sign up for a house for sale and it's empty."

I said, "That would be good!" I did not particularly want to live close to any of Frank's relatives, but the fact of the matter was Box Hill was a reasonably comfortable suburb and had good transport and good roads. We didn't want to settle in Brunswick, we couldn't have Elsternwick or Ormond, definitely not Oakleigh (as his older sister Terry lived there, which would have been a disaster) but I could manage the younger one, she wasn't so obnoxious.

I rang the agent there and then and the next day he came down and showed us the house. It had the same layout as theirs, a brick veneer house on a corner, three bedrooms, a garage and had plenty of storage downstairs. They wanted $200,000 for it. After some negotiation, I got it down to $182,000, for cash, settlement in 30 days. The owner needed the money, because he'd bought a business. We could move in straight away, because the house was empty. The owner was willing to give us the key to the place. So, once again, I bought the house (in an evening) and the money we had covered all our expenses. Everyone was impressed and complemented me on a 'good buy'. Frank complained that we could have done better. We had spent an awful lot of money on the flat in Vienna, but that was a different story, it was worth it to have the comfort.

So we had three weeks to get the house ready before the furniture arrived: the settlement would be in June. It was end of May so we got the keys for the house. It had ceramic tiles through the whole house except the bedrooms, which had horrible old carpet. It also needed painting.

We teamed up with Frank the brother-in-law to help me, as my Frank virtually didn't do anything. He just walked around with a bottle in his hand and gave orders. I worked with the other Frank he got a labourer to help us get rid of the tiles, build in the fireplace and I bought new carpets. The place needed painting, but my husband argued against it and as we didn't have a lot of time, so we just washed everything down. The girls, and even Panni come to help, to clean and fix up as much as we could.

On the 17th June 1988, (on the girls' birthday) the final settlement occurred and the following day the container was delivered to the house. It was dumped in front of the garage for us to unpack. We had three days to do this before they took the container back!

There was a lot of work to do.

I wanted a second sort of a sitting room, where Frank could be put away, where he could spend his days and make a mess, without having the rest of the house looking like a tip all the time. After weeks of hard work, renovating and making everything work the way I wanted it to, we settled in to live finally in Australia!

Georgie came home for 'their' 30th birthday. She came back to Melbourne from Perth, to surprise her sister, so they could be together for their thirtieth birthday as twins. She didn't get a very friendly welcome from her sister, which was unfortunate, because at that stage Pearly was involved with Jehovah's Witnesses and apparently they don't celebrate birthdays. (I don't know why but that's how it is). Anyway Georgie spent a little bit of time with us, even though we hadn't really settled in yet. I think about six or eight weeks later she decided to come back from Perth to live in Melbourne, and because we had the extra bedroom she stayed with us, but not for very long, perhaps six months or so. She certainly didn't appreciate the atmosphere, which I can fully understand.

17

I hadn't worked for 6-7 months, so it was time for me to look for a new job. I got one at a small accounting firm, just near the Box Hill Station. Frank was obviously just his usual self, sitting home, doing absolutely nothing, and drinking himself into oblivion. I worked in this accountancy for a while, but it wasn't really what I wanted to do. I was looking to buy a canteen, or a sandwich bar, that was operating in business hours only and situated in an area where there were factories or an office building. But unfortunately by this time, prices had risen for businesses of this kind, since we were last here 17 years ago.

The sandwich bar business really was blossoming: everybody wanted to do sandwich bars or canteens or whatever you call it. Anyway, it would have needed about a hundred thousand dollars to invest in one, and Frank definitely refused. He wouldn't allow it. Well, I mean I suppose I could have done it without his approval, but because the money was in both our names I didn't want to do the wrong thing and use his share.

I also knew that I wouldn't be able to rely on him for any help or any assistance whatsoever, it would have needed a co-worker, so it wasn't possible. The company where I worked was taken over by another firm and my wages weren't really that spectacular. I was disgusted when I realised what the accountants were charging for all the work we were doing, and we were paid just a fraction of it.

Somebody mentioned that it would be possible to apply for a job with one of the big insurance companies, to be trained and work there on insurance sales. In a way, that would be like running your business, working for commission. As it turned out, I am not a salesperson. I am a service person. I do personal service and I am very good at that. I can do retail sales behind a fixed counter, where the client says I want this or that, but that's different to sales where you go out and cold call on businesses and private people.

I applied and was accepted at National Mutual, in their office in Doncaster, which was just around the corner from the house, so it was handy. I could pop home during the day to check out if everything was okay. So I did some training and I was doing reasonably okay: I did the training for 'financial advisor' as well.

It was about the second year that things were getting really bad at home. Georgie moved out because it was the best thing for her to do. She was constantly in disagreement with Frank. He was not just demanding and rude but also unpredictable in his behaviour.

I was left with him alone in the house. He was

spending his days reading every paper that was published, watching television and smoking and drinking. It didn't matter that I refused to buy drinks: his sister and brother-in-law would bring it to him. He had money obviously: we drew a certain amount of money each week for housekeeping and for general needs. All the money that was invested, plus the interest, went into the bank. The rent from the flat went into the bank into joint names. I always managed all our finances, but if they said, well, I needed to give them a hundred dollars or whatever, because they'd bought things for Frank, I gave it to them. I did ask them not to get alcohol for Frank, but they ignored me. I couldn't go into detail about how they shouldn't be buying him alcohol, as I didn't want to publicise the situation we were living in.

At times we went across to his sister's place, but by the end of the evening, the three of them were virtually paralytic. Then when the other sister came along, they were all just hopeless. Frank was sleeping most of the day, like he had nothing to do. He would not help in the house or do some gardening even. At night time he'd wake me with questions and ideas, his dementia was really getting worse. He couldn't remember anything. He would ask me things fifty times; I had broken sleep for possibly 6-7 years thanks to Frank.

Working in insurance was quite demanding. I had to travel a lot, go out to places after hours, visiting clients. So I didn't spend an awful lot of time in the office. I was out on the road, trying to drum up business and wasn't very well paid. I wasn't getting very far, because the company's method of selling to a client wasn't always ethical as far as I was concerned. The idea was just sell them anything, life insurance, income protection, anything, even if they really couldn't afford it and get paid the commission. I couldn't do it very well, it wasn't within my capabilities and my ethics.

I was getting desperately worried. One of my bosses said to me, "Helen you are servicing your clients to death, and if you don't watch out, you are going to starve to death." So, I started to concentrate more on house and content insurance, which was fairly straightforward. I bought a register, (that already existed) and just had to keep it going and service it to receive a regular income from that. Anyway, I was managing, but wasn't doing extremely well at the same time. I was so worn out and desperate, I didn't know what to do. I had days where I just parked the car somewhere off-road, near a park or somewhere and slept a couple of hours in the park. Because I just couldn't drag myself any longer.

It was getting to the point when I virtually thought I really have to end my life. I coulnd't carry on like this, but of course, the fact remained that I couldn't do that to my girls. They had a pretty tough childhood as it was and to commit suicide and leave them here with Frank and his family would take even more away from them. And emotionally, it wouldn't be possible. I didn't want to distress them, or create trouble for them, but taking my life looked the most attractive solution to me at times, even though I could not bring myself to do it, for the above reasons.

I joined a group that was called SWAP (Salespeople With a Purpose). We had morning meetings to hype us up for the daily grind of doing door-to-door selling. I think that's the hardest possible life you can think of doing: cold calling and selling. I made good friends in that group. Quite a few of them are still in my life and been very helpful true the years.

But, anyway, I persevered with the work for nearly five years. So as I said, it didn't give me very much income. But I thought I had to give it a proper go.

In the meantime, Pearly's marriage had broken down, but her husband still expected to be getting money from us all the time, which wasn't going to happen. She had a very good hairdressing business in the City, which was virtually ruined by her husband (who had negotiated the rental of the premises). He didn't sign a contract, just got a verbal agreement and it was "sealed" with a handshake with the landlord, an old man. The landlord sold off the property and they lost a lot of money and a promising business, because of that. Pearl then found another place, sharing another hairdressing salon with someone else and she also worked in the post office at nights. She was doing it really tough. But her husband had so many debts and she wasn't going to pay them anymore, so he wanted a divorce and money.

The first few years had been good in that the girls and I felt that we were closer with each other. We were having nice times together. Pearly visited every Saturday; we did our shopping together and spent the afternoon with each other. Georgie, if she didn't had to work was at home too, so we had a really, really good relationship at that time.

I would try to hide as much as possible the misery that was my life, so as not to distress them too much. But I finally got to the point where I really couldn't do it any longer. I mentioned a few things to Panni, my friend and she virtually couldn't believe her ears.

She said that she'd been envious of me that I had such a nice marriage. "You always talked to one another nicely, you never had arguments in front of anybody."

I said, "No we didn't." I kept the facade up and he had enough sense from that side that he would't do any hysterics or behave badly in front of others. He was always a perfect gentleman and great companion, a caring husband, when there was an audience. So it was a Jekyll and Hyde lifestyle.

By this time his drinking was absolutely disastrous. He was having fits of jealousy. When I went to work, he decided I was out after men and anybody I talked to was suddenly my boyfriend. He also said I was cheating him with the money as well. It didn't matter how often I produced bank statements and showed him what was happening and how much we spent and how much money we had left and so forth, he had forgotten within half an hour and then it started all over again.

He'd always been a very fussy eater and now he became incredibly demanding. Whatever I cooked was never good enough. He demanded soup, had one spoonful and said it wasn't good enough or he wasn't hungry. Ten minutes; half an hour later, he raided the fridge for ham and cold cuts and sausages. I was spending half of the housekeeping money on cold cuts because that's all he would eat.

He complained constantly of aches and pains, and that he was sick, he needed the doctor's attention. I took him to doctors, had him checked out, and they recommended psychiatric treatment. He would not go there. Eventually his sister took him in for some counselling. Then I took him for follow-up the appointments for three months: he had a half a dozen sessions with a psychiatrist. By that time they figured out that there was nothing really wrong with him physically, except he was putting it on most of the time. I knew that he did have dementia and sometimes if he would go outside the door and you turned him around, he couldn't find his way back. But he was also very cunning: I took him to four or five different doctors, for counselling or assessment, but after a few visits he would refuse to go because, "The doctor doesn't understand me." Or, "He's an idiot, he doesn't know what he is talking about" etc.

Sometimes his symptoms were made up and the episodes of dementia were not always real. I reckon half the time he was putting it on, just to annoy me. The paranoia was getting out of hand. Then he started to go to his sister (who lived a few streets away) virtually every day to eat, because by this point he'd decided I must have been poisoning him. I was throwing out food by the tons, because I cooked, shopped, had a fridge full of food and he wouldn't eat it. He would go to his sister to get a sandwich and he'd tell her I have nothing at home to eat – but the fridge was full. He told them I mixed up his medication, that's why he was unwell.

The last psychiatrist I took him to was a Hungarian man, so he understood Hungarian. Frank often pretended that he didn't know English well enough and that was the reason the other doctors couldn't help him. After a few visits, there were problems with this one as well. Then the doctor, asked me to come along for a meeting alone, which I did. He said, "Look, Helen, there's nothing really wrong with Frank, he's hysterical, he's alcoholic, he knows that, but I can't really do much for him unless he goes into a hospital and has himself totally checked out. They need to assess his emotional state and work out what and how we can treat him. We can't give him medication because as you say he is drinking, so we can't mix medication and the drink. But, I do think you are the one who needs some help."

I had to hide all the medications in the house from him and only give him what the doctor ordered. He was mixing them up and was threatening to drink and take all the tablets or what have you. When I told him that the doctor recommended "an inpatient assessment," he accused me of wanting to put him away in a mental institution for good, so I could have a good life.

A few days after that, I went to the bank and

wanted to draw out some money to pay bills or whatever was needed, the usual stuff. The ATM showed zero balance. So I went into the bank and they told me that the account was closed. I said, "What do you mean closed?"

"Well, Mr Nemeth has closed the account!"

I asked, "Was he here personally?"

They could not say. But it was a joint account and he had no right to close it without my signature!

Apparently Frank had given 'Power of Attorney' to his nephew and he in turn had taken over everything and closed the account. When I questioned him, he boldly told me that he had all the documents and, "If you make a list of how much and what you needed the money for," he would send it to me if he approved!!!!!!.

I said to him: "Hang on a minute, that account was a joint account and half of the rent that comes in is mine, half of the pension is mine because I am keeping him and the interest that comes in, half of that is mine, as well as my earnings are also in that account, so you have no right to close off the account".

I made an awful hassle at the bank, about closing a joint account with neither of our signatures involved. I was brushed off as 'not relevant' because he is the man!

Next I rang the solicitor and said, "Don't you dare give a penny out to anybody until I sort this out. The interest from the account must not be distributed. No more money to go into any account and that's the end of it."

I also had my work commissions going into that

account as well. I was really quite desperate at the time, with bills to pay and no money in the bank. They eventually sent some money back, but definitely not what I was entitled to.

Next thing I knew was that Frank decided to stay with his older sister in Oakleigh. He said he was going over to stay there for a few days, until we worked out something. All right that was good, I got a bit of reprieve, but I came home one afternoon unexpectedly and here was his sister and the brother-in-law (the ones that lived close by) packing things into the car. He wanted his things with him.

I was absolutely surprised but secretly relieved. Well fine, if he wants to move out good, that's a good idea, get him out. I asked them why they couldn't have done this when I was home, there was no need to do it behind my back. There was of course no real answer, it was, "He just asked us." The brother-in-law was quite sheepish about it all, he was just doing what he was told, so they took away two suitcases.

I thought well, good idea, I rang the locksmith and changed the locks on the house. It he wanted to move out, so be it. Later on, I found out that while I wasn't at home (on earlier occasions) his eldest niece of the family, had made an inventory of my house. They knew exactly how many books I had, how many tablecloths I had, how many crochet doilies I had, linen, pillows and just about everything. They knew much better than I did what was in the house. They also took away documents and things that were not wholly his, but I did not find this out until much later, when I needed them.

Our solicitor would not take the case, their excuse was because they previously represented us as a couple, and could not represent one party over another. I then found out that all the documents that I had, including titles, his will (we had a will both signing to the other,) every document worth anything, was also taken.

By that time I was really, really desperate and physically, emotionally and mentally a total wreck. I found a reasonably cheap solicitor to try to work out some kind of settlement. First, they wanted me to sign the house over to Frank so he could stay in the house and for me to take the unit, because the unit and the house at that time was approximately the same value.

I said no, "I am not moving out of the house. I made my home here. This is my home I made it as such and I am not moving out. I am working around here. I have no reason to move into a flat. I never wanted to live in a flat anyway, and what would he do with the house? He doesn't even bother to wash his cup; the house would be filthy within two days. He leaves the dirty dishes everywhere in the house, he never does anything, so how do you think he will manage in the house on his own. No way, I'm not moving from the house, the house is mine."

So anyway there was a settlement made that I kept the house and he took the flat. I didn't know they had already transferred some of the investment money out and whatever was left was shared equally, but I finished up with very, very little, after a lifetime of hard work.

I had all the expenses and I couldn't afford any more solicitors. My income wasn't that much and I wasn't in the emotional shape to be able to really work harder or earn more money. I didn't know what I was going to do and I didn't want to have the girls involved much. I didn't say too much I just told them that he'd moved into his sister's place.

Then I found out, after about three weeks, his sister had organized for him to live with a Hungarian woman, who first thought that he would be a good catch. He had some money and he had property and his pension from Austria. Of course he was 'a good catch' because I had organised his pension and the income from the flat. He was boarding with her originally, but she was thinking long term. Within six weeks she took his measurement and kicked him out and wouldn't have anything more to do with him or his sister after that.

As neither of his sisters wanted him around, his family decided to send him back to Hungary, but he could not get medical clearance to travel alone. For that purpose, they recruited his ex-wife. She had eventually turned up in Melbourne, many years earlier and became great bosom-buddies with his elder sister. Her boyfriend left her very well off, when he passed on. She was a merry widow and a couple of times, on big family occasions, they tried to throw them together. They even invited his ex-wife to Frank's 70th birthday (we had in a restaurant) at my expense.

I don't know what they were hoping would happen to them perhaps that they may get back together! But I heard (because there are always good friends that will tell you the gossip) that he made such a nuisance of himself and upset this woman so badly, that by the time they got to Singapore, she was threatening to put him back on the plane and send him back to Australia.

Anyway she did take him home to Hungary and handed him over to his sisters. Of course neither of them wanted him to live with them. They had their own lives, they didn't want a lame brother to run around and wipe his nose every five minutes, they didn't need that.

So they sent him off to his youngest brother's family, to Farad, (his birthplace) to his brother's widow, because she lived in the old family home. My poor sister-in-law Rozsi had already lost her husband and was thanking God for the relief. She now at least started to have some peace and quiet, because the sisters had done the same treatment to her, exactly as they did to me. The two sisters had got her husband to write a will, leaving the 'family home' to only the two grandsons.

They got the old house (that originally was their grandparents') under the justification that they had looked after their mother for years. After the mother's death they paid out the rest of the family for their shares. The house payments however were mostly paid by my sister-in-law, as my brother-in-law had managed to drink away most of his income. There were some very nasty things done in this family, to rob the people who had worked the hardest.

Eventually, she was left in peace to live there as the grandchildren decided to decline because that was the right thing to do.

However, now the sisters wanted her to look after Frank for the rest of his life! Well, of course, she couldn't possibly take him on: she was glad to get rid of one drunken bastard, she did not need to have another one foisted on her and besides he was not her problem. Also, after a few days he was starting to behave inappropriately to her.

He tried it on with quite a few 'friends' and I don't know and I don't care if he was ever unfaithful. But I certainly was very upset about him propositioning my sister-in-law Rozsi in that way. She is one of the best people I know: she has a golden heart and is the hardest working-woman I ever have known in my life.

Thank goodness her son, after a two weeks, had enough guts to stand up and say, "No uncle you can't stay here. You have to go" He showed him the door, thank God for that.

Frank finished up in a retirement home. That only lasted for two months because he was annoying all the other residents and they wouldn't put up with him. So they had to take him somewhere else and he recreated the same situation all over again.

Two or three months later, they refused him residency so his sister apparently arranged for one of the cleaning women from the home, who lived in a country house) to take him on as a boarder for the rest of his life. Obviously they had to pay her well to look after him but I have no idea about the arrangements they made. But his Austrian pension would have covered it very well, so that would have at least doubled what an average wage was in Hungary at the time for this woman. He also had the interest from the flat, plus the money they appropriated.

Eventually I found out, they sold the flat to one of the ex-business partners of my brother-in-law Stephen. They sold it to them officially for $80,000. In 1996, about a year after Frank left, that flat at that time was worth about $250,000. That was the official price reported, but obviously, the rest was paid cash under the table, tax-free. So then his nephew, niece and sister travelled back and forth to Hungary, which was easy to do on my money.

My house needed a lot of repairs and renovations, which Frank refused to have done when he lived here – he only wanted that which would increase his comfort. So I could have the heating system put in, because that was for his benefit. But other than that there was no work done. He would agree to nothing. He wouldn't allow me to spend. It is a funny word 'allowing' when I managed all the money. I earned most of the money, but he didn't 'allow it'. I always thought that marriage was a joint venture for 'life', sharing everything. To me, it wasn't right to do something behind his back. Mind you, that did not have the same meaning for him at all, and certainly didn't stop him cheating me! But what a mess: in 1988 we'd come back, and by 1993-94, he'd moved out and gone back to Hungary.

There were horror stories coming back from Hungary about his behaviour. The brother-in-law that lived nearby told me a few things afterwards, but I did not want to keep the family connections, with either of them, and I certainly didn't needed the gossip. As far as I was concerned, they knew where I was if they wanted to talk, but obviously his oldest nephew and oldest niece were 'written off' in my book. The nephew is an accountant; he worked with a firm that had solicitors and accountants in it. They are the ones who caused me so much financial pain. I had to mortgage the house to be able to fight them. It was a high price to pay, but now I have my peace and sanity.

I have my little house. Once he left, I spent a week virtually fumigating the house. I washed everything and I cleaned out or threw out everything to get rid of the smell of smoke and alcohol from the place. I found bottles everywhere: hidden behind the fridge, under the couch, unopened bottles of drinks everywhere, which lasted me nearly twenty years. I didn't need to buy any drinks. I still had Frank's bottles of alcohol for any visitors that came. My peace of mind was really worth it, every bit of it. Okay I did have to work much, much harder to try and maintain and provide something for myself. I managed to keep the house, which is my only asset, it's not fully mine anymore but I am still here.

I think that part of the story I better finish off before the memories get to me again because after all these years it still upsets me.

18

By the time Frank finally left, my physical and emotional state was in a very precarious situation. Physically I was totally worn out, emotionally drained and without any real fight left in me. I really just existed from day to day.

All my energy went towards maintaining my job, which wasn't a very satisfactory situation, with National Mutual. Their requirements were getting more complex and that meant more study needed. I was questioning how far I could go with that. I wasn't earning sufficient money to maintain the house and myself.

Things went from bad to worse. The settlement was a kind of arrangement, which forced my hands, because I was virtually happy to sign anything just to get some peace into my life.

I had great disappointment and heartache the way that Frank's nephew and niece were treating me. They were discussing how many tablecloths I would have, how many crochet doilies I could have and what proportion of it was Frank's. At one stage, I really lost my cool: I told his niece that if she wanted crochet tablecloth and doilies and embroidered stuff, she'd better make it herself, because what I have here is all my work!

Her reply was that Frank's money had paid for some of the materials. I told her that his money didn't pay for anything. Virtually what he had earned he'd puffed into the air by smoking or put down the loo from the grog he'd drunk! He had contributed very little to our life and finances over the years and had no right to any of my handiwork. Most of our savings were my efforts. My work provided the security we had, and now it was being taken away from me. I found it very, very difficult to deal with it all, I was really devastated.

Pearly's marriage had broken up shortly before my life collapsed. He needed money and wanted a divorce. He insisted on selling the house, despite virtually never putting a penny into it or helping with any maintenance. But by law, he was entitled to 50%, so after paying out the loan for the mortgage, there was very little left, as they'd only had the house for about 3-4 years.

One day I came home to find Frank sitting in the kitchen when I got back from work. I just popped in from work to see how things were going at home and he was sitting, drinking with Terry, (Pearly's ex-husband) who was loudly rubbishing Pearly, as to how lazy she was. He maintained she didn't clean or cook and all that.

Naturally I got very upset. How dare he come here into my house, sit at my table and rubbish my daughter? She'd been working two jobs, running a business that his lack of foresight ruined for her in the end.

I said, "I will not listen to anyone rubbishing my daughter, especially you when I know you are the laziest bastard in this world. You, who has used her all these years. Don't you ever come here again, I don't ever want to see you in my house!"

I also had a big fight with Frank as to what kind of a 'father' he was, letting his daughter be rubbished like that in our own home, when he knew that it wasn't true. I told Frank, "Don't you dare ever let this guy set foot into my house, ever again."

Well that was one story, which I didn't want to share with my daughter, because she still cared for her husband, regardless of how he treated her.

Of course after Frank left, she turned on me, saying it was all my fault. I was ruining the family as well, she hasn't got a marriage and now she hasn't got a family either and what am I doing to this poor, sick man?

That 'poor sick man,' who hadn't really loved her or looked after her at all. That 'poor sick man' who'd been rubbishing her (along with her husband) and that really hurt.

For Pearly, it didn't matter that they'd separated, he was still her life. He'd used her, he'd abused her, but he was still 'the top of her priority list', so it was very painful on top of everything else.

So I just carried on the best as I could and worked for another year or so with NM. My only solace was belonging to this group SWAP. There were a lot of good friends there (still are, even today) they gave me moral and emotional support. Though I didn't tell anybody how difficult things truly were.

I also joined Rotary and made some very good friends there as well. I always felt that giving back is a really worthwhile way of living and Rotary do provide a lot of support for good causes. These organisations also helped me by providing good friends for the rest of my life, as well as social activities.

I had to spend quite a bit, on the house maintenance and things that needed doing.

The neighbouring house was rented; after some years of nice people, the new tenant was often screaming and yelling at his wife. It got to the point where I had to call the police a couple of times, so he came to the front door and threatened me, so I had to call the police again

The police took him away to sober up for the night. The result was that he kicked down the dividing fence one drunken night and I had to urgently have new fences put up. This was more money I had to find. I was afraid to go into the backyard, and the garage was at the back of the house, so I organized to have a fence done urgently.

A little while later they skipped without paying any rent. They disappeared overnight which was a blessing for me. After that, very nice young people bought it, and lived next door, so I was lucky in that respect and life went on.

I worked day and night trying to do the best I could, while trying to support the girls as much as I could. I couldn't do it financially, but I tried emotionally, by providing a happy home when they came to see me.

Georgie, came back home to live, after working in Tasmania for a while. She also had some disappointment, which was very unfortunate, but we got over that too.

I got some bookkeeping work. In the meantime I resigned from National Mutual. Basically their requirements were really unacceptable as far as I concerned. Their sales method was just sell, sell, and sell. Insurance sales people were getting a very bad reputation. Financial advising got to the point where I was told just to reassess their portfolio every twelve months and get some movement in there, because we only got paid when there was a sale of of assets or they bought assets, and some of those sales were definitely not to the benefit of the client.

I just couldn't, I wouldn't do it. I can't sell something that I don't one hundred per cent believe in. I'm no good at cold calls, so it was very, very difficult.

I applied for the Government's New Start programme. This meant I went back to study, to do a course in small business management, so I could set up a bookkeeping service, which worked to a certain extent. I got a couple of clients, but of course that's not enough to make the world turn around. I had done some bookkeeping temporarily here and there, but it involved driving from place to place, which was tiring, always new rules to learn etc.

One of the young women I met through that course said I should start my own business, rather than rely on the agency. She had a stonemason client who was a great worker, but horrible at administration, and as she was moving away, she suggested I take him on. So I got working with New Age Stone and Richard was the most generous man, but so unreliable as far as paperwork was concerned.

He was always doing deals where the paperwork was questionable. So it was quite hard work to get it straightened out and get things on even keel: to give his workers the proper wages, do the correct tax payment and so forth, and to get the accountant to finalise his taxes. I got on very well with Richard and worked with him about 2-3 days a week to keep his business running. Keeping a lookout for more opportunities, I researched computer cleaning, and worked part time with a company for a short while, until I managed to get a couple of clients on my own. So I was bookkeeping and cleaning computers.

As things grew, I hired people to help me with cleaning the computers when big jobs came in. But it wasn't always steady. There would be quite a lot of downtime between jobs, and then all of a sudden, there would be too much work for us to do and I'd have to find more people.

I was doing it for about three years, it seemed to be getting to the point where growing the business became harder to manage as I had to hire more people. Then came new tax regulations with superannuation: Work-cover came in and this needed to be paid to casual workers as well. My business was so small, I would have to register for Work-cover and Superannuation. I couldn't employ somebody as a part-time contractor as that would have made it an absolute nightmare to administer, as well as being financially unviable.

Friends that were in business were telling me all their problems they had with their workers and so I thought. "Oh really? I can't possibly do that!" So I just had to gradually let it slide right down to nothing.

In those years, I'd also done night cleaning with a cleaning company. I've done all sorts of temporary jobs this way or that way, trying to get something going, that I could really keep on doing, to provide some security, as I wasn't getting younger.

Three and a half years after Frank left, he passed on, and then the problems started again. I believed that I should get back whatever was left from his assets, but apparently he had made a new will. His old will was taken by his niece and nephew, when he moved out.

The solicitors who made the Will (and were custodians of the Will) had merged a few times in these years and became a very large firm. One of the partners that wrote our Will was also a co-executor of both of our Wills. He told me that they could not find our Wills, which was in their safe keeping. That is professional negligence in my book.

So there was no chance that they would help me as I believed they worked with Frank's nephew's company as well. They did not take any responsibility for losing the Wills.

The new Will that was produced was hand written, which, in my opinion and in the handwriting expert's opinion, was written by his sister. He bequeathed whatever was left of his monies to his village church and to his nephew for looking after him.

I tried to find solicitors in Hungary as well as here. I had to work in two countries, one because he was in Hungary, and two, there were no probates lodged here, as he did not have any more Australian investments in his name.

When Frank left, he took some valuable books that belonged to my family: my cousin had given them to us, but it also included a very special bible, (the original was printed one thousand years ago), commemorating Hungary turning one thousand years old. A replica was printed in original format. This 'Bible', which I ordered and paid for, was quite valuable.

A couple of years after his death, I was alerted by friends about an article in a Hungarian newspaper, that "Mrs B" (who was his eldest sister,) had donated this very valuable Bible to the Hungarian Reform church.

I was really, really so annoyed, because first of all, it wasn't hers to donate, it should have been donated in her brother's name, and anyway, originally I paid for it and it was mine.

So I rang the church and complained and told them that I want that corrected. I rang the newspaper and told them too, I want that corrected, that it is not Mrs B. who donated it, but me! Not out of my free will, but if it was going somewhere, it should go to the Hungarian church. I am happy about that, but not under her name as her donation.

This kind of under-handedness was happening all the time. All valuable things that they took from my home, finished up at the sister's place and eventually in the rubbish because nobody really wanted them. But they didn't want me to have them either. So that was the story of the most unbelievable meanness and selfishness. It still puzzles me, even today! Why? Because, I have never ever said a wrong word or did anything, other than provide assistance, help and friendship to them all.

As far as Christmas presents or any occasion where gifts or a thank you was needed, over all the years, it was all my doing because Frank couldn't care two hoots about anybody. He didn't bother about anybody's birthday or Christmas, or anything. It was all about what he wanted, when he wanted it and what suited him. I did not hurt anybody intentionally, I did not say a bad word about anybody. I don't understand why they did it. That's life I suppose and even today, there has never been any real effort by anybody from his family, to try to make amends in any way, for what they did to me and mine.

I find it really, really hard to reconcile the fact that Ilse, (Georgie's girlfriend,) of all the people, (she had married Frank's nephew) who had been such a part of my family, who enjoyed so much benefit from knowing me over the years, would not acknowledge me. I understand she has loyalty to her husband, but she would go and visit Panni, talk to her and thank her for what she's done for her (she gave her board when she arrived here, for about six weeks) but she doesn't acknowledge me. That is not something that you reconcile very easily. I must have done something wrong in her eyes. I don't know and I probably will go to the end not knowing what I did to anybody that just used me up completely, without a thought.

I suppose that is the story of my life, trying to make a living, create a home and support my girls as much as I could: that's about all, that is and ever was my intention.

In the meantime, I got quite involved with learning about the world and studying natural therapies, which I always believed is best, rather than all the artificial stuff. I did courses in meditation, EFT, colour therapy, massage, reflexology, you name it, I did it. That has taken up a lot of my energy and funds, but I never begrudge that at all, there is no price too high for education. This has been something that really gave me a grounding that I could put my faith and energy into. I was, at one stage, thinking about setting up a massage service, unfortunately my hands are not strong enough, to really maintain this work.

I've done heavy physical work all my life, from our time in the milk bar and after, so my back and hands are not that strong. I set up the second bedroom as a treatment room, (which would have been quite handy,) but then again I started thinking about allowing total strangers to come into my home. A woman on her own? How would I know my customers intentions? I could be in strife in some situations.

I was thinking about when I learned colour therapy: that was really very, very exciting and I enjoyed it immensely. Colour therapy does not require physical strength but it was the same deal, having a treatment room in your home, when you're on your own not really advisable.

I did have some renovations on the house to make, take out the window in the second bedroom and put in a sliding door instead, and also put stairs to go into the front yard.

If that business had worked out practically, I could have client coming in from that side door, directly into the treatment room and that would be safer, but it didn't work out.

So my best and great friend 'soul mate' Marilyn used it. I met her and her husband, through the SWAP group. Marilyn her husband Frank (another one) and Graeme, we were the 'four musketeers' in SWAP we organised functions and also enjoyed spending time together. Marilyn and I became very, very close friends. She was very understanding about all these therapies: she had done a lot of reading and research on them. She and her husband had a bookshop that specialized in self-improvement and motivational books, so we had a great time. I accumulated all these books and studies we'd did quite a lot together and she was an absolute angel.

Unfortunately they diagnosed her with breast cancer and within two years she passed on. This was in 1998, it was a great heartbreak for me and truly a very big loss: it's a very, very sad memory to think of

Marilyn. She was an absolutely great woman, very hard working and very straightforward a sincere, true friend.

We were talking one day and I was saying that my mother is getting on and it would be a good idea I suppose to go and see her. I hadn't been back to Hungary since we left (nearly ten years) I thought well, it would be good to go back to see her, but I didn't have the money for it.

I really couldn't afford to go gallivanting off to Europe and take the time off work. At that stage, I was in limbo, between businesses, with half a dozen things on my mind. None of them terribly successful, so in '97, I was talking with Marilyn (she was in hospital), and she said, "Helen, don't carry on, just go get your ticket, you've got a credit card, extend the limit on it and go and visit your mother. You can pay it off when you come back, money doesn't matter." How right she was! (Mum passed on the following year.)

But Marilyn was not really well by this time, she'd been through hell and back with various operations and I was honestly too scared that if I left she might pass on while I was away.

Anyway, she talked me into it and I booked and in September 1997 I packed my bag and went back to Hungary to see my mother. I stayed with friends in Vienna for a couple of days, then with my cousin Jancso in Hungary. We had lost touch, these friends and I. It's hard to keep up friendships from distance; life leads us away, into different interests.

So anyway, I hired a car in Vienna, because I knew I would have to travel quite a bit and went to Hungary. I wanted to see my sister-in-law in Farad and her family, she is really the only part of the Nemeth family that I really love and respect. They were the only ones that went through exactly the same things as I did with Frank and his sisters, so we understand and respect one another. I definitely wanted to spend a few days with them then I went on to stay with my cousin in Kiskunfélegyháza so I'd be close to my mother. My mother by that time was in a retirement home there.

As an aside, after we came back to Australia, I kept contact with my mother as much as was possible. I was hoping that she might let herself be talked into coming and living with us here, instead of staying in Hungary, but she would not leave my brother or miss the opportunity that they visit her.

But by that time, my brother had two children and he wasn't happy with me at all. He didn't like the idea that I wasn't available for providing them with everything and looking after them. When they wanted to visit Hungary, we were a good rest stop, offering help and assistance whenever he may have wanted it.

He complained to my mother constantly about it and by that time, the boys were about 3-4 years old, so there were grandchildren close by, and travelling to Australia was a long journey.

As I said, she'd had a job as a tea lady in an office and she loved it. When I hadn't heard from her for a while, I tried to ring the neighbours, but she wasn't home. I got very concerned that my letters weren't answered and I wasn't able to contact her. As it happened, the neighbours were not available for quite some time, maybe a couple of months. I think the lady was unwell and was away in hospital, so there was no contact.

Finally when I managed to catch up with her, when she was back at home she said, "Your mother moved away." I said, "Where to?" She said, "We don't know. Your brother packed her up and took her away."

She spent most of her life 40-50 years virtually in that house, in that area and all her friends were very upset: they had no idea what had happened to her. She just disappeared. I rang my brother, I tried to get in contact with him, but couldn't find him either. So I got my cousin to try to find out what happened to my mother. Then eventually, I got a letter from my mother to say that she is living in a small town, not too far from Pest, with the sister-in-law's sister and her family.

When I rang my brother to ask why he'd done it, he said, "Well Mum nearly 80, it's not good enough for her to need to work, and she shouldn't be working."

He said she needed someone to look after her, and as I was 'so heartless' to come to Australia and not care about our mother, he arranged for her to move to his sister-in-laws.

At this time I wasn't getting much news from Mum, she never was a good letter writer but now, there were only short meaningless notes. I was worried!

My cousin went to see her and she wasn't well at all by that time, her legs were very bad. She was of course, always a bit heavy, her knees were giving her trouble, so she couldn't walk very far.

And that village is on a hilly area, the house didn't offer much comfort and she didn't know anyone, I could not do much for her from this distance.

Then, all of sudden all communications ceased again. I didn't hear from her again from her again and couldn't find her. Letters I sent had no reply and my brother didn't answer the phone. So again, I got my cousin to look into it, to find out where my mother had gone. Some days later, he found my mother in a strange hospital, about seventy kilometres away, from where they were living.

Virtually on the brink of death as it turned out: they mixed up her medication and caused a small heart attack, took her into the hospital, left her there, with nobody to visit. She wasn't given any clothes or anything she may have needed.

In Hungary you have to have your own things with you. You have to pay (under the table) to get the nurses and doctors to look after you, otherwise the care is not forthcoming and luckily, one doctor took pity on her and made sure that she stayed alive. She was close to death and by the time my cousin found her, she was getting better. They told my cousin she was brought in, covered with bruises. She had nothing with her and nobody came to visit her and the cause was definitely mixed medication.

The people who brought her in told the hospital that they didn't want to take her back and they were told that they had to find her a Hospice, she needed constant care and they were unable to do that. So my cousin made arrangements with the doctor to get her well, so she was strong enough to travel, in an ambulance and he took her 150 km's away to where he lived in Kiskunfélegyháza. He was the district medical officer there, so he put her in hospital there to fully recover.

When she got her physical health back, there was nothing wrong with her. They said she had Alzheimer's as she couldn't remember anything etc.

Anyway he told me all about it, so he found a nursing home close by and got a room for my mother there. Well naturally, I sent the money for her care. I sent money to get her settled into the home. I had to buy into the nursing home, and to pledge to pay her care fees, which was not a problem. I would have paid it anyway. But she was there with nothing, one night-gown and a very grubby, torn dressing gown and an old pair of slippers. They had not given her anything at all, none of her own clothes or things. I had to arrange to buy sheets pillowcases, underwear, clothes: everything that she needed to move into the home. They had not given her any of her own things.

I rang my brother and bitterly complained to him about the treatment our mother received. He said she was useless, she didn't do anything and anyway all her things had been used up.

That wasn't possible, because my mother had enough linen for two households when I'd left home. When I got back, she had clothes galore: she had jewellery and she had money. She got money from me regularly - as well as her pension plus the pay she received from working the few hours.

Turns out, when they moved her over, they sold her flat. They had taken away all her things and made her a bed in a kitchen. While she could, she cooked for four adults and kept the house and when she slowed down, she was making them noodles every single day, which they went and sold in a market.

She didn't get the money from that. She cooked, she washed, and she looked after them, because they all worked. Officially they were all going out to work and when my mother wasn't able to maintain her workload, she was discarded. There was nowhere and no one in that village that she could go to. She didn't know anybody. She didn't have any money. She didn't have any friends. So they totally isolated her. I don't know what they did with all her things, but they were all gone. Furniture, linen, her household equipment, her personal things all gone!

They didn't even give her back her Bible and my father's picture, which I had made for her. It was an enlargement from a passport photo. My father didn't have a lot of photos; he hated photographs. I'd had this photo framed and had given it to my mother, years and years before. They wouldn't give her my father's photo. They grudgingly gave her two little photo albums, which had mainly my children's photos in it and some of the wedding photos.

They just didn't give her anything of hers. I found out also, that my brother exhumed my father's ashes from where he was buried in Budapest.

When we first went back to Hungary, (another regression painfully pops up); I went to visit my father's grave. There was no grave there, but I found the 'plaque' from his cross, at the plot, that was just left there.

My mother had changed from the burial ground

into an urn, because she couldn't walk to his grave - it was too far away. Mum decided (or my brother decided I don't know,) to get father's ashes into the urn and put it into the memorial wall, with a new plaque in the front. But they did not tell me.

Anyway I bought the plaque back with me and it's still here in the garden. Not his ashes but his memories are with me. Anyway I was quite upset about that at the time, but there was nothing I could do about it.

Then, I also found out that my brother picked up the urn from Budapest and took it into the cemetery where his sister-in-law lives, into that village cemetery.

The trouble was that mother couldn't visit the plaque because it was on the hill and she couldn't walk that far.

So once my mother settled into this retirement home in Kiskunfélegyháza and everything was organized, she was quite happy. Family was close by: my cousin and his family, her sister and her children so she had her family around and she was back in her birthplace. Everybody loved her in that retirement home.

When I went back in 1997 and visited the home, she was very well loved and cared for, she had as much as I could possibly provide for her. She wanted my father's ashes back with her and she wanted to make sure that she had a grave where she will be put in, (when the time comes to be cremated.) so they would be together.

I went to organize the plot in the cemetery, (which is close to my cousin) and to the retirement home where she was. She could walk to the place to visit. I bought a plot, I organized for my father's ashes to be picked up from that village cemetery, then we had a ceremony and a mass was said. I put my father to rest there, in the town he was born. We had a gravestone made, just how my mother wanted as well.

And while I was in Hungary visiting her every day and taking her to places, I took her in the car to Budapest, to visit her old flat, her neighbours and friends. She was really very happy, she had a great time and so did I. I really enjoyed our two weeks together; it was possibly the happiest time that I'd ever spent with my mother.

My mother was determined that we phone my brother, as she hadn't heard from him in such a long time. He didn't come visiting there. I arranged for a late afternoon call to Germany to my brother, from the nursing home.

As he picked up the phone, after I said my name, the response was: "What you want?"

I said, "I don't want anything Mum wants to talk to you."

"What does she want?"

"Well hang on a minute." I handed over the phone to Mum.

"My darling boy why don't you call? Where are you? What you doing? When are you coming to visit me?"

I didn't hear what he was saying at the other end, all I know is the next minute Mum was saying something and the phone clicked.

He'd put the phone down on her!

She was heartbroken! But what could I say, what could I do? I couldn't do anything. I couldn't say anything to make it better for her. He didn't want to talk to me. That was the last time, and then I said goodbye and left Hungary.

My aunty wanted to have a good old whinge about her bad luck. I tried to be as diplomatic as I could be and I said; "Now look, I can't do anything about it. It's nothing to do with me."

Her son was drinking badly and her daughter had her family. She was in a small flat and she wasn't happy about it: she was used to having big spaces and everything, so she wasn't happy with anything unless she was calling the shots.

So we didn't part as adversaries, but we had a fairly cool goodbye.

Anyway I left Hungary, came back home and within about three weeks Marilyn passed away.

It was a relief for her because she was suffering an awful lot by then. But it was for me a great loss to know that she's was not around anymore. My only solace was that I got back and could still see her and say good bye.

I was really glad that I had gone to see my mother because the following year in June, all of a sudden, she got a bad cold, went to hospital and passed away within three days. So virtually I think she gave up.

Her funeral was paid for; everything was paid for in the end. My brother was supposed to contribute to her monthly retirement village costs, (which he seldom paid.) I made the last payment.

But his payment I think was three months overdue and the retirement village sent a letter of demand to my brother (after my mother's passing) and he refused to pay.

I told my cousin, "Tell them that I'll pay it, don't worry about it, I'll pay for it, I didn't want any bad feelings around the people that were so good to Mum."

But he said: "No, no they don't want it from you, they want it from *him*." So they sent him a solicitor's letter to pay it. I presumed he paid it because I never heard any more about it.

My mother didn't have very much left there, except a few things: the two albums, her prayer book and a song book (which I bought for her because she didn't have her old one) and my father's photos, that's the whole lot, which was my inheritance from my mother. My brother had all her assets and stuff beforehand.

A couple of months later, I really wanted my mother's wedding ring, because she had the two wedding rings joined after my father passed, and she wore it all the time. But when we got her to the retirement home, she didn't even have her wedding ring on. She had nothing. I knew that my brother had it all, so I wrote a letter to my brother to say I don't care what he'd taken from mother, could he please give me my mother's wedding ring. It was a very short, unemotional and plain letter.

Quite sometime later, I was thinking I might have to do something more drastic than that. I received a letter from my sister-in-law. My darling brother didn't even have the decency to write it himself. She wrote that my mother had given all her jewellery to him, and he was her son too and he wanted the wedding ring. I knew that wasn't right, like so many other things. He just didn't want to give it to me, so I never got it. And that was the last time I heard from my brother and that was in 1998. Obviously, he didn't need anything further from me.

I don't think I'll ever hear from them and I don't really want to. It was officially part of my life but it was severed about 40-50 years ago and it's never going to be resurrected, unless he needs me for something. But by now, he's nearing eighty years old, so I doubt it, I don't even know if he's still alive.

So that's my family!

19

In my life I have learned as much as I can. I've tried to work with various people, in different businesses. I don't know, it just didn't seem to pan out. After Frank N. died, and I realised I couldn't get any of my money back, I reported his death to the Austrian authorities.

I made sure I was eligible for the widow's pension and also so his family couldn't keep on receiving Frank's pension anymore, because months after his death they still hadn't informed the Austrian government about his death, which meant they'd kept getting his pension. By rights, you need to inform the authorities within six weeks if your circumstances change. They had taken enough from me already.

I was entitled to the widows' pension, which was not very much, but at least it's something to help me out. Then after I reached sixty-eight years, I applied for my own pension, which I am receiving still, thank

God for that. That's the one thing that keeps me going, day to day.

I ran the bookkeeping service for Richard until 2000 when the GST (Goods and Services Tax) came in … that's when I decided to take some time out for myself. And with the help of Graeme who has been a very, very good friend, and great support (we met at SWAP many, many years ago) and with many others, they kept me going and helped me out. Sometimes it was just with advice or by listening when things were going pear-shaped.

Graeme had a camper van, which he'd had for many years and wasn't using very much. I asked him if he would lend me the van as I longed to go on a road trip around Australia. Then I told Richard I had to stop work - he wasn't too upset, as he was closing up shop himself. He was quite a few years older than me and had worked very hard all his life.

So with that decision made, off I went to do something different and set off in the campervan. I fixed it up a little bit, cleaned it up and set out, going up the east coast as far as I could go. I'd stop wherever, in camping places and various spots. Georgie, by that time, had been living with me for some years, so she was looking after the house.

In the camper, I headed down to Geelong to visit a

friend who'd moved down there from Richmond. After catching up with her, it was time to hit the road in earnest, so I drove towards Canberra, then further north to the Blue Mountains and across the Blue Mountains. This was quite an experience, because when I got to the top of the mountain it was getting late in the day. There was a camping ground where I stayed for the night, before I descended down into Sydney. That night, the camping ground was freezing. It had been a beautiful day, but by next morning the taps were frozen, the ground all around was frosted and white and I wasn't really prepared for how cold it was! It was a shock.

Anyway, I got up, got myself together and started down the mountain and drove into Sydney. I had arranged with Graeme that he would meet me in Sydney, as he had business there. I would spend a couple of days in Sydney, and then we would drive around exploring nearby towns and countryside together. After two days, I would put Graeme on the train in Cootamundra and go on my merry way.

I drove all the way up to Queensland, stopping in various places, little towns, big towns, beaches and camping grounds. I'd get to a town, set myself up for the night in the camping ground and then have a look around the town. I drove all the way north to Townsville and was thinking about going further north. There were beautiful mountains everywhere, but the locals advised me against taking the little camper through the hills, as it might not make it. Little did they know how tough she was, and so was I.

Unfortunately, I couldn't always avoid the hills. Especially in one place when I took a wrong turn in a town and was caught in peak-hour traffic. There was nowhere to pull over, the van was stuck in first gear, and the hill was really, really steep, straight up, about 70 degrees.

My calves were burning as I pressed down on the pedal, but I couldn't get the van into second gear. I was afraid that any minute the van would start going backwards and topple down the hill. The traffic behind me was furious, their horns were going, but there wasn't anything I could do. Finally, I found a cut-in place to pull over and let the traffic pass. I was exhausted! As I drove on, I couldn't see any camping grounds, but there was a small town pub, so I asked them where the nearest camping ground was. They didn't know, but they said I could park out in their back yard!

It was perfect! I cleaned up and had dinner in the pub. I was the only woman in there, but everyone was very friendly, so no comparison to my first pub experience! Then I slept in the camper. In the morning I was up early and I drove on.

So there were a couple of other memorable experiences: one Sunday, I got to a sleepy little town, it was getting hot (after lunch) and I just couldn't see any camping places. The road was close to the sea, the highway was following the shoreline and I was just driving along the main road, hoping to find some sign of life or a camping place. I pulled into a side road and saw a bit desolate spot, with a sign 'camping'.

Thinking 'better than nothing' I drove in to find a camping spot: no one was at the office when I drove in. An old chap walked up to me and said, "You want to camp love?" and I said, "Yeah, I'd love to."

He said, "Okay, drive in, the boss won't come until the morning, you can fix him up then, before you leave. Just go around and come back on the second line, close to the office building there. I'm sure you will find a spot just opposite the laundry. Just don't stop down the back, that's the black's area, quite a few Aborigines living there." There I was; it was a camping place but eighty per cent were permanent residents. So I parked in a spot that was free, with one empty spot on either side, in between the permanent shacks. One was an old van with a tent over the side: it looked like it had been there forever.

I settled in, and a young girl came up and wanted to talk, so we had a chat: she was about 8-9 y.o. She showed me where the laundry was, so I did my laundry and got it dried which was good. I got myself organized for dinner and cooked. Then in the next door shack, about 3-4 people were sitting around having a smoke and beers. Having a leisurely Sunday afternoon. They invited me to come and join them. So after I had a meal I went over, I didn't have a beer of course, I didn't have any beer with me, I had some soft drinks.

So I took a soft drink and they told me all sorts of stories about the area and were getting pretty boisterous. I don't know what else they were having beside the drinks. Anyway, I said, "Look, guys, I am sorry but I have to go. I want to start off early in the morning." I wanted to get into Brisbane. Brisbane was still a fair way to go, I wasn't going to get there the next day, but anyway I said, "Goodnight," and got into the van and closed up.

Just as I'm about to drop off to sleep, about eleven o'clock, there was somebody rattling on the window. I didn't open the door, I just pulled the window open and there was the chap from next door. He was pretty high on the beer (whatever!); he wanted to give me a gift for remembrance, (a souvenir from a two dollar shop, a little embroidered wall hanging thing, that you could buy at the time for fifty cents). He gave it to me as a souvenir, because I was such a nice woman and was so courageous to be travelling on my own.

He kept on talking for a while, until I told him, "Sorry I am too tired, I need to rest." So I just closed the window and tried to go to sleep, but there wasn't much sleep until about two o'clock in the morning, when they finally all settled down Next morning by eight o'clock, I was ready. They weren't awake, so I just got up quickly and went and paid my dues at the office and left the camping place. Normally, it could have been quite scary, (they looked scary), but they were all absolutely the most friendly, caring and accommodating people in every way. That was an experience, certainly an unusual one, but a really good experience. You can't go by appearances.

Some of the camping places I stopped at, were all very educational. Usually you find the 'grey nomad' couples in caravans, around the camping places. But I found that being on my own, always some men would try to be helpful and come over to offer a hand. A few minutes later, the wife would come out and say something like, "Jim come here and help me with this." I got a couple of very funny looks from the ladies: they where all very protective of their men. If they only knew how safe they were! I had absolutely no intention of having anything to do with anybody's man: but I suppose it wasn't written on my face, 'Don't want a man'.

I just enjoyed the holiday, enjoyed the time being on my own; able to do whatever I wanted to do. If I wanted to drive, I drove. If I stopped, I stopped. I ate when I was hungry. I could please myself and it was very, very beneficial.

I really, really enjoyed this time. I managed to get my mind into a calmer place and became more settled into my situation. That was truly my time, helping me get over the last ten years of horrors and everything else that wasn't pleasant.

From Townsville, I drove across the desert to the Stuart Highway. Unfortunately, on the last leg, a Kangaroo hit me, on the passenger side. He messed up my door, luckily no damage was done to the motor, and the car was okay to drive, but it did look pretty messy. Unfortunately, at Tennant Creek there was no panel beater, only a roadhouse.

At the petrol station, people suggested I drive to Darwin to get it fixed, but that I should be OK to get there.

We patched the door as much as we could and tied it up so it wouldn't open.

Then I drove up to Katherine, as they'd given me

the address of a panel beater in this town. He serviced the van and replaced the door, but we didn't have time to have it painted. They couldn't have painted it the same colour anyway. The door was replaced, it worked and the colour wasn't too different!

I needed to get to Darwin, as I'd arranged to meet with Graeme again. He was flying up as he wanted to see the city. So I got myself into a rental apartment, like a motel, but they called them apartments there. So I met Graeme at the airport and we spent about 4-5 days in Darwin, looking around at everything, enjoying the different feel of the town. It was also nice to have company to explore, and then we drove to Alice Springs.

He certainly did not enjoy the long drive back on the Stuart Highway, because of the arrow-straight road for hundreds of miles ahead. You have to make sure that you have enough petrol to get to the next petrol station. I think it was about eight hundred kilometres of road. He spent most of the time sleeping in the back. Anyway, we got to Alice Springs and stopped at a camping ground near Uluru. We got on a small plane to fly over the Rock and the Olgas: it was very interesting. We went quadbike riding on the salt planes, super fun. Then to Coober Pedy, and onto Adelaide. In Adelaide, Graeme got the plane back to Melbourne. I came back along the coast, along the Great Ocean Road, from Adelaide to Melbourne.

I was away for fifteen weeks and drove fifteen thousand kilometres: it was a really remarkable time. I look back on it, and realise it was the best time of my life. It was remarkable to see so much of Australia - the eastern half. I plan to go back and go down from

Darwin to Perth but it hasn't happened yet. As it stands, I know now that it won't happen, but it's something to dream about.

I've been very, very grateful that I had the opportunity to do it, and beside the petrol cost and the food, it wasn't expensive. I camped in places that were pretty cheap most of the time, it was a couple of dollars for the night and so it wasn't an expensive trip. It was very, very exciting and emotionally, it was a relief to let everyday problems go.

Every now and again I would call back home to let them know where I was and what's happening. Nothing major happened back home, so there was nothing to worry about.

When I came home, I went back to work for Richard for a little while, more to help him close down the business. I was now on the Australian pension and earned a bit of extra, here and there, I was also getting my widow's pension.

For a couple of years, I was still working with a financial advisory group. I was doing mortgage and brokering. A friend of mine, Leslie, was telling me that her father had to move into an old peoples' home and then he'd passed away. She had to sell his house, which was in Springvale Road.

I thought if I could get credit to buy it and the girls could help with the interest payments, we could build three units. Each daughter would have her own home and by selling one of the units, it would settle most of the costs. I got the girls to sit down and look at the idea. The old house was solid and the land was a good size. Pearly was renting in Malvern and Georgie was living in Castlemaine. If we pull together and work with it, it could provide security for both of them.

Well, I thought we agreed on principal that we do it together. I arranged to mortgage my house and so finance the purchase, and started the proceedings for a building permit and plans. Unfortunately, it did not work out as I hoped and things became difficult.

That has I believe, also contributed to problems and resentments from the girls.

Finally, after two-and-a-bit years of planning, I got the permit! I just did not have any money or credit left to proceed with the building. So, the only option I had was to put the house on the market, with the 'building permit' (which was easier to sell) and hope I'd recoup some of the costs. Builders were looking for these kind of properties, so the sale happened fairly quickly. That put an end to my ambition to provide the girls with a home of their own. By the time I cleared up most of the debts, there wasn't any profit left on the house. Really it was just an exercise in trying to do something, to advance all our lives: just didn't work out.

Around 2006 I had a small heart attack, so I was in hospital for a couple of weeks. I had to take it easy afterwards and had to think what could I do to earn a living.

Then I was given an idea about getting some

vending machines that I would be able to service. It would only be for a few days a week and it would be like 'running the Milk Bar' in miniature. I bought five vending machines, with soft drinks, chips and chocolates that were placed in offices. I planned that the profits would help pay off the existing mortgage.

This unfortunately didn't work out, because the person who sold me the business had totally misrepresented it. I didn't really do enough research, so the figures that they gave me were untrue and the profit on it was negligible. It was only five machines, but it was very hard work, carrying the soft drinks and stocks etc. The machines were in the city and I had to find new places for them. As the contracts out, the companies changed, which was also very difficult, so I ended up putting some in the garage. I really didn't have sufficient energy for this kind of work; I wasn't well enough anymore, so I virtually finished up selling off the machines at a loss.

I also got some lolly machines, which were reasonably profitable, but I was also hoping that Pearly would help me with it, as she had put some money into it. When I sold them off eventually, she got her money back, with interest. The lolly machines were also eventually sold off for a loss, because I couldn't keep it up, it was just too much and such heavy work.

So by that time I was seventy-four, and I thought, "This is it!" I stopped chasing my tail, and left the struggles behind of trying to pay back all my debts. I'm managing on what the pension gives me and when I need extras, I can use my overdraft on the house and leave it at that. I'm just doing it the best way I know how.

At least I know that Georgie is settled in her little two bedroom house in Harcourt. (145km away) which she managed to buy. It needs a lot of work, and she is not well, but hopefully she will manage okay. Pearly also bought her two bedroom little unit, in Hastings (76km away). At least both of them are not paying rent to other people, but paying off their own homes and have that security.

There have been hard times and with sickness benefits, it's not easy to manage, but I know both of my girls will do the best they can.

This is the end of my story for now. I just know, that all my life I did the best I could and tried to manage the best I knew how, with whatever life has thrown at me. Unfortunately, my energy is not as great as it used to be, after open-heart surgery. Life is finally catching up with me and I have to slow down. I am just so thankful that I am now nearing the end and all the major troubles are behind me.

Before the final curtain call, I thought it would be a good idea to write a little bit about what my life was like, what I went through, so it will be a kind of memoir for my girls. They may be interested in how my life's journey has unfolded and how I came to be here, to be their mother and to be me, as I am.

Finally many and sincere thanks to all the people that helped and guided me on this long road. All, friends and foes that took this road with me, and taught me all my life lessons. I will always be grateful that the Universe had gifted me my wonderful daughters, even the bumpy roads we travelled together. And to the Universe that guided me into this country, that gave me the opportunity to meet so many wonderful people and to learn to be myself, (even if it has taken a long time) I always feel blessed and thankful.

ACKNOWLEDGMENTS

My sincere and total gratitude to Ebony McKenna, the talented author and teacher whose hard work on my behalf has helped this story come to completion.

A very special thank you to Barbara Stone, who encouraged me and started me off with the first audio-taping of my story and guided me all the way. Encourage me in this mammoth task, and finally spent a lot of time correcting all my mistakes and spellings.

Many thanks also to all my dear friends who encouraged me to do it and their patience with me.

My sincere thanks to all the wonderful and lovely people in all my life, too many to list, you know who you are; who have supported and encouraged me all through this journey.

Blessings to you all!

www.ingramcontent.com/pod-product-compliance
Lightning Source LLC
Chambersburg PA
CBHW070728020526
44107CB00077B/2093